My Reminiscences of
East Africa

GENERAL VON LETTOW-VORBECK

My Reminiscences of East Africa

East Africa

The East Africa Campaign of the First World War
by the Most Notable German Commander

Paul Emil von Lettow-Vorbeck

LEONAUR

My Reminiscences of East Africa
The East Africa Campaign of the First World War
by the Most Notable German Commander
By Paul Emil von Lettow-Vorbeck

First published under the title
My Reminiscences of East Africa

Leonaur is an imprint of Oakpast Ltd

ISBN: 978-0-85706-417-2 (hardcover)
ISBN: 978-0-85706-418-9 (softcover)

http://www.leonaur.com

Publisher's Notes

Contents

Preface

In all the German colonies, though but a few decades old, a life full of promise was discernible. We were beginning to understand the national value of our colonial possessions; settlers and capital were venturing in; industries and factories were beginning to flourish. Compared with that of other nations, the colonizing process of Germany had progressed peacefully and steadily, and the inhabitants had confidence in the justice of German administration. This development had barely commenced when it was destroyed by the world war. In spite of all tangible proofs to the contrary, an unjustifiable campaign of falsehood is being conducted in order to make the world believe that the Germans lacked colonizing talent and were cruel to the natives.

A small force, mainly composed of these very natives, opposed this development. Almost without any external means of coercion, even without immediate payment, this force, with its numerous native followers, faithfully followed its German leaders throughout the whole of the prolonged war against a more than hundredfold superiority. When the armistice came it was still fit to fight, and imbued with the best soldierly spirit. That is a fact which cannot be controverted, and is in itself a sufficient answer to the hostile misstatements.

It has not been possible for me to give an exhaustive account of the operations of the German East African Protective Force. The existing material is insufficient, much has been lost, and even now I am unacquainted with various events, the actors in which have not yet returned home. My own records have for the most part been lost, and I had not the leisure to prepare a detailed description of the campaign in East Africa in addition to my other duties. My account is therefore necessarily incomplete. In the main I must rely upon my memory and on my personal experiences. Errors in detail are unavoidable.

But in spite of this, the following account may not be without value, nor perhaps without interest, since it shows how what is up to the present the greatest drama in our colonial history was enacted in the head of him who was destined to conduct the military side of it. I have endeavoured to set down my recollections of East Africa as they actually are, and thus at least to present what is subjectively correct.

CHAPTER 1

Before the Outbreak of War

When I landed at Dar-es-Salaam in January, 1914, I hardly suspected the nature of the task that was to confront me in a few months' time. But during the past ten years the universal war had more than once seemed so imminent that I was obliged seriously to consider whether the force under my command would be called upon to take any part in that conflict, and, if so, what its task might be. Owing to the position of the Colony and the weakness of the existing forces—the peace establishment was but little more than two thousand—we could only play a subsidiary part. I knew that the fate of the colonies, as of all other German possessions, would only be decided on the battlefields of Europe. To this decision every German, regardless of where he might be at the moment, must contribute his share.

In the Colony also it was our duty, in case of universal war, to do all in our power for our country. The question was whether it was possible for us in our subsidiary theatre of war to exercise any influence on the great decision at home. Could we, with our small forces, prevent considerable numbers of the enemy from intervening in Europe, or in other more important theatres, or inflict on our enemies any loss of personnel or war material worth mentioning? At that time I answered this question in the affirmative. It is true, however, that I did not succeed in interesting all authorities in this idea to such an extent as to cause all preparations which a war of this kind rendered desirable to be carried out.

It was to be considered that hostile troops would allow themselves to be held only if we attacked, or at least threatened, the enemy at some really sensitive point. It was further to be remembered that, with the means available, protection of the Colony could not be ensured even by purely defensive tactics, since the total length of land frontier and coast-line was about equal to that of Germany. From these considerations it followed that it was necessary, not to split up our small available forces in local defence, but, on the contrary, to keep them together, to grip the enemy by the throat and force him to employ his forces for self-defence. If this idea could be successfully carried out, we should at the same time protect our coast and our infinitely long land frontier in the most effective manner.

In examining the question where to find a point so vital to the enemy as to afford us the prospect of a successful attack, or, at any rate, of a threat of such an attack, one thought at once of the frontier between German and British East Africa. Parallel with it, at a distance of a few marches, runs the main artery of the British territory, the Uganda Railway, an object which, with a length of quite 440 miles, was extremely difficult for the enemy to protect, and would, therefore, if effectively threatened, require a large part of his troops for the purpose.

On my first journey of reconnaissance and inspection, commenced in January, 1914, I went by sea from Dar-es-Salaam to Tanga, thence to Usambara, and then on into the country round Kilima Njaro and Meru Mountain. At Usambara I met an old friend whom I had known well since our military college days (*Kriegschule*), Captain von Prince (retired). He was an enthusiastic supporter of the idea that, in case of a war with England, we East Africans should not remain idle spectators, but should take a hand if there should be even a trace of a prospect of relieving the pressure in Europe. At the same time, he was in a position to inform me that in the Usambara country, round Kilima Njaro, and near Meru Mountain, Volunteer Rifle Corps were being formed, which in a short time would probably include all the Germans capable of bearing arms in these northern territories. In view of the density of the settlements in those parts, this was a fact of great importance.

The main contingent of the three thousand Europeans whom we were able to enrol in the Protective Force during the course of the war was furnished from these very territories lying along the Usambara Railway. It was, indeed, difficult to introduce a workable military organization among these voluntary associations, and to make effective use of their abundant good will. Still, it was, on the whole, successfully arranged that all, even those not legally obliged to do so, should be ready in case of war to act under the orders of the Protective Force. The District Commissioners also manifested the greatest sympathy; but they also expressed the, unfortunately well-founded,

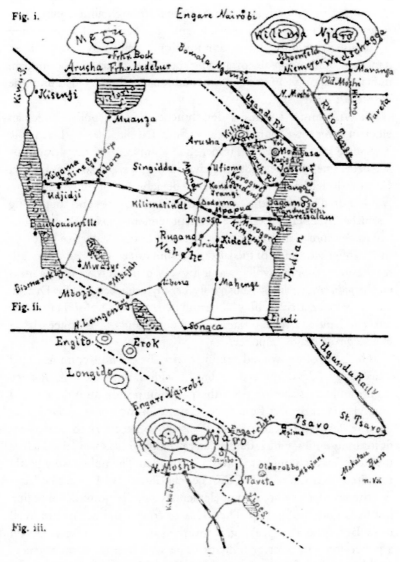

Fig. i.

Engare Nairobi

Meru

F.hr. Bock
Arusha F.hr. Ledebur

Bonala Ngonge

Kilima Njaro

Schoenfeld
Niemeyer W. di Tchagga
N. Moshi   Old Moshi
Mavanga

Kiwu-S. Kisenji

Uganda Ry

Rio Tsavo

Taveta

Muanza

Arusha Kilima

Vol Mombasa
Saristu Jasini
Tanga

Kigoma Tabora
Taline Gottorp

Singidda
Ufiome
Kondoa
Irangi
Dodoma
Dagamojo
Morogoro Handwetchi
Dar es salam

Udjidji

Kilimatinde Mpapua

Kilossa Morogor Kinganja
Pugu

Baudouinville

Rugano
Wahehe
Iringa Kidodi

Indian

Mwaya
Mbejah

Songea

Dismarcks
Mbozi

Mahenge

Libena

N. Langenbg

Lindi

Fig. ii.

Engito Erok

Longido

Ugundu Raily

Engare Nairobi

Tsavo St. Tsavo
Apima

Kilima Njaro
Zauna

N. Moshi
Olderobbo Anjani
Mahatan Buru

Taveta
m. Vol

Fig. iii.

FIG. I. AND III. KILIMA NJARO
FIG. II. GERMAN EAST AFRICA. THE CENTRAL RAILWAY.

doubt whether, in a universal war which could certainly cut us off completely from the home country and leave us to our own resources, such voluntary organizations would possess the requisite cohesion.

The armament was also in a bad way; although almost every European possessed a useful sporting rifle, the variety of patterns and the consequent difficulty of ammunition supply had not yet been remedied. The proposals for arming these rifle clubs with a uniform military weapon were still pending, and remained undecided until the outbreak of war.

At Wilhelmstal I found a detachment of native police under an efficient sergeant-major, who came from Ditmarschen. Whereas the Protective Force proper was under the Commandant, the various police detachments were under the civil authorities, and so each District Commissioner had under his orders a detachment of one hundred to two hundred men, for the purpose of collecting taxes and supporting his authority. There prevailed a constant tendency to increase this police force more and more, to the detriment of the Protective Force. In this manner, alongside of the latter, a second force of the same strength had come into being which was in its very nature a travesty of a military organization, and could hardly be anything better. The District Commissioner, a civil official, often understood little of military matters, and handed over the training and command of his Police-*Askari* to a sergeant-major of police.

The latter often worked zealously, with the old non-commissioned officer's usual devotion to duty; but he seldom received any guidance from a military superior, since the police inspector, an officer, could only visit each district from time to time. So the Police-*Askari* often became slack, and lacked the strict discipline necessary to keep them fit for their duties, which demanded reliability. To this was added a further defect which ought to have been avoided. The police were partly recruited from the native N.C.O.'s of the Protective Force. The latter was thereby deprived of its best elements, who, after joining the police, lost their good military qualities. This, of course, did not obtain in all cases. But, generally speaking, it was the case that, in order to obtain a police force of inferior military value which in the circumstances could never be of any real use, the quality of the Protective Force was steadily impaired.

From New Moshi, the terminus of the Usambara Railway, I proceeded *via* Marangu, where an English planter lived and where I met the English Consul King, of Dar-es-Salaam, to the Kilima Njaro country, and thence to Arusha. Several German planters, some of them former officers, whom I visited at their estates during the march, assured me that the German settlers in those parts formed a valuable source of military power.

At that time I made the acquaintance of the charming estate of Commander Niemeyer (retired), whose wife entertained us with excellent home-grown coffee. Later on she rather hindered us on one occasion: when, during the war, her husband was in Engara-Nairobi Camp, north-west of Kilima Njaro, we had temporarily lent her a telephone, so that she could call up her husband. Immediately afterwards the whole telephone service stopped, and after a long, long search, we at last discovered that our kind former hostess had not switched off her instrument and displayed no intention of doing so.

Close by was the plantation of Lieutenant-Commander Schoenfeld (retired), who hospitably offered us a glass of very fine Moselle wine, and did so with a military tone like a word of command which even then characterized him as the energetic leader who was later to defend the mouth of the Rufiji River against a superior enemy with such stubbornness. Just short of Arusha we came to the coffee-plantation of my old brother-cadet Freiherr von Ledebur, where at table I met the charming old retired Lieutenant-Colonel Freiherr von Bock. We talked about the Volunteer Rifle Corps which were being formed near Meru Mountain, and I did not dream that a few months later this old gentleman of over sixty would be one of our toughest patrol leaders on the east side of Kilima Njaro, and would often with his few men, who were mostly recruits, successfully engage several companies of the enemy. His true chivalry and fatherly care soon won him the hearts of his black comrades, to such a degree that he was in their eyes the bravest of all Germans, and they clung to him with touching loyalty.

At Arusha the first inspection of a company of *Askari* was held. The spirit and discipline of the black unit revealed the admirable education they had received at the hands of my predecessor, Colonel Freiherr von Schleuntz; but, in accordance with the hitherto accepted principles of their employment, their training for fighting against an enemy with modern armament had been developed to a lesser degree. Like the majority of the *Askari* companies, this company was still armed with the old 1871 pattern rifle, using smoky powder. The opinion was widely held that for black troops this was more suitable than a modern rifle with smokeless powder, for they had hitherto never been employed against an opponent with modern armament, but only in native warfare, where the larger calibre is an advantage, while the disadvantage of smoke is of no consequence.

After the outbreak of war, indeed, the enthusiastic supporters of the 1871 rifle changed their minds. Against an enemy provided with modern smokeless equipment the smoky rifle was, not only at the long ranges obtaining in the open plain, but also in bush-fighting, where the combatants are often but a few paces apart, decidedly inferior. The man using smokeless powder remains invisible, while the cloud of smoke betrays the enemy with rapidity and certainty, not only to the sharp eye of the native *Askari*, but even to the European accustomed to office work. Thus, at the beginning of the war, the greatest reward which could be earned by an *Askari* was to give him a modern captured rifle in place of his old smoky one.

In distributing the force by companies throughout the country it had been necessary to accept the disadvantage that in many cases it was impossible to employ them in large formations, or to train the senior officers in this respect. It was evident that in war the movement and leading in battle of forces greater than a company would be attended with great difficulty and friction. According to my view, the force had the double duty of preparing to meet an enemy from outside with modern armament, as well as a native enemy within our borders; their training for battle had therefore to take account of two distinct sets of conditions. The exercises in native warfare presented a spectacle which differed widely from our European inspections.

At Arusha, on this occasion, the company marched through thick bush, the "*Pori*," and was in native fashion surprised on the march. The enemy was represented by Meru warriors, who, arrayed in full war-dress, with spears and head-dress of ostrich feathers, remained concealed, and then at only a few paces distance fell upon the Safari, the column of route, with loud war cries. A fight at such close quarters, like the one in which Zelewski's expedition had been overwhelmed in 1891 at Iringa, is decided at short range and in a very few minutes. The troops quickly rally round their leaders and rush the enemy. In accordance with this whole character of native warfare, careful and thorough musketry training in the modern sense had hitherto been unnecessary.

It was, indeed, at a pretty low level, and it may interest the soldier to hear that in some companies the average at two hundred yards standing without rest barely attained Ring 3, and that only a few companies got beyond Ring 5. Neither did the nature of native warfare provide a sufficient inducement for thorough training with the machine gun. Fortunately, however, I soon discovered among all Europeans of the force a complete understanding of the importance of this arm, in particular in modern battle. In spite of this not particularly high standard of training, the results of field-firing, even at long ranges, were not unsatisfactory, and in this the *Askari* profited in a high degree by his sharp eyesight, which enabled him to observe his fire and correct his aim accordingly.

The journey was continued *via* Ufiome Mission, where the excellent Father Dürr was settled, to Kondoa-Irangi, Kilimatinde and back to Dar-es-Salaam. The impression left by this first inspection was that from a military point of view there was still a great deal to be done if we wished to be properly prepared in case the English should make war on us. Unfortunately I did not succeed in arousing sufficient interest in the matter on the part of the authorities. The ruling opinion was that we were on exceptionally good terms with the English, and that a war, if it came at all, was still in the distant future. Thus it happened that when war actually did break out but a few months later we were unprepared.

For me, a newcomer in East Africa, the journey had not only been of military interest. At Boma la Ngombe, a place between Moshi and Arusha, a number of old *Askari* had been settled by the late Lieutenant-Colonel Johannes; they were mainly engaged in cattle-dealing, and had become well-to-do. The news of my coming had preceded me, and the people appeared in full strength to greet me on my arrival. I had the impression that this was not a mere show of loyalty; the people not only told me enthusiastically of Germans under whom they had previously served, but after the outbreak of war, unasked and without the slightest pressure, they placed a large sum of money at our disposal to help the force.

In that district I also saw the first Masai, who, in contrast to the majority of the East African tribes, are pure Hamites, and live in a special reservation. It may be mentioned that Merker, the best authority on the Masai,[1] considers them to be the original Jews. They possess to a marked degree the characteristics of the pure inhabitant of the prairie. Occasionally, one of these tall, slim, and very swift men acted as my guide on hunting expeditions; their vision and skill as trackers are astonishing. In addition, the Masai is intelligent, and, at any rate

1. M. Marker, *Die Masai,* Berlin, 1904 (2nd Edition, 1910).

towards strangers, an extraordinary liar. He lives in closed villages of mud huts, and, like all nomads, wanders with his herds over the prairie. He seldom enlists in the force.

In agriculture the Masai engages hardly at all, whereas among the other tribes this forms the chief occupation and is a necessary condition for close settlement. Thus the banana districts on the eastern slopes of Kilima Njaro support a native Wajagga population of some twenty-five thousand souls, and this number could easily be increased. The great wealth of cattle in the neighbourhood of Arusha, on the Masai prairie, and near Kondoa-Irangi, showed me that the tsetse fly, the principal enemy of African cattle, is comparatively rare in those parts. As a comparison, I may state that the cattle in the single district of Arusha are estimated to be more numerous than in the whole of South-West Africa. At Kondoa-Irangi and Singida the people had come from a great distance, and had lined the road to greet me. No traveller who visits these countries can fail to observe that in the fertile, elevated interior there is room for the settlement of hundreds of thousands of Europeans. Here I would like to record an impression which I only obtained later, during the war.

At times we passed through fertile districts which were completely forsaken by the inhabitants, but which were known not to have been occupied even in the previous year. They had simply moved away, had settled somewhere else in the abundantly available, empty and fertile country, and had there begun to cultivate fresh fields. If the country capable of cultivation were fully utilized, it would probably be possible to support in German East Africa, which has hitherto been inhabited by about eight millions only, a population barely less than that of Germany. An Englishman captured during the war at Mahenge remarked that it would be possible to make East Africa into a second India, and I think he was right. My experience in the war has confirmed my opinion that there exist many possibilities of economic development, of which we had hardly an inkling before the war.

At Singida I saw one of the stud-farms of the country. For breeding purposes there were two horse stallions, no mares, a few Muscat donkey stallions, and mainly country-bred donkey mares. Of the objects it was sought to attain I could get no clear idea; in any case, the crossing of horse stallions and donkey mares had produced no results. But the district is extraordinarily suitable for horse-breeding, and the Government Veterinary Officer Hiffmeister, who was stationed there, was very inclined to settle in the country as a private farmer and horse-breeder. Similar stud-farms existed at Kilimatinde, Iringa and Ubena. From Singida to Kilimatinde I followed the Mpondi River; the sportsman will be interested to know that this is the district in which the best buffaloes in East Africa are said to be found. A few days before I had successfully hunted buffalo, but I had not succeeded in getting a shot at a powerful bull, and so, as far as time permitted, I was out for buffalo.

Besides a native boy, I had as trackers two excellent *Askari* of the Konda Company. As soon as I arrived in camp at the end of a march and dismounted from my mule, I would ask *Kadunda,* one of these *Askari,* who had done the march on foot, whether he was ready to hunt. He always agreed with the greatest enthusiasm, and away we went through the bush, which was sometimes so dense that one had to crawl under the branches in order to get through at all. For the European not yet accustomed to the African climate it is extraordinarily fatiguing to follow a trail through dense bush and high grass reaching over one's head for hours on end in the blazing sun.

The wounded buffalo is considered to be the most dangerous game in East Africa; he often charges at once with great determination. At Mpondi, a short time before, a wounded buffalo had attacked a hunter so suddenly that the latter did indeed find himself seated on its neck, but would hardly have escaped with his life unless at the critical moment his sun-helmet had fallen off. The animal then proceeded to attack the helmet, and the man managed to get a shot at its heart. From this and similar tales it will be understood that as the trail gets warmer and warmer, one's excitement becomes intense and one's senses more acute.

But although I often heard the buffalo breathing only a few paces from me, the bush was so thick that I could not get a shot. I had already abandoned all hope of success and had marched off with my caravan for good and all, when at seven in the morning we crossed a perfectly fresh buffalo trail. At this point the forest was clearer, and the guides seemed keen to follow the tracks. So we let the caravan go on, and after four hours of exhausting tracking got a sight of the buffalo. In a clearing, at one hundred yards, I raised my rifle, but Kadunda would not allow it, and insisted on our stalking the quarry, which was passing us in quite open wood without undergrowth, up to within thirty yards. Luckily the bullet cut the main artery; the buffalo fell at once, and so any further possible developments of the episode were cut short. As often happens, we discovered in the animal's body a bullet from a native gun. Besides this buffalo I had got a large number of antelope and gazelle of various kinds; lions we often heard, but never caught sight of.

On this march through the "*Pori*" I learned, to my astonishment, that even in the interior of Africa it is no easy matter to disappear without a trace. I had marched off without leaving word what road I intended to take. Suddenly, in the heart of the bush, a native met us on the march, and handed me the oversea mail. The fact is that in their interchange of information the inhabitants tell each other everything that happens in their vicinity. Calls, fire signals, and the signal drums serve to exchange and quickly spread all news. The incredible way in which the innumerable rumours spread abroad, with which I became acquainted later on, is mainly due to this communicativeness.

After returning to Dar-es-Salaam from the first journey of inspection, I immediately made arrangements for re-arming three more companies; up to date only three companies had been equipped with modern rifles. It subsequently became a factor of the greatest importance that, at any rate, these arms, with the necessary ammunition, reached the Colony just in time for the outbreak of war.

During a tour of inspection in April to Lindi, where I saw the Third Field Company, I fell into a rocky hole and got water on the knee so that I could not start my next long journey till the end of May. Although the Central Railway was open for public traffic only as far as Tabora, the construction had proceeded so far that I could reach Kigoma (on Lake Tanganyika) by rail, and was thus already enabled to acquire a superficial knowledge of this important means of communication which connected our coast directly with the lake and the rich countries bordering on it, and indirectly with the Congo basin.

At Kigoma the steamer *Coetzen* was still building, and to reach Bismarckburg I made use of the small steamer *Hedwig von Wissman*. At Baudouinville, in the Congo Territory, I paid a short visit to the Bishop of the White Fathers, without suspecting how soon we would be at war with that country. The wonderful church would be an ornament to any of our towns. It had been built by the Fathers themselves and the interior was decorated with rich carvings. Extensive, splendid orchards surround the station. The plague of lions must, however, be very great; the Fathers told me that a short time before a lion had one night jumped the wall into the court and killed an ox.

Our reception was very friendly, and we were made welcome with a glass of fine Algerian wine. We were also well received at Mwasyl

18

Mission Station in German territory, where there were also White Fathers mostly Belgians. During the war, however, we captured correspondence which proved that the French missionaries, who also lived at stations in the Tanganyika country, by no means confined themselves to spreading Christianity but intentionally carried on a national propaganda as well. One missionary's letter defines the difference between a *missionnaire catholique* and a *missionnaire français*, remarking that the latter is bound, in addition to spreading the Christian faith, to carry on French national propaganda. It is well known that this national propaganda is a work from which the German missionaries generally refrained.

These missions, which are naturally to be found in the densely populated and well-cultivated countries, exercise a remarkable influence on the education of the natives. The missionary is mostly the only permanently settled white man; he becomes well acquainted with the country and people, and wins their confidence. The missions have deserved extremely well by introducing European handicrafts; everywhere one finds carpenters' shops, shoemakers' shops and brickworks.

My later tours disclosed that the extremely fertile country around Langenburg and Ssonga, where there are many wheat-fields (the density of population is indicated even on the map by the numerous mission stations), was protected by only one company, which was not even connected by a direct wire. A telegram could only reach Langenburg from Dar-es-Salaam by the English line through South Africa. The communication by heliograph from Iringa to Langenburg was too unreliable to be considered an efficient substitute. It may be mentioned that in that country the natives have not only been educated up to agriculture by the Missions and by the German Administration, but that considerable native industries have been indigenous there for a long time past.

Where iron occurs one finds numerous forges, the bellows being made in the primitive manner out of hides and perforated branches. Very beautiful are the native weavers' products; basket-work is also done here as almost everywhere else in the Colony, and the work not only shows good taste, but is so close that the natives use wickerwork cups for drinking. The large herds owned by a few European farmers suffered, owing to the poorly developed communications, from the difficulty of reaching a market; this is especially the case with Mbeya Farm, between Lake Nyassa and Tanganyika.

I camped at Mbosi Mission, and the local missionary, Bachmann, who had known the country and the people intimately for many years past, told me that a striking change was taking place in the views of the natives. Foreign Arabs and Swahili were appearing in the country, and were telling the people that the Germans would soon be going, and that the English would take possession of the land; that was in June, 1914.

The continuation of my journey to Iringa brought me to the places where the great chief Kwawa had defied the Germans in the early days, and at Rugeno some of the many assembled natives were able to relate to me what they had witnessed of the annihilation of Zelewski's expedition on the spot.

In the short period of peace-work that was vouchsafed to me, my endeavours to obtain a thorough grip of all my duties in East Africa could not produce results sufficient to secure me great personal authority among Africans of long standing. I was still considered a raw hand. All the same, my career in the service had prepared me to some extent for the work that Fate had in store for me.

It was probably about the time when, as a cadet who had been transplanted at an early age from my home in Pomerania, I was studying Caesar's Gallic War, that the German Fatherland was presented by Bismarck with its first colonies. In the year 1899-1900, when employed on the General Staff, I studied our own colonies as well as many foreign ones. During the troubles in China (1900-1901) I made the acquaintance, both officially and socially, of all the contingents engaged with us in East Asia, particularly the English. The Herero and Hottentot Rebellion in South-West Africa (1904-1906) introduced me to the peculiarities of bush warfare. At that time I gained abundant personal experience, not only of natives, but also of Boers, both on the Staff of General von Botha and as an independent Company and Detachment Commander. The excellent qualities of this Low German race, that had for generations made its home on the African *veld*, commanded my respect. That the Boers would later take a decisive— and in a sense tragic—part in anglicizing the German part of Africa I never dreamt.

In 1906, in South-West Africa, I was wounded. This brought me to Cape Town, so that I also acquired a superficial knowledge of Cape Colony. On my return journey I also touched at the future scene of my work, German East Africa, for the first time.

Later, my position as Commander of the Marine Battalion at Wilhelmshaven afforded me an insight into the inner life of our thriving and growing navy, which was so closely connected with German work overseas. I took part in exercises and cruises on large and small ships, in naval manoeuvres, and in a visit by the Fleet to Norway, during which new views of general and military life continually presented themselves.

Even after my return to the Army the alternation between regimental and staff employment afforded me much inducement and opportunity for comparison. In this manner my development had rendered me capable of rapidly accommodating myself to new conditions. Grateful as I was for every expansion of my horizon, I owe the best of all to the Army at home, in which I had the privilege, under the guidance of admirable commanders, of learning to know the spirit of military life and true discipline, a spirit which was then properly understood.

CHAPTER 2

The Beginning of the War

Early in August, 1914, when on my way *via* the heliograph station of Kidodi towards Kilossa, a special messenger brought me a telegram from the Governor, to say I was to return immediately to Dar-es-Salaam; and on the following day I received the news that His Majesty had ordered mobilization, but that the state of war did not extend to the overseas possessions. A telegram from the Secretary of State of the Imperial Colonial Office called upon us to reassure the settlers.

In contrast to this a wireless message from the Admiralty Staff mentioned England also among our probable enemies.

At Kilossa I managed to catch a goods train, and so arrived at Dar-es-Salaam on the 3rd August. Here everyone was busy the declaration of war had arrived in the middle of the preparations for a big exhibition, in the programme of which was included the ceremonial opening of the Tanganyika Railway; numerous Germans had come on a visit to Dar-es-Salaam and were now unable to get away. In order to assist in the preparations for the exhibition, Captain von Hammerstein, commanding the 6th Field Company in Ujiru, had also arrived there, and it was very fortunate that I was able at once to employ this energetic officer, who not only shared my views, but to whom I was also cordially attached, for the work of mobilization.

The question which immediately forced itself upon us was whether, in the now obviously imminent universal war in which England would almost certainly join, the Colony would remain neutral or not. As I have already explained, I considered it to be our military object to detain enemy, that is English forces if it could by any means be accomplished. This, however, was impossible if we remained neutral. In that case the situation would be that we, who did not command the sea, would have to remain inactive, with a force which, though

22

small at the moment, had behind it a loyal, very efficient population of eight millions suitable for military service. England, on the other hand, would have no need to employ a single man in East Africa on our account; it would be able to take away the very last fit *Askari*, after providing for internal security, for employment in other theatres more important than East Africa. It would, therefore, obviously have been an advantage for England if any agreement had existed which condemned us to neutrality.

But this was not the case: the Congo Act, which deals with the Equatorial territories, only says that in case of conflict between two of the Powers concerned, a third Power may offer its good services as a mediator. But as far as I know this step was not taken by any Power. We were therefore not obliged to restrict our operations out of regard for any agreement. From a military point of view it was a disadvantage, not for us, but for England, if war occurred in East Africa. The fact that we were not obliged to remain neutral enabled us to make use of our favourable coast as a base and refuge for the German cruiser operations in the Indian Ocean. But, above all, we were able, with our few thousand men, to contain throughout the whole duration of the war an enormously superior force of the enemy.

At the outbreak of war the Protective Force consisted of 216 Europeans (from whom a part must be deducted as on leave) and 2,540 *Askari*; there were, further, in the Police Force, 45 Europeans and 2,154 *Askari*; these were later increased by the ships' company of the *Königsberg* (which had put to sea), 322 men, and of the *Möve*, 102 men. The total numbers enrolled in the Force during the war were about 3,000 Europeans and 11,000 *Askari*.

These figures include all non–combatants, such as those employed on police duty, medical personnel, supply and maintenance services, etc. How many milliards it cost to try and crush our diminutive force the English themselves will presumably someday tell us. We, on the other hand, could probably have continued the war for years to come.

For the hostile strengths no authentic figures are at my disposal; I quote from the statements of English officers and Press reports, and they must bear the responsibility for them. According to them over 130 generals took the field against us, the total strength of the hostile troops was about 300,000, the losses in European and Indian dead amounted to 20,000; horses and mules, 140,000. These numbers, especially those of the general officers, seem even to me rather exaggerated; I can therefore only repeat that they are taken from English sources. In any event, however, their losses were very considerable; and considering that the number of black soldiers who were killed or died is not given, the total number of enemy dead can hardly be under 60,000.

We should have been compelled, if a cruiser had sought shelter in our harbours, to refuse to admit her, by reason of our neutrality, whereas the favourable position and coastal development of East Africa made it the natural hiding-place in cruiser warfare in the Indian Ocean. As regards the agreements laid down in the Congo Act, it should be borne in mind what it would have meant for our Navy if our colonies had been declared neutral.

At Dar-es-Salaam it was very interesting during those days of tension to watch the proceedings of the English Consul King. He was to be seen everywhere, either in the Officers' Club at a game of bridge, or at the post office where our telegrams were handed in. The standing orders of the English Expeditionary Force, which were subsequently captured at Tanga, and which were mainly based on King's reports, showed how active this man had been in the time before the war, and how excellently he was informed as to the internal conditions in our Colony. His judgment on relevant matters extended so far that he even compared the relative fighting value of the Europeans in different districts, and credited those of Dar-es-Salaam with little "stomach for fighting." To be honest, it must be admitted that in the case of a large number of the Germans in that place (and even of the local Government authorities) it actually did take some time before they were imbued with that warlike spirit without which the fulfilment of our task was simply impossible.

Very difficult was the position of the coast towns, which were inhabited by numerous Europeans (among them many women and children), and which were of course exposed to bombardment by English men-of-war at any minute. The Governor maintained that such a bombardment must be avoided under all circumstances. According to an ordinance, which certainly did not contemplate the case of foreign war, the supreme military power in the Colony was in the hands of the Governor, and communication with home having ceased, it was anyhow physically impossible to get this altered. So I was obliged to make the best of this, from a military point of view, very serious difficulty and to reckon with the possibility that, if the Governor's instructions were faithfully executed, Dar-es-Salaam and

Tanga for instance, the termini of our railways and the obvious bases for hostile operations from the coast towards the interior, would fall into the enemy's hands without a struggle.

My view was that we would best protect our colony by threatening the enemy in his own territory. We could very effectively tackle him at a sensitive point, the Uganda Railway, and one might almost say that the numerous German settlers in the country traversed by our Northern Railway (Tanga-Moshi) were already deployed for this object. The Governor, however, did not agree with the proposal I had already previously put forward in case of war, namely, to concentrate our forces in the North near Kilima Njaro. But, in order to act at all, it was obviously necessary to collect our troops, who were scattered all over the country. As this could not be effected in the Kilima Njaro country, as I wished, the concentration took place on the heights of Pugu, a day's march west of Dar-es-Salaam.

At this place the Dar-es-Salaam Company met those from Kilimatinde, Tabora, Ujiji, Usambara and Kissendji, which came partly by march routes and partly by rail. The police, who, in accordance with the scanty preparations already made, were to join the Protective Force immediately, were in part, at any rate, placed at my disposal, a number of old *Askari* were called up, and in this way four new companies (No.'s 15 to 18) were at once formed. The German Reservists were mobilized as required, and each company was brought up to an establishment of about 16 Europeans, 160 *Askari* and 2 machine guns.

In some cases difficulties occurred in calling the Europeans to the colours. By mistake, the crews of a few ships of the East African Line, lying in the harbour of Dar-es-Salaam, were informed, in response to their application, by the officer in command at the railway station, that there was no room for them in the Protective Force. Then, at the suggestion of the governor's representative, a declaration was submitted to them, according to which they were to engage in writing to remain neutral during the war. Later on the men saw that this constituted an offence against the law relating to liability for service, and their own sound feeling was opposed to it. They appealed to me, setting forth the circumstances; I had had no inkling of these proceedings, and fortunately, as the declaration had not yet fallen into the hands of the enemy, the intended decision could be reserved.

The number of carriers allotted to each company varied, and may have averaged about 250. The stores of arms, ammunition and other war-material, which were lying unprotected in the harbour of Dar-es-Salaam, were distributed among various places in the interior along the railway, where depots were established. The training of the troops was at once vigorously proceeded with, and even then we realized the value of rendering our head-dress unrecognizable by means of grass and leaves, a measure proposed by a practical company commander, Captain Tafel.

The question of course was whether we, with our *Askari*, would be able to fight modern troops; it was denied by many an experienced hand. But from what I had seen during the revolt in South-West Africa, from 1904 to 1906, I believed that courage and military efficiency could be awakened in the East African native also, who belongs to that same great family the Bantu, as the Herero. That certainly was a proof; but the matter was greatly simplified by the fact that there was no possible alternative.

All questions of organization, which are usually carefully prepared and considered in time of peace, had now to be dealt with and decided on the spur of the moment. One of them was the extraordinarily important one of establishing a service of subsistence and a complete system of supply from the rear. The main point was to consider, in the first place, the main roads, which were also important in a military sense. Which roads might these be? It was immediately found how disadvantageous was the absence of railway communication between the Central and Usambara Railways. In time of peace, communication had been effected by sea between Dar-es-Salaam and Tanga; this was now impossible. Obviously the importance of a military use of the lines had not been thought of.

As a substitute, we had to develop a road between Morogoro and Korogwe, on the Northern Railway. The second road ran past the western side of the Masai Reservation, from Dodoma via Kondoa-Irangi, and Ufiome to Arusha, and the third from the rich district of Tabora, the capital of the Wanyamwesi country, to Muansa, on Lake Victoria, into the country of the Wassukume, who were recognized even by Consul King as the most important of our tribes. This road was also valuable because by it we could draw on the rice crops of Lake Victoria as well as on the abundant stocks of cattle. Other roads connected Kilossa with the rich territory of Mahenge, Iringa, and even Langenburg, which last provided us with a large part of our requirements in wheat flour.

The provisional organization of the supply system having been fixed in broad and general outline, it was not possible for the details of its development to be worked out at Headquarters. Someone had to be found whose past military career rendered him capable of working the system, not only from the administrative point of view, but also in accordance with the sometimes very urgent military requirements, and of adapting it to them.

Major-General Wahle, a retired officer, who happened to have arrived on the 2nd August, on a visit to his son, and to see the Dar-es-Salaam Exhibition, at once placed himself at the disposal of the Force, and at my request took charge of the Lines of Communication. His task was particularly difficult, because where there were no railways, the bulk of the work had to be performed by native carriers. I have at my disposal no figures showing the total number of carriers employed for the service of the troops, and it is very difficult to arrive at it at all definitely. It included men who only carried the loads from one place to another before the permanent carriers took them over, but I am sure I do not exaggerate in saying that, on the whole, hundreds of thousands of carriers worked for the troops; and all of them had to be fed and medically looked after.

Of our many other difficulties one of a special nature may here be mentioned. The peacetime existence of the Europeans in tropical colonies had, even for reasons of health, accustomed them to a certain degree of comfort. When on *safari* (a journey) in East Africa, it is generally impossible to buy European food; but few Europeans had learnt to live on the vegetable products supplied by the natives or by Nature. Shelter is rarely to be had. Against mosquitoes it is, however, imperative to protect oneself. So the white official or soldier seldom travelled with less than eleven carriers, who, besides his tent, camp-bed and clothing, also carried a considerable quantity of food.

Such large numbers of carriers were, however, impossible for a force which was to be mobile. Another difficulty was that nearly every *Askari* had a boy. With these simple people, whose predilection for their ancient traditions and customs is further confirmed by Islam, and who are besides very proud and vain, it is particularly difficult to interfere with such *dusturis* (customs). In individual cases it was not always easy for a company commander to find the happy mean.

In the tropical warfare which was before us medical care is one of the most important factors. Generally speaking, the native is in a great measure immune against malaria, and it does not often happen that an *Askari* gets really ill with it; some tribes, however, like the Wajagga, on Kilima Njaro, who inhabit elevated, non-malarial districts, and are therefore not immune from early youth, suffer severely from malaria as soon as they come down to the plains. From the evening until well into the morning mechanical protection against the malaria mosquito (anopheles), by means of a mosquito net, was strictly enforced for every European. For many months I slept on the ground, and even then the mosquito-net afforded me a high degree of protection; even so I had malaria ten times, for in the field it is not always possible to employ preventive measures to the extent that is desirable from a hygienic point of view. In our endeavour to attach a medical officer to every company we received most welcome assistance from the fact that there was a considerable number of them on Lake Tanganyika, and in the Southern territories on the Rovuma, who had come out to study and combat sleeping-sickness.

The work entailed by all this business of mobilization not only kept us going day and night, but also the native telephonist at Pugu, and it was extraordinary to see the skill with which the black man worked his instrument, both there and elsewhere. His great technical talent proved of the greatest value to us. Of difficulties there was, of course, an infinity. During the early days it happened that cattle coming from the country north of Tabora for the civilian population at Dar-es-Salaam met other cattle going in the opposite direction to feed the troops. To this day I feel something of a physical shock when I think of a collision at Pugu, between a train laden with the finest show cattle going at full speed, and another one, which nearly produced a serious reduction in the personnel required for working out our mobilization scheme.

Our place of concentration at Pugu is some twelve miles inland from Dar-es-Salaam. Our camp was situated on the slopes of the Pugu Mountains. The forest is extremely thick, and the country densely covered by plantations of natives and Europeans. In spite of its somewhat elevated position, Pugu is quite in the hot coastal area, and although in August we were still in the cold season, the temperature was still what we describe as "tropical;" it is that oppressive, somewhat damp heat, which makes long marches so exhausting for the European.

At that time we had tents for the Europeans and a camp-bed with the inevitable mosquito net for everyone, so that in this respect there were no difficulties. In case of sickness we had established a provisional field hospital in the neighbouring Wichmann Plantations. Our horses did not suffer unduly. But one after another all our animals went down with tsetse. In camp it was not possible to provide them, as we could at Dar-es-Salaam, with tsetse proof stables, fitted with wire gauze similar to fly-proof windows.

Chapter 3

The First Actions

In this manner we were fully employed in the camp at Pugu, when, on the morning of the 8th August, we heard heavy artillery fire from the direction of Dar-es-Salaam. According to reports which soon reached us, it emanated from two English light cruisers, *Astræa* and *Pegasus*, who were aiming at the wireless tower. This tower had been erected in this exposed position because on the coast it could reach further out to sea; it was of importance to us because the high-power station at Tabora was not yet finished, and the two smaller ones at Muansa and Bukoba were of only local use. The tower was not hit by the English, but blown up by us, from a rather excessive fear of its falling into the enemy's hands.

A short time later an observation officer reported that the enemy was apparently preparing to land at Konduchi, a day's march north of Dar-es-Salaam. The formation of the coast rendered it not unlikely. I therefore immediately ordered the seven companies of *Askari*[1] available to march off, so as to seize the favourable opportunity of surprising the enemy in the act of landing.

Before they marched off I had a conversation at Pugu Station with the Governor, Dr. Schnee, who was passing through by train to Morogoro. He seemed quite surprised by the English hostilities, and entirely agreed with my proposal to attack them at Konduchi. On the way there I met two gentlemen belonging to the government at Dar-es-Salaam, who showed me a document dealing with negotiations for surrendering Dar-es-Salaam to the English. As the governor had said nothing to me about it, and I was also rather in a hurry, I only glanced superficially at it. It did not occur to me that this might be any kind of

---

1. *Askari* are "soldiers," not a distinct tribe.

agreement drawn up with the consent of the governor.

But when, during the night, the force had reached a mountain ten miles north of Dar-es-Salaam, and on the next morning we obtained a view of the harbour and the English cruisers lying off it, it became clear that the report of an attempted landing at Konduchi was a mistake. We were able to establish the fact that the English ships had communicated with the shore, and now it did appear to me probable that negotiations with the enemy had taken place. I now advanced on the town, and, as I could not but fear that in the confusion of the moment a disadvantageous agreement might be concluded at Dar-es-Salaam, I sent Captain Tafel on ahead. He was to announce that I was taking over the executive power, and that negotiations with the enemy must be conducted through me alone.

It was only from Captain Tafel that I learned that by order of the governor negotiations for surrender had actually taken place. My intervention was not approved by the Governor, in whose hands, according to a Protective Force Ordinance intended to meet quite different conditions, supreme military power was actually placed. For the moment this had no practical consequences. Only a few English marines had landed, and had already gone on board again. But for a soldier it was not inspiring to find that here, under the very eyes of a thousand good troops, an agreement had been concluded which forbade us to undertake any hostile act in Dar-es-Salaam, while the enemy was not so bound, and that we had received no information of a step of such great military importance.

The *Königsberg* had already put to sea from Dar-es-Salaam several days before, and the surveying vessel *Möve*, which was in harbour, had been blown up by us on the 9th August. This brought the land forces a valuable military increase, as the captain of the *Möve*, Lieut.-Commander Zimmer, now came under my orders. Lieutenant Horn at once proceeded with a few seamen to Kigoma, where he manned and armed the small steamer *Hedwig von Wissmann*. On Lake Tanganyika he chased the Belgian steamer *Delcommune*, which he surprised and shot to pieces after a few days, thereby securing to us the extremely important command of the lake. The ability rapidly to transfer troops from the Central Railway towards Bismarckburg or Usambara depended entirely upon unimpeded transport on Tanganyika, and played a part in the later course of the operations.

In the north of the Colony, the 1st Company at Arusha had been reinforced by the 13th Company, coming by rapid marches from Kondoa, and by another company formed at Moshi from Police *Askari*. Further, a large part of the Europeans of the northern districts had combined to form a detachment under Captain von Prince. Most of those troops were in the neighbourhood of Moshi. Taveta, which lies to the eastward, in English territory, was held by the enemy, who thereby secured a valuable sally-port against our European settlements in the north; it was, therefore, an urgent matter for us to capture this important point without delay. It took considerable time before we were able to set the force in motion for this purpose.

Many people believed that on the strength of the Congo Act we were bound to remain neutral, and naturally had little confidence in the instructions they received from the new commandant. It was not until the 15th August that the weakly-held place was taken. The course of the fight proved that the force still required much further training to render it fit to carry out combined operations in unison in the dense bush. In this area the command was assumed by Major Kraut, who happened to be in the north-eastern frontier district for the purpose of frontier delimitations. During the next few days the holder of the supreme military power was successfully persuaded to agree to moving the bulk of our forces to the Northern Railway. Simple as was this movement in itself, under the conditions then existing, it required considerable preparations.

There were few Germans to be found who were so well acquainted with the whole country between Dar-es-Salaam and Morogoro on one side, and Tanga and Mombo on the other, that they could give reliable information about roads and conditions of subsistence It was necessary to send out reconnaissance officers in order to determine the roads on which a suitable quantity of supplies could be found. But we could not afford to await the results of all these reconnaissances; the marches had to be begun. According to European ideas the country was sparsely populated; and on the existing maps the only notes as to water and food showed whether the supplies available would suffice for bodies of a strength equal to a company at most.

Without preparation one could therefore hardly put more than one company on each road without distribution in depth; the training and skill in the collection of supplies which the force had acquired by the end of the war were at that time non-existent. Taking it all round, it came to this, that the march and supply of a single company in the conditions there prevailing required about the same consideration as would a division in Germany. It was also necessary in this move to take into account the risk arising from the fact that companies would for a prolonged period be out of reach of orders. The only telegraphic communication between the Central Railway and the north ran close along the coast, and could therefore be interrupted whenever the enemy intended to do so.

However, the Director of the Postal Service, Rothe, and Secretary Krüger displayed such adaptability in meeting the wishes of the troops, and such energy in starting work on the new line Morogoro-Handeni-Korogwe, and, under the pressure of circumstances, temporarily overcame the normal torpor of the Tropics with such success, that the line was completed in only a few weeks. Owing to the destructiveness of the termites (white ants) it is the rule in time of peace to employ iron telegraph poles, which, owing to the prevalence of giraffe in this particular district, have to be very tall and carry very heavy conductors. In the first instance, however, the construction in this case had to be of a provisional nature, and this, and the use of cable, caused continual breakdowns and repairs.

In the meantime I received reports of the advance of small hostile detachments at Jassini, two marches north of Tanga, and this confirmed me in the belief that the enemy intended to land in that district, and would then rapidly advance into the interior along the Northern Railway. Consequently, the various companies had marched off from different points on the line Dar-es-Salaam-Mpapua, and were for the most part converging on Handeni, while some were directed on other points on the line Tanga-Korogwe, when I was called up on the telephone at Pugu on the afternoon of August 23rd, by Lieutenant von Chappuis, who was encamped at Bagamoyo with the 17th Field Company.

He reported that an English light cruiser was lying off Bagamoyo, and had called upon the local Civil Administrator to destroy the telegraph station, threatening to bombard the place in case of refusal. I ordered him to assume control of the executive and to prevent a hostile landing by force of arms. A boat from the man-of-war that attempted to land under the white flag was therefore sent back, and the place was bombarded in consequence, to the great amusement of the company and the native inhabitants, since the enemy scored practically no hits.

At the end of August, Headquarters moved by rail to Kirnamba, near Morogoro. On the way, General von Wahle, who was directing the service on the Lines of Communication from Morogoro, wished me the best of luck in the decisive action which we expected in the neighbourhood of Handeni, and to which his son was also proceeding. From there Headquarters travelled on towards Handeni in two requisitioned motors. After about twenty miles we had to leave them, as the improvement of this road had not been completed beyond that point. Captain von Hammerstein and I went on on bicycles, and gradually caught up the companies on the march. The anticipated landing of the enemy did not take place, and early in September we reached Korogwe. In the meantime an English cruiser had appeared at Tanga and towed away some lighters lying there.

Our next duty was to organize the supply and transport services in the north. Captain Schmid, who had until then directed them as Field *Intendant*, had become sick, and it was difficult to find a suitable successor. Fortunately we discovered one in Captain Feilke, of the *Landwehr*, who had for many years directed the Prince Albrecht Plantations in Usambara, a man of great experience. He was at the time in the vicinity of Tanga, and had placed himself at the disposal of the force. He had formerly been adjutant of the 8th Jäger Battalion, was fifty-two years of age, a man of much knowledge of the world and a skilful officer; he thus combined in the happiest manner the military knowledge and business talent necessary for the difficult post of *Intendant*. He came immediately, and we drove to New Moshi together.

There I met Captain Kraut. On Kilima Njaro preparations had been made for guerrilla warfare by establishing supply depots, our patrols were pushing beyond Taveta towards the British Uganda Railway, and numerous minor encounters had already taken place. At that time, however, the force lacked the experience necessary for carrying out distant patrols like those which at a later stage led so successfully to interruptions of the line. The first patrols had arrived at the Uganda Railway in a half-starved condition and had been captured. From New Moshi I went to Himo Camp, where Captain von Prince was holding a fortified position. He accompanied me to Taveta, which was held by an advanced post under an officer.

Now we could discuss on the spot the problem of transferring the main body of the Northern Force to Taveta. The local native population was very numerous and placed entire confidence in the European administrators appointed by the force: they continued to sell their products in the market, and our mutual relationship was completely satisfactory.

Directly war broke out the fear of a native rising had been expressed in many quarters. Along the Central Railway there were wild rumours about a revolt of the Wahehe—the warlike tribe who had so long defied German authority in the Iringa country—and around Kilima Njaro a rising of the Wajagga was feared. The authorities also thought that the large number of black labourers on the European settlements in the north were unreliable on account of difficulties of subsistence. But none of these fears turned out to be justified. Later, a very intelligent captured Belgian *Askari* told me outright: "You know quite well that the natives always side with the stronger party," and an English Masai admitted frankly: "It is all the same to us whether the English or the Germans are our masters."

It was not till later, after the enemy had penetrated the country, that the native became a real danger to us: and then it was, indeed, very great. The native has a fine sense of the transfer of real power from one hand to the other.

After returning for a short time to Korogwe, Headquarters moved to New Moshi, and shortly afterwards to Taveta. Three companies who had reached the Northern Railway from the Central Railway were concentrated at Tanga, the remaining five were moved into the Kilima Njaro country. At Dar-es-Salaam there remained for the moment only Captain von Kornatzki with the newly-formed 18th Field Company.

During the following period several enterprises were carried out by flying columns, of the strength of one company each, the intention being to drive away the hostile detachments who were reported to be guarding the watering-places in the adjoining English territory, to inflict losses upon them, and so to open the way for our patrols to operate against the Uganda and Magad Railway. Thus, at the end of September, Captain Schulz had marched with his company from Kilima Njaro down the Tsavo River to the Uganda Railway, where he had met an enemy detachment of several companies, who had probably been concentrated by means of the railway. North of Kilima Njaro Captain Tafel had with his company and a detachment of fifty Europeans pursued a column of English Horse, but had then been attacked by the latter in his camp in the dense bush on Engito Mountain.

This was the first serious engagement fought by our *Askari* in the north. Although the enemy consisted of English and Boer farmers, who were therefore good horsemen and good shots, our *Askari* attacked them with the bayonet with such dash, that out of a strength of eighty Europeans some twenty dead were left behind, and their total

GENERAL MAP OF THE CAMPAIGN IN EAST AFRICA.
—— TRACK OF THE GERMAN MAIN FORCE, 1916–1918.

THE FALLEN.
DRAWN BY GENERAL VON LETTOW-VORBECK'S ADJUTANT.

casualties may therefore be estimated at half their number.

In the same way the expeditions undertaken by Captain Baumstark, who commanded the three companies at Tanga, led to fighting in the frontier districts between Jassini and Mombasa. An equally important object of all these enterprises was to secure the most indispensable information about this theatre of operations, as it had not been reconnoitred in time of peace, and the conditions as to water-supply and cultivation were unknown to us. In this manner we gradually obtained a clear idea of the country and its inhabitants. Along the coast the English frontier district was well settled and highly cultivated. Further inland it is a dry desert covered with thorn scrub and partly with thick bush.

Out of the desert rise a number of mountain ranges, which often attain the character of steep masses of rock. The troops were quartered in several fortified camps east of Kilima Njaro, but, owing to the difficulty of communication from Taveta, Headquarters were moved back to Moshi. Later, when the Director of the Field Postal Service arrived, and I asked him what he thought of the line between Moshi and Taveta, he could only describe it as "pretty." The insulators were made from knocked off bottle-necks, fastened to poles or branches of trees, the wire had been taken from the fences of the plantations. But the breakdowns really were so frequent that the great volume of reports and information in connection with the working of Headquarters could not have been carried on this line for a prolonged period.

Since the outbreak of war our communication with the outside world had been to all intents and purposes cut off; at first, indeed, we did pick up wireless messages from Kamina (in Togo), and then occasionally, under favourable weather conditions, from Nauen (Germany); but otherwise we had to depend for fresh news on picking up enemy wireless messages, or on obtaining possession of enemy mails or other papers.

The November Actions at Tanga

Captured English newspapers stated that it would be particularly painful to Germany to lose her beloved colonies, its "little chicks," and that German East Africa was the most valuable mouthful. Captured mails spoke of an impending attack by an Indian expeditionary force of 10,000 men, and, as I had from general considerations always expected a hostile attack on a large scale in the neighbourhood of Tanga, I went there at the end of October, drove all over the country in a car I had brought with me, and discussed the matter on the spot with Captain Adler, commanding the 17th Company, and with District Commissioner Auracher.

I was pleased to find that the latter was of my opinion that, in the event of Tanga being seriously threatened, the prime necessity would be unity of action, and I assured him that I would, of course, undertake the responsibility for any consequences that might ensue. This was particularly important for the reason that, according to the Governor's instructions, a bombardment of Tanga was to be avoided under all circumstances. Opinions as to what should be done or left undone in any given case might therefore differ very widely.

On the 2nd November, a few days after my return to New Moshi, a wire from Tanga informed me that fourteen hostile transports and two cruisers had appeared off the place. They demanded unconditional surrender of the town; the negotiations were protracted, as District Commissioner Auracher, who had gone on board, pointed out that he must obtain special instructions, and prevented the threatened bombardment by remarking that Tanga was an open and undefended place. Captain Baumstark, who was with two companies in the frontier district north of Tanga, was at once moved off towards Tanga. Similarly the two companies of Europeans and the *Askari* companies were moved by forced marches from near Taveta and Kilima Njaro to New Moshi. Two lorries which were employed on supply work between New Moshi and Taveta rendered valuable service in this move.

My intention to collect all available troops as rapidly as possible, to meet the obviously impending landing at Tanga, could only be executed, in spite of the long marches expected of the troops, if the Northern Railway exerted its capacity to the utmost limit, and this, with only eight locomotives, was asking a great deal. The railway is a narrow gauge line of 190 miles, on which, in a fully-loaded train of 24 to 32 axles, only one company could be carried with complete baggage, or two companies without either baggage or carriers. That the transport of the troops could be carried out at all is entirely due to the willingness of all those connected with it—I specially mention Railway Commissary Kröber, who had been called up to the Force as a 2nd Lieutenant, and the traffic director Kühlwein—who at Tanga conducted the trains up on to the actual battlefield under fire.

As early as the 2nd November the troops actually at New Moshi, one and a half companies, were pushed off by train, followed on the morning of the 3rd by Headquarters and another company. Three other companies followed later. Similarly, all the smaller detachments employed on railway protection duty were moved to Tanga. The spirit of the departing troops was magnificent, but this may have been due, not so much to the fact that the *Askari* clearly understood the gravity of the situation, as that for him a trip in a railway train is at all times a great delight.

Headquarters reached Korogwe in the evening of the 3rd November. I went to the hospital that had been established there and talked to the wounded who had come in from the action at Tanga on the 3rd. One of them, Lieutenant Merensky, of the *Landwehr*, reported to me that on the 2nd November, outpost and patrol encounters had taken place near Ras–Kasone, and that on the 3rd the enemy, apparently several thousand strong, who had landed at Ras–Kasone, had attacked the Company east of Tanga. The latter, reinforced by the Europeans and Police *Askari* from Tanga under Lieutenant Auracher, had withstood the attack until the first one and a half companies coming from New Moshi joined in, rushing at once to attack the left flank of the enemy and driving him back.

Lieutenant Merensky had the impression that the enemy was completely defeated, and that the attack was unlikely to be repeated. The telegrams coming in piecemeal during the railway journey had not afforded me a clear idea of the situation, when at 3 a.m. on the 4th November, Headquarters left the railway four miles west of Tanga, where we met Captain Baumstark. He had formed a different estimate of the situation, and believed that, owing to the great superiority of the enemy, Tanga could not be held against another attack. He had, therefore, on the evening of the 3rd November, collected his own two companies coming from the north, and the troops who had that day been in action at Tanga, at a point four miles west of the town, leaving patrols only in the place itself.

Whether Tanga was held by the enemy or not was not certain. Strong officers' patrols were at once pushed forward beyond Tanga towards Ras-Kasone. Luckily Headquarters had brought a few bicycles, and so, in order to satisfy myself quickly by personal observation, I was able to go off at once with Captain von Hammerstein and Volunteer Dr. Dessel to the railway station at Tanga, where I found an advanced post of the 6th Field Company. They, however, could give no accurate information about the enemy, and so I rode on through the empty streets of the town. It was completely deserted, and the white houses of the Europeans reflected the brilliant rays of the moon into the streets which we traversed.

So we reached the harbour at the further edge of the town. Tanga was therefore clear of the enemy. A quarter of a mile out lay the transports, a blaze of lights, and full of noise : there was no doubt that the landing was about to commence at once. I much regretted that our artillery—we had two guns of 1873 pattern—was not yet up. Here, in the brilliant moonlight, at such close range, their effect would have been annihilating, the hostile cruisers notwithstanding.

We then rode on towards Ras-Kasone, left our bicycles in the German Government Hospital, and went on foot to the beach, close to which, right in front of us, lay an English cruiser. On the way back, at the hospital, we were challenged, apparently by an Indian sentry—we did not understand the language—but saw nothing. We got on our cycles again and rode back. Day began to break, and on our left we heard the first shots. This was the officers' patrol under 2nd Lieutenant Bergmann, of the 6th Field Company, who had met hostile patrols west of Ras-Kasone.

One of my cyclists now brought Captain Baumstark the order to advance at once with all the troops to Tanga Station. For the manner in which I proposed to fight the action, which was now to be expected with certainty, the nature of the country was one of the

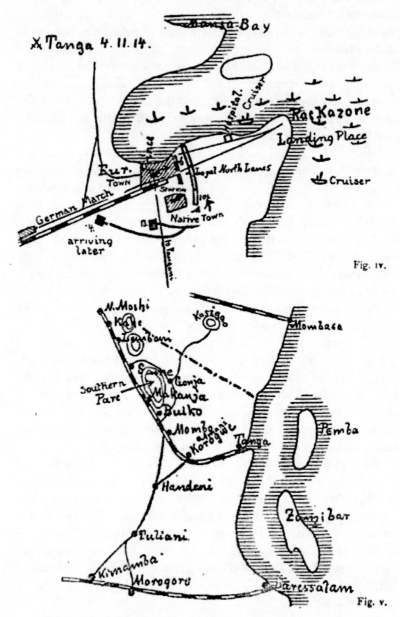

FIG. IV. BATTLE OF TANGA. FIG. V. THE NORTHERN RAILWAY.

decisive factors. In the north, the houses of the European
harbour provided cover from view, and therefore also from
the cruisers close by. The town was surrounded by contin
nut and rubber plantations, which extended almost to
and in which, besides the native town, a few native patch
tion were scattered about. Undergrowth occurred along a few points
and the ground was absolutely flat. It was probable that the enemy,
whether he landed at Ras-Kasone only, or simultaneously at several
points, such as Mwambani, for instance, would press upon our south,
or right, wing. Here, to the south of Tanga, the ground afforded us also
the prospect of greater power of manoeuvre. I decided to meet the
attack, which I expected with certainty, on the eastern edge of Tanga,
and to *echelon* strong reserves behind our right wing for a counter-
attack against the enemy's flank.

In allotting the various duties it was necessary to consider the peculiarities of the different units. At that time each company had different
characteristics, according to its composition and its state of training.
The good 6th Field Company, which had in time of peace received a
careful training at Ujiji with both rifle and machine-gun, was ordered
to hold the eastern edge of Tanga on a broad front. On its right rear,
outside Tanga, was *echeloned* Baumstark's battalion, consisting of the
16th and 17th Companies, formed from the police, and several small
units amalgamated into one company. To the right rear again, on the
telegraph-road Tanga-Pangani, I kept three good companies at my
own disposal, the 7th and 8th Rifle Companies, with three machine-
guns, composed of Europeans, and the 13th Field Company with its
four machine-guns.

Headquarters remained for the present on the Tanga-Pangani road
and connected up to the telegraph line there. The 4th and 9th Field
Companies and the two field guns (Captain Bering's Battery) were
still on the way, and the time of their arrival was uncertain. So the
situation remained essentially until the afternoon. In the hot sun of
the coast area we suffered not a little from thirst, but quenched it with
the milk of the young cocoanuts. There were other drinks as well in
Tanga at that time; we still had wine and soda-water. Master-butcher
Grabow even brought the troops hot sausages.

The proceedings on board the hostile ships were kept under constant close observation. We saw every boat that left them, and its load.
I estimated the total troops landed up to midday at 6,000. But even
on this too low estimate I had to ask myself whether I dared risk a

·cisive engagement with my thousand rifles. For various reasons I decided that I would do so. It was too important to prevent the enemy from gaining a firm footing in Tanga. Otherwise we should abandon to him the best base for operations against the Northern territories; in his advance the Northern Railway would afford him an admirable line of communication, and he would be enabled continually to surprise us by bringing up and pushing forward fresh troops and stores. Then it was certain that we would be unable to hold the Northern Railway any longer and that we would be obliged to abandon our hitherto so successful method of warfare. Against these all-important practical reasons, limited considerations such as the Governor's order to avoid a bombardment of Tanga under all circumstances could not prevail.

A few circumstances there were that favoured us. For one thing, from personal experience in East Asia, I knew the clumsiness with which English troops were moved and led in battle, and it was certain that in the very close and completely unknown country in which the enemy would find himself directly he landed, these difficulties would grow to infinity. The slightest disorder was bound to have far-reaching consequences. With my troops, of whom the Europeans were well acquainted with the country round Tanga, while the *Askari* were at home in the bush, I had a reasonable prospect of taking advantage of the enemy's weak points by skilful and rapid manoeuvre.

On the other hand, if the affair miscarried, it would be a bad business. Already my method of waging active war had met with disapproval. If on top of that we were to suffer a severe defeat the confidence of the troops would probably be gone, and it was certain that my superiors would place insuperable difficulties in the way of my exercising command. My decision was not easy, and as if the military situation alone did not render it difficult enough, it was made unnecessarily harder by the fact that the regulations did not allow sufficient freedom to the responsible commander. But there was nothing for it : to gain all we must risk all.

The same morning I personally ordered Captain von Prince to move into Tanga with his two companies of Europeans, so that, in case of an attack on the *Askari* Company holding the eastern edge of the place, he could intervene rapidly without orders. I had already begun to doubt whether the enemy would attack at all on the 4th November, when at 3 p.m. an *Askari* reported to me in his simple, smart way: "*Adui tayari.*" (The enemy is ready.) Those two short words I shall

44

never forget. The next moment the rifle fire opened along the whole front, and one could only judge of the rapid development and the ebb and flow of the action from the direction of the firing. One heard the fire draw in from the eastern edge of the town to the middle: so the 6th Company had been driven back at this point.

The enemy, with odds twenty to one in his favour, had penetrated close up to the station and into the town. Captain von Prince had immediately rushed up his two companies of Europeans and at once prevailed upon the brave *Askari* to stand and then to advance once more. The British North Lancashire Regiment, consisting only of long-service Europeans, 800 strong, was driven back with heavy losses, and the houses captured by the Indian Brigade (Kashmir Rifles), who were advancing between that regiment and the beach, were retaken in stubborn street-fighting. But on the south side of Tanga Captain Baumstark had also brought his companies into action on the front, and after about one hour's fighting I observed the *Askari* at this point retiring through the palmtrees to the Tanga-Pangani road. The European members of Headquarters at once ran there and stopped them.

To this day I can see the fiery and determined Captain von Hammerstein, full of fury, throwing an empty bottle at the head of a retreating *Askari*. After all, they were for the most part young companies, only just formed, who were fighting at this point, and they had been staggered by the intensity of the enemy's fire. But when we Europeans got in front of them and laughed at them they quickly recovered themselves and saw that every bullet did not hit. But on the whole the pressure on our front was so strong that I thought I could not delay the decision any longer and must start my counter-stroke. For this I had now but one company available, but it was the good 13th Field Company. The 4th Company, whose arrival I was most anxiously awaiting every minute, had not yet arrived.

The course of the action up till now had shown that the enemy's front, of which the flank was unprotected, did not reach further south than the right wing of our own. Here, therefore, the counter-stroke must prove annihilating, and no witness will forget the moment when the machine-guns of the 13th Company opened a continuous fire at this point and completely reversed the situation. The whole front jumped up and dashed forward with enthusiastic cheers. In the meantime the 4th Company had arrived; although, in consequence of a misunderstanding, it did not prolong the outer flank of the 13th, but pushed in between the latter and our front, still it did take an effective part in the battle before dark.

In wild disorder the enemy fled in dense masses, and our machine-guns, converging on them from front and flanks, mowed down whole companies to the last man. Several *Askari* came in beaming with delight with several captured English rifles on their backs and an Indian prisoner in each hand. The handcuffs, however, which we found in their possession for use with German prisoners, were not used on them by any of us.

At this time, in the dense forest, all units, and in many in stances friend and foe, were mixed up together, everybody was shouting at once in all sorts of languages, darkness was rapidly setting in; it is only necessary to conjure up this scene in imagination in order to understand how it was that the pursuit which I set in motion failed completely. I had been stationed on the right wing, and had quickly despatched such units as were within reach at the moment to push with energy towards Ras-Kasone. Then I had gone to the left wing. There I found hardly any of our people at all; it was not till some time afterwards, in the night, that I heard the sound of the nailed boots of a party of *Askari*. I was glad at last to have a force in hand, but was somewhat disappointed to find it was a detachment of the right wing, under 2nd Lieutenant Langen, who had missed the way to Ras-Kasone and had thus got on to our left wing.

But even these difficulties were not all. In some inexplicable way the troops imagined a Headquarter order had been issued that they were to return to their old camp west of Tanga. Only during the course of the night, at Tanga Railway Station, did it become clear to me that nearly all the companies had marched off for that destination. Of course they were ordered to return at once. But unfortunately this caused so much delay that it was impossible to bring Hering's Battery, which had arrived later, into action by moonlight against the ships.

The troops, whose great exhaustion was quite comprehensible, did not get back to Tanga until the morning of the 5th November, and occupied essentially the same position as the day before. It was not now advisable to advance with all our forces against the enemy, who was re-embarking at Ras-Kasone, as the country there was entirely open, and commanded by the cruisers lying in its immediate vicinity. All the same, the strong patrols and individual companies, who advanced towards Ras-Kasone, in order to harass the enemy, succeeded in surprising him by machine-gun fire directed on various detachments, a few boats, and even the decks of the cruiser lying close to the hospital. During the day, the impression that the enemy had suffered a tremendous defeat grew stronger and stronger.

It is true, the full extent of his losses did not become known to us all at once; but the many places where hundreds and hundreds of dead were piled up in heaps, and the smell of putrefaction which the tropical sun brought out all over the district, gave us some indication. Very cautiously we estimated the killed at about 800, but I believe this number to be far too low. A senior English officer, who had accurate knowledge of the details, told me later, on the occasion of an action in which he stated the English casualties to have been 1,500, that the losses at Tanga had been considerably greater. I now think that even 2,000 is too low an estimate. Even greater was the enemy's loss in *moral*. He almost began to believe in spirits and spooks; years afterwards I was asked by English officers whether we had used trained bees at Tanga but I may now perhaps betray the fact that at the decisive moment all the machine-guns of one of our companies were put out of action by these same "trained bees," so that we suffered from this new "training" quite as much as the English.

The enemy felt himself completely defeated, and he was. His troops had fled in wild confusion and thrown themselves head over heels into the lighters. The possibility of renewing the attack was not even considered. From prisoners' statements and captured official English documents it was ascertained that the whole Anglo-Indian Expeditionary Force of 8,000 men had been thus decisively beaten by our force of little more than 1,000 men. Not till the evening did we realize the magnitude of this victory, when an English officer, Captain Meinertshagen, came under a flag of truce to negotiate with Captain von Hammerstein, my representative, for the handing over of the wounded. Captain von Hammerstein proceeded to the hospital, which was full of severely wounded English officers, and in my name agreed to their being removed by the English on giving their word of honour not to fight against us again in this war.

The booty in arms enabled us to re-arm more than three companies with modern weapons, for which the sixteen machine-guns were particularly welcome. The moral of the force and its confidence in its leaders had enormously increased, and at one blow I was delivered from a great part of the difficulties which so greatly impeded the conduct of operations. The continuous fire of the ships' guns, which the closeness of the country had rendered ineffective, had lost its terrors for our brave blacks. The quantity of stores captured was also considerable; besides 600,000 rounds of small-arm ammunition the enemy had left behind the whole of his telephone gear and such quantities of clothing and equipment that we were able to meet all our requirements, especially in warm coats and blankets, for at least a year.

Our own losses, painful though they were, were numerically insignificant. About fifteen (?) Europeans, among them the splendid Captain von Prince, and fifty-four (?) *Askari* and machine-gun carriers, had fallen. The Europeans were buried in a worthy warriors' grave in the shade of a fine *Buyu* tree, where a simple memorial tablet is inscribed with their names. The work of clearing up the battlefield and burying the dead meant several days of most strenuous work for the whole force, as the streets were literally strewn with dead and badly wounded. In unknown tongues they begged for help which, with the best will in the world, could not always be accorded at once.

At our main dressing station, in Tanga itself, our male and female nursing personnel had conscientiously cared for friend and foe even under the fire of the heavy guns of the ships. As recently as the evening of the 4th November I had been to see the wounded. I little thought that Lieutenant Schottstaedt, who was sitting there on a chair with a severe wound in the chest, had but a few minutes to live. The English Lieutenant Cook, of the 101st Indian Grenadiers, lay there with a bad gunshot wound in the leg. This bright young officer, who had fallen into our hands in the hottest part of the fight on the Indian left wing, maintained his cheerfulness in spite of his wound. With the bulk of the other wounded, he was treated for nine months in the Field Hospital at Korogwe by our best surgeon, *Stabsarzt* Dr. Müller. He was already walking about once more, when an unfortunate fall on the stairs caused his death.

The fighting at Tanga was the first occasion on which heavy demands were made on our arrangements for the care of the wounded. For this purpose, hospitals had been established at Korogwe and at various other points on the Northern Railway, to which the sick could be taken by rail without being transferred from one method of transport to another. No special hospital arrangements of a permanent nature had been made for transport, but we never had any difficulty in improvising what was necessary.

In spite of their undoubted defeat at Tanga it was probable that British determination would not accept this decision as final. Even after his defeat the enemy was still several times as strong as we were, and would not improbably attempt another landing elsewhere. But a cycle ride on the 6th November to Mansa Bay, in the North, convinced me that the hostile ships had run in there only for the purpose of attending to their wounded and burying their dead and had no intention of landing. And the ships actually did steam off towards Zanzibar soon after. At that time it was interesting to me to visit our Government Hospital near Ras-Kasone, which had in the meantime been evacuated by the English wounded released on parole.

Among others I saw here two German officers who had been wounded at Tanga on the 3rd November, and others who had been wounded in an earlier action; from the hospital they had been able to observe events behind the English front on the 4th November, the day when the principal fighting took place. With the greatest excitement they had watched the landing at Ras-Kasone and the advance on Tanga; in the afternoon they had heard the opening of our decisive machine-gun fire and the bombardment by the ships' guns, and had then witnessed the wild flight of the enemy close by the hospital. The numerous shells that had fallen near the hospital had fortunately done no damage.

Quite early on the 5th November they had suddenly heard guns firing again, this time from the direction of Tanga; they realized that they must be German guns. They were in fact our two 1873 pattern field-guns, which, though too late to deal with the English transports by moonlight, had at least managed to secure a few hits after daybreak. A prolonged fire for effect was now unfortunately impossible, as the smoke disclosed the positions of the guns at once and drew the fire of the ships.

In the meantime it had become evident that the attack at Tanga was not an isolated enterprise, but had been intended to form part of a simultaneous operation on a large scale. Suddenly in the morning mist, on the 3rd November, English troops appeared north-west of Kilima Njaro, at Longido Mountain, which was held by Captain Kraut with three Companies of *Askari* and a Mounted Company of Europeans. Just as orders reached Longido Mountain by heliograph directing Captain Kraut to move off to Moshi, the first shell arrived. The enemy, about 1,000 strong, had ascended the great mountain, which lies by itself in the open plain, at several points, being guided by Masai, who called out to the outposts: "We belong to Captain Kraut's men."

But our three Field Companies deployed rapidly and succeeded in working round the enemy detachment in the rocky ground and quickly repelled them. A hostile detachment of mounted Europeans who became visible in the plain at the foot of the mountain, and apparently intended to ascend it from the south, or to act against our communications, was fired upon with effect and quickly driven off.

Probably in connection with these events on the Northern Railway, hostile enterprises took place on Lake Victoria. At the end of October numerous Waganda warriors had penetrated from the North into the Bukoba district. To meet this menace, a force of 570 rifles, 4 machine-guns, and 2 guns left Muanza on the 31st October on board the small steamer *Muanza*, with 2 tugs and 10 *dhows* (boats). Soon after the landing these transports were attacked by English steamers, but got back to Muanza without damage. An English attempt to land at Kayense, north of Muanza, broke down under the fire of our detachment posted there.

Thus, at the beginning of November we were confronted with a concentric attack on our Colony, planned on a large scale. Its failure made everyone expect that we would be able to hold our own as long as the home country could do so. But such scanty information as we could get from there gave us confidence. At the time of the action at Tanga we had, indeed, not heard the name of Hindenburg; but on the other hand we knew nothing of our reverse on the Marne, and were still buoyed up by the impression created by our victorious invasion of France.

CHAPTER 5

Awaiting Further Events

The danger threatening the Kilima Njaro country appeared to me to be by itself a sufficient reason for rapidly moving the troops back to the vicinity of New Moshi after the decisive success of Tanga, which in any event could not be further exploited. The joy of the Northern settlers, who, it should be noted, had furnished the bulk of the Europeans who fought at Tanga, was indescribable. The first train, which carried the European Company, returned to New Moshi bedecked with flowers. I myself had still enough to do at Tanga, and did not follow the troops to New Moshi for several days, where Headquarters was reopened. Shortage of personnel prevented us from having separate people for each duty.

Officers of Headquarters had sometimes in an emergency to act as riflemen or cyclists, the *Intendant* occasionally did duty as an orderly, the clerk went into action with a rifle and acted as orderly in battle. The work was greatly facilitated by the fact that the railway station, constructed on European lines, afforded us accommodation which, in spite of being rather small, enabled us to settle most matters affecting the Staff only by word of mouth. We had good telephone and telegraph installations, and were situated centrally as the telephone and road systems, which we had either made or perfected, and which led out in both directions towards Tanga, Taveta, East Kilima Njaro, West Kilima Njaro and Longido, as well as to Arusha. Sometimes the work would go on for a week at a time almost as in peace, although the volume of work to be dealt with was greater. But although hardly anybody at Headquarters was either trained or prepared for his functions, harmonious and successful co-operation was secured. It was based upon the best spirit, devotion to the cause, and the support of good comradeship.

I myself went by car—for we had made a motor-road right up to Longido Mountain—to the Engare-Nairobi (cold river), a small stream rising on the northern slopes of Kilima Njaro, and flowing between it and Longido through the prairie in a north-westerly direction. In this country a number of Boer families were settled on farms. Kraut's detachment had moved their camp there, as their supplies, if they had remained on Longido Mountain, would have had to make a two-days' march across the prairie, where they could not be protected, and were, therefore, too uncertain. I satisfied myself that there was at this time no opportunity for any enterprises north of Kilima Njaro, and returned to New Moshi.

The distance from New Moshi, where we collected a large proportion of the supplies coming from Usambara and the country further south by rail to Taveta, is thirty miles. Although we had available only a few motors, namely, three cars and three lorries all told, they were in the circumstances a considerable help. The road being well made, the three-ton lorries could do the trip out and back in one day in dry weather. As carriers took at least four days for the same journey a calculation showed that one lorry could do the work of six hundred carriers, who required subsistence in addition. The principle, later maintained by the English, of replacing carriers and pack-animals by mechanical transport, is further supported by the fact that men and animals suffered severely from tropical diseases, whereas mosquitoes are powerless against automobiles.

We, however, could not derive full benefit from this advantage, since we had so few motors. Even in this period, which, as far as transport was concerned, was one of quiet and regularity, we had constantly to fall back upon carriers. To this day I remember the joy of the *Intendant* when a column of six hundred Wassukuma carriers arrived at New Moshi from about Muanza; they brought rice, which was urgently needed, from Lake Victoria, *via* Kondoa-Irangi to Kilima Njaro. If one remembers that this march required at least thirty days, that the carrier needs one kg. (two lbs.) of food a day, and that his maximum load is twenty-five kg. (fifty-five lbs.), it is clear that these marches have to be arranged with great care and directed through well populated and fertile districts if this method of transport is to be of any value.

If, in spite of these disadvantages, carrier transport had to be resorted to on a large scale, it only shows up the supply-difficulties we had to contend with. The *Intendant*, Captain Feilke, was, however, a past master in handling the men and looking after them. The carriers felt that they were well cared for, and the word "*Kommando*," which some of them took as a personal name, became quite common. I myself was able, by means of the motors, to carry out many reconnaissances and inspections of the troops. I could reach Taveta, to which place some of the troops from Tanga returned, in two hours from New Moshi; this would otherwise have taken four days; later on I drove in one day from New Moshi to the Engare-Nairobi, round the west side of the whole of Meru Mountain, and back to New Moshi, a journey which could hardly have been accomplished with carriers in less than ten days.

The success at Tanga called forth and revived the determination to resist all over the Colony.

At Morogoro, on the 26th November, the Inspector of Lines of Communication, Major-General Wahle, succeeded in obtaining the Governor's consent to the defence of Dar-es-Salaam in case of attack. As luck would have it, this consent was given just in time. On the 28th, two men-of-war, a transport and a tug, appeared off Dar-es-Salaam, and demanded to inspect our ships lying in the harbour. Among others, there was the *Tabora*, of the German East African Line, which had been converted into a hospital-ship. As the English had on a previous occasion declared that they did not consider themselves bound by any agreement about Dar-es-Salaam, fresh negotiations would have been necessary every tune we wanted to escape a threatened bombardment. Thus an endless screw was created.

I now wired that the entry into the harbour of a *pinnace*, demanded by the English, was to be resisted by force of arms. Unfortunately, however, it had been conceded by the German civil authority, against my opinion, and the Senior Officer present at Dar-es-Salaam felt himself bound. The English, however, came in, not with the one *pinnace* which had been agreed to, but with several small vessels, and then proceeded to carry out demolitions on board the *Tabora*, and even took some of her crew prisoners. This made it only too evident, even to those who had hitherto been doubtful, how misplaced our previous compliance had been.

Captain von Kornatzky was just in time to open effective machine-gun fire on the small English vessels as they passed out by the narrow English harbour entrance. Unfortunately, on this occasion, one of the German prisoners was also hit. The necessary defensive measures had simply not been adopted in time. This is a small example of the dangers and disadvantages that arise when, in time of war, the military commander is constantly interfered with in his decisions, and in the execution of operations which are in the nature of things inevitable.

And, after all, the subsequent bombardment of Dar-es-Salaam did no harm worth mentioning, for the damage done to a few houses can hardly be considered as serious.

During the time of comparatively sedentary warfare at New Moshi the material side of life was also pleasant. The Europeans, who mostly belonged to the settler community of the northern territories, provided most of their subsistence themselves; abundant supplies of rice, wheat-flour, bananas, pineapples, European fruit, coffee and potatoes, came in from the plantations. Sugar was provided by the numerous factories, and our principal supply of salt came from the Gottorp salt works, on the Central Railway, between Tabora and Lake Tanganyika. Many plantations devoted themselves entirely to supplying the troops, and, owing to the abundant labour available this change in production caused no difficulties. But the transport system had also to work at high pressure. The great road leading from Kimamba to Mombo and Korogwe, on the Northern Railway, was continuously improved, so as to carry the transport of the products from the area of the Tanganyika Railway and further South, to the North.

On this line alone at least eight thousand carriers were continuously employed. It soon proved to be practical not to make the carriers do the whole distance of a hundred and ninety miles, but to distribute them on different stages. This made it possible to quarter them permanently and to look after their health. Experts in hygiene travelled up and down the road, and did what was humanly possible for the health of the carriers, especially against dysentery and typhoid. In this manner we established along this very frequented route permanent carrier-camps a day's march apart, in which the men were accommodated at first in extemporized huts, which were later properly completed. Camp discipline was strictly regulated.

In order to provide also for the many Europeans passing through, small houses with concrete floors were put up; and individuals were enabled to subsist on the supplies held on the line of communication, without having to burden themselves with provisions to last for a prolonged period, as is customary on journeys in Africa. The work on this line of supply was the object of constant attention. Both Europeans and natives had still to learn how to ensure the co-operation of such masses of men, and to understand the importance of order and discipline in the working of the transport for the health of all concerned.

At New Moshi Station both telephone and telegraph were working day and night. Where the whole organization had to be improvised friction was not altogether unavoidable. All the members of Headquarters were extraordinarily hard-worked. But we did have bright intervals during the strenuous work. The abundance of creature comforts enjoyed by the Europeans in the North was shared by us at Headquarters. We were literally spoilt by the number of gifts sent us by private individuals. If one of us travelled on the Northern Railway, on which in time of peace it was difficult to obtain a little food for love or money, he was now cared for by someone at almost every station.

I remember when Lieut. Freiherr von Schroetter returned to New Moshi, very famished, after carrying out some very exhausting patrols in the country north of Erok Mountain. After having, according to normal ideas, been thoroughly well fed from seven o'clock till eleven, he shyly asked if he might have some supper. The next morning he started on fourteen days' leave to his plantation in Usambara, in order to recuperate and attend to his business. After breakfast we gave him coffee, bread, butter and meat, to take with him in the train, and had warned the various railway stations to look after this completely famished patroller.

So, after half an hour, the station guard at Kahe offered him another breakfast, at Lembeni the charming wife of the Station Commandant had baked him a cake, and at Lame he was looked after by the commander of the local Recruit Depot, Sergt.-Major Reinhardt. At Makanya the guard, Planter Baroy, who belonged to the country, brought him home-made chocolate and bullocks' hearts—a fruit the size of a melon—at Buiko the hospitable traffic manager of the Northern Railway, Kuehlwein, who had so often entertained us in passing through, had prepared him a delicate meal. At Mombo, where the supplies from the Usambara Mountains were collected, and where we had established most of our work-shops, our *protégé* was met by Warrant Officer Meyer, of the Navy, with a sustaining supper. But then we got a telegram:

Please do not order any more, I can't eat any more.

Although this continuous feeding shows a spirit of sympathetic chaff at the expense of the starving subaltern, it also proves, better than any theoretical dissertations, how intimately all classes of the population of the northern districts worked in with the troops, and how they tried to anticipate our every wish. This co-operation continued as long as the troops remained in the North.

Whenever duty gave us a chance we arranged for change and re-cuperation. On Sundays we often went out together near New Moshi for a cheery day's shooting. Both carriers and *Askari* soon picked up their business as beaters, and drove the game towards us in exemplary order, with loud shouts of *"Huyu, huyu."* "There he is." For variety of game the country provided more than one would be likely to find anywhere in Europe: hare, various dwarf antelopes, guinea-fowl several relatives of the partridge, duck, bush-buck, water-buck lynx, several kinds of wild boar, small kudu, jackal and many other kinds of game abounded.

Once, I remember, to my astonishment, a lion silently appeared fifteen paces in front of me. Unfortunately I had my gun in my hand, and before I could put up my rifle, which was on my knees, he had as silently disappeared. In the teeming Kilima Njaro country, and even more east of Taveta, our shooting expeditions provided a welcome increase to our meat supply. But in the main this depended on the cattle which the Masai brought us from the Kilima Njaro and Meru country, but which also came from far away near Lake Victoria.

CHAPTER 6

Further Heavy Fighting in the North-East

By the time we kept Christmas in the Mission Church at New Moshi, and afterwards in our mess in the Railway Station, the military situation north of Tanga had become sufficiently acute to indicate that decisive events in this quarter were probable. During the last days of December, our patrols, who in that district were on British territory, had been gradually pushed back, and had concentrated south of Jassini, on German territory. The combined force amounted to two companies and a corps of some two hundred Arabs. The enemy had obviously been reinforced, and occupied the buildings of the German plantation of Jassini. It looked as though he intended to push gradually forward along the coast to Tanga, securing the occupied country by a system of block-houses.

In order to investigate matters on the spot, I travelled early in January with Capt. von Hammerstein to Tanga, and thence by car to Capt. Adler's camp at Mwurnoni, using the newly-completed coast road to the north, a distance of thirty-eight miles. Lieut. Bleeck, of the Reserve, whose numerous successful patrols in that country rendered him particularly suitable for the purpose, accompanied me on my reconnaissance, from which I learned that the country for miles round Jassini consisted principally of a cocoanut plantation belonging to the German East African Company, which was also planted with *sisal*, a species of *agave* with sharp thorns. This *sisal*, which formed a dense undergrowth among the palms, was in many places so interlaced that one could only force one's way through by enduring a quantity of very unpleasant pricks.

It is, of course, always difficult to make plans for an action in country so totally unknown to one without the aid of a map, and relying only on the reports of patrols. In this case we got over the difficulty as Lieut. Schaefer, of the Reserve, who had been called to the colours, had for years held the post of Assistant on this plantation, and could therefore furnish exact information. A tolerably accurate sketch was prepared, and the battle-names allotted to various localities were entered on it.

The general situation appeared to be that Jassini was an advanced post, and that the main body of the enemy was in fortified camps further north. It was to be assumed that an attack on the advanced post of Jassini would entice the main body to leave its camps and fight in the open (*sic!*). My plan was to take advantage of this possibility. In order to engage the enemy while hurrying from his places of assembly to the assistance of the advanced post, in favourable tactical conditions, I intended to place my troops in readiness on his probable lines of advance, in such a manner that he would have to run up against them.

In this closely-settled country supply presented no difficulty, and the necessary carriers could be provided by the numerous European plantations. So the companies ordered up by telegraph from New Moshi had only to be accompanied by their machine-gun and ammunition carriers, a considerable advantage in arranging for their railway journey. This was accomplished rapidly and without friction, thanks to the proved capacity of the Commandant of the Line, Lieutenant Kroeber, retired, of the *Landwehr,* and the understanding and consuming zeal with which the whole personnel of the railway bore the unavoidable strain without a murmur.

By the 16th January the companies from New Moshi had detrained a couple of miles west of Tanga, and at once marched off towards Jassini, as well as the troops from Tanga, for the immediate protection of which only one company was left behind. On the evening of the 17th January the force of nine companies, with two guns, was assembled at Totohown plantation, seven miles south of Jassini, and orders for the attack were issued for the following morning. Major Kepler, with two companies, was directed to attack the village of Jassini, working round by the right, and Captain Adler, with two more companies, had a similar task on the left.

To the north-west, on the road from Semanya, was posted the Arab corps. Captain Otto, with the 9th Company, advanced frontally by the main road on Jassini, followed immediately by Headquarters and the main body, consisting of the European Company, three *Askari*

Companies, and two guns. The marches were so arranged that the attacks on Jassini should take place simultaneously at daybreak, and that all columns should mutually support each other by pushing on with energy. Even before daybreak the first shots fell in the vicinity of Kepler's column, a few minutes later firing began in front of us with Otto's column, and then became general.

It was impossible in the endless dense palm forest to obtain an even approximate idea of what was really happening. We were, however, already so close up to the hostile position at Jassini, that the enemy seemed to be surprised, in spite of his excellent intelligence service. This supposition was afterwards, in part at least, confirmed. Of our rapid concentration south of Jassini, and our immediate attack with such strong forces, the enemy had actually had no idea.

Otto's column quickly drove back an entrenched post in its front, and Headquarters now made a circuit to the left through the forest, where first one, and then two more companies, were put in so as to outflank Jassini. What seemed curious was that in this move we came under a very well-aimed fire at short range, possibly no more than 200 yards; and it was not till much later that we learned that the enemy had not only a weak post in Jassini, but that four companies of Indians were also established there in a strongly constructed and excellently concealed fort. Suddenly Captain von Hammerstein, who was walking behind me, collapsed; he had been shot in the abdomen. Deeply as this affected me, at the moment I had to leave my badly-wounded comrade in the hands of the doctor. A few days later the death of this excellent officer tore a gap in the ranks of our Staff which was hard to fill.

The fighting had become very hot. Two companies, although their commanders, Lieuts. Gerlich and Spalding, had fallen had quickly captured the fortified buildings of Jassini by a brilliant charge, and had now established themselves close in front of the enemy's position. Soon the intervention of the enemy's main force made itself felt. From the direction of Wanga, in the north-east, strong hostile columns arrived and suddenly appeared close in front of our companies, lying close to the fortifications of Jassini. The enemy made three strong attacks at this point and was each time repulsed. Hostile columns also arrived from the north and north-west.

Against that from the west the Arab corps had done badly; the day before many of them had urgently demanded their discharge. Now, when they were to lie in ambush on the enemy's road of advance, the tension became too great for them. Instead of surprising the enemy by an annihilating fire, they fired blindly into the air and then bolted. But luckily these hostile columns then came on Captain Adler's two companies, and were repulsed with slaughter. Up till then the whole action had been in the nature of an energetic assault; even the last reserve, the European Company, had, at its urgent request, been sent into action. Towards noon the fighting had everywhere become stationary before the strong defences of the enemy. We had, as a matter of fact, no means of making a sufficient impression on them, and even our field-guns, which we placed in position at two hundred yards, produced no decisive effect.

The heat was insupportable, and, as at Tanga, everyone quenched his thirst with young cocoanuts. I myself went with Lieut. Bleeck to the right wing, to find out how things were going with Major Kepler's column. At that time I had not yet obtained a clear idea of the enemy's defences, and so, on the sands of a clear and open creek, which was then dry, we again came under a very well-aimed fire. From a distance of five hundred yards the bullets fell close to us, and the spurts of sand they threw up made correction easy. The sand was so deep and the heat so great that one could only run, or even walk quickly, for a few paces at a time. Most of the time we had to walk slowly across the open and bear the unpleasant fire as best we could. Fortunately it did no serious harm, although one bullet through my hat and another through my arm showed that it was well meant.

On the way back from the right wing our thirst and exhaustion were so great that several gentlemen, who were usually by no means on bad terms with each other, had a serious difference of opinion about a cocoanut, although it would not have been difficult to get more from the countless trees all round us.

Headquarters had now returned to the Totohown-Jassini road. Along this ran a light railway for the work of the plantation, the wagons of which were now continuously employed in taking wounded back to Totohown, where a hospital had been established in the European buildings. Ammunition—of which the *Askari* carried about 150 rounds—began to run short, and reports from the firing line that they could not hold on longer became more frequent. Slightly wounded who had been tied up and a mass of stragglers collected at Headquarters, whole platoons had completely lost themselves, or had for other reasons left the places assigned to them. All these men were collected and re-organized, and thus a fresh reserve was made available. The ammunition in the machine-gun belts was to a great extent expended, and fresh supplies came up from Totohown by the light railway.

The belt-filling machines were fixed to the palmtrees and kept incessantly at work. It was evident that we had already suffered considerable casualties. A few wished to break off the action, as there seemed no prospect of capturing the enemy's defences. But the thought of the unpleasant situation of the enemy, shut up in his works, without water, and having to carry on all the occupations of daily existence in a confined space, in a burning sun and under hostile fire, made it appear that if we only held on with determination we might yet achieve success.

The afternoon and night passed in incessant fighting; as is always the case in such critical situations, all sorts of rumours arose. It was said that the garrison of the enemy's works consisted of South African Europeans, who were excellent marksmen; some people even declared they had understood their speech perfectly. It was indeed still very difficult to form a clear idea. My orderly, Ombasha (Lance-Corporal) Rayabu, at once volunteered to make a close reconnaissance, crawled close up to the enemy's line, and was killed there. The native, who is at all times easily excitable, was doubly so in this critical situation at night, and I frequently had to take the men severely to task for firing blindly into the air.

Early on the 19th January the fire broke out again with the greatest intensity. The enemy, who was surrounded on all sides, made a sortie, which failed, and soon after hoisted the white flag. Four Indian companies, with European officers and N.C.O.'s, fell into our hands. We all remarked the warlike pride with which our *Askari* regarded the enemy; I never thought our black fellows could look so distinguished.

Both friend and foe had been in an unpleasant situation, and were near the end of their nervous strength. That is usually the case with any soldier who takes his duty seriously. But the *Askari* now learned that one must overcome one's own feelings in order to obtain the superior moral force necessary for victory.

I estimated the enemy's casualties at 700 at least; the captured documents gave a clear indication of his strength, which was more than double our own. According to them, General Tighe, commanding the troops in British East Africa, who had landed a short time before at Wanga, had more than twenty companies assembled at and near Jassini, most of whom had come by march route along the coast from the direction of Mombasa. They were to push forward towards Tanga.

With the aid of the mechanical transport and the *rickshaws* which worked between the Field Hospital at Totohown and Tanga, the wounded were moved from Jassini to the hospitals on the Northern Railway quite easily in a few days. These rickshaws, small spring-carts (like dog-carts), drawn by one man, which take the place of cabs at Tanga, had been requisitioned for carrying wounded by the Senior Medical Officer. The enemy had withdrawn into his fortified camps north of the frontier, and a fresh attack on them did not seem to me very promising. We immediately commenced patrol operations, as a support to which we left a detachment of a few companies at Jassini; the bulk of the troops was moved off again to the Kilima Njaro country.

On the march to the entraining station on the Northern Railway the troops passed through Amboni Plantation. There the inhabitants of Tanga had voluntarily provided food and refreshments; and after the tremendous exertions entailed by the expedition to Jassini, with its continuous forced marches, the exhausting heat, and the uninterrupted fighting by day and night, the sulphur-laden Sigi stream was soon alive with white and black bathers. All our toil was forgotten, and our spirits rose to the highest pitch on receiving at this very moment, after a rather long interval, another wireless message from home. It indicated that news of the fighting at Tanga had probably just reached Germany, and contained His Majesty's appreciation of the success we had gained there.

CHAPTER 7

Guerilla Warfare and
Further Preparations

Documents which we captured later proved by figures that the enemy moved troops from Lake Victoria towards Kilima Njaro. So the battle actually did relieve other, far distant theatres. This observation bore out the original contention that the best protection of the whole territory consisted in taking a firm hold of the enemy at one point. Whether the remainder of the Colony was also locally protected with energy was not as important. All the same, I was greatly rejoiced when in February, 1915, the Governor was persuaded to issue the order that the coast towns were to be defended if threatened by the enemy. The successes obtained hitherto had demonstrated that this local defence was not hopeless, even against the fire of ships' guns.

Although the attack carried out at Jassini with nine companies had been completely successful, it showed that such heavy losses as we also had suffered could only be borne in exceptional cases. We had to economize our forces in order to last out a long war. Of the regular officers, Major Kepler, Lieuts. Spalding and Gerlich, Second-Lieuts. Kaufmann and Erdmann were killed; Captain von Hammerstein had died of his wound. The loss of these professional soldiers—about one seventh of the regular officers present—could not be replaced.

The expenditure of 200,000 rounds also proved that with the means at my disposal I could at the most fight three more actions of this nature. The need to strike great blows only quite exceptionally, and to restrict myself principally to guerrilla warfare, was evidently imperative.

The guiding principle of constantly operating against the Uganda Railway could, however, be resumed, as here it was in any case impossible to act with larger forces. For it was necessary to make marches of several days' duration through the great, waterless and thinly populated desert, which provided little sustenance beyond occasional game. Not only food, but water had to be carried. This alone limited the size of the force to be employed. Such expeditions through districts providing neither water nor food require a degree of experience on the part of the troops which could not possibly exist at that stage of the war. A company even was too large a force to send across this desert, and if, after several days of marching, it really had reached some point on the railway, it would have had to come back again, because it could not be supplied. However, these conditions improved as the troops became better trained, and as our knowledge of the country, which was at first mainly *terra incognita*, increased.

So there was nothing for it but to seek to attain our object by means of small detachments, or patrols. To these patrols we afterwards attached the greatest importance. Starting from the Engare-Nairobi, small detachments of eight to ten men, Europeans and *Askaris*, rode round the rear of the enemy's camps, which had been pushed up as far as the Longido, and attacked their communications. They made use of telephones we had captured at Tanga, tapping in on the English telephone-lines; then they waited for large or small hostile detachments or columns of ox-wagons to pass. From their ambush they opened fire on the enemy at thirty yards' range, captured prisoners and booty, and then disappeared again in the boundless desert. Thus, at that time, we captured rifles, ammunition, and war material of all kinds. One of these patrols had observed near Erok Mountain that the enemy sent his riding-horses to water at a certain time.

Ten of our horsemen at once started out, and, after a two days' ride through the desert, camped close to the enemy. Six men went back with the horses; the four others each took a saddle, and crept at a distance of a few paces past the enemy's sentries close up to the watering-place, which lay behind the camp. An English soldier was driving the horses, when suddenly two men of our patrol confronted him out of the bush and covering him with their rifles ordered "Hands up!" In his surprise he dropped his clay pipe out of his mouth.

At once he was asked: "Where are the missing four horses?" for our conscientious patrol had noticed that there were only fifty-seven, whereas the day before they had counted sixty-one! These four needed light treatment and had been left in camp. The leading horse and a few others were quickly saddled, mounted, and off they went at a gallop round the enemy's camp towards the German lines. Even in the captured Englishman, who had to take part in this *safari* on a bare horse, without much comfort, the innate sporting instinct of his nation came out. With great humour he shouted: "I should just like to see my Captain's face now!" and when the animals had arrived safely in the German camp he remarked: "It was a damned good piece of work."

This capture, increased by a number of other horses and mules we had picked up, enabled us to form a second mounted company. We now had two mounted companies, composed of *Askari* and Europeans mixed, an organization which proved successful. They provided us with the means of sweeping the extensive desert north of Kilima Njaro with strong patrols who went out for several days at a time; they penetrated even as far as the Uganda and Magad Railways, destroyed bridges, surprised guards posted on the railways, mined the permanent way and carried out raids of all kinds on the land communications between the railways and the enemy's camps.

In these enterprises our own people did not get off scot free. One patrol had brilliantly surprised two companies of Indians by rifle fire, but had then lost their horses, which had been left behind in hiding, by the fire of the enemy; they had to make their way back across the desert on foot, which took four days, and they had no food. Luckily they found milk and cattle in a Masai *kraal*, and later on saved themselves from starvation by killing an elephant. But success whetted the spirit of adventure, and the requests to be sent on patrol, mounted or on foot, increased.

The patrols that went out from the Kilima Njaro in a more easterly direction were of a different character. They had to work on foot through the dense bush for days on end. The patrols sent out to destroy the railway were mostly weak: one or two Europeans, two to four *Askari*, and five to seven carriers. They had to worm their way through the enemy's pickets and were often betrayed by native scouts. In spite of this they mostly reached their objective and were sometimes away for more than a fortnight. For such a small party a bit of game or a small quantity of booty afforded a considerable reserve of rations. But the fatigue and thirst in the burning sun were so great that several men died of thirst, and even Europeans drank urine.

It was a bad business when anyone fell ill or was wounded, with the best will in the world it was often impossible to bring him along. To carry a severely wounded man from the Uganda Railway right across the desert to the German camps, as was occasionally done, is a tremendous performance. Even the blacks understood that, and cases did occur in which a wounded *Askari*, well knowing that he was lost without hope, and a prey to the numerous lions, did not complain when he had to be left in the bush, but of his own accord gave his comrades his rifle and ammunition, so that they at least might be saved.

The working of these patrols became more and more perfect. Knowledge of the desert improved, and in addition to patrols for destruction and intelligence work, we developed a system of fighting patrols. The latter, consisting of twenty to thirty *Askari*, or even more, and sometimes equipped with one or two machine-guns, went out to look for the enemy and inflict losses upon him. In the thick bush the combatants came upon each other at such close quarters and so unexpectedly, that our *Askari* sometimes literally jumped over their prone adversaries and so got behind them again. The influence of these expeditions on the self-reliance and enterprise of both Europeans and natives was so great that it would be difficult to find a force imbued with a better spirit.

Some disadvantages were, however, unavoidable. In particular, our small supply of ammunition did not enable us to attain such a degree of marksmanship as to enable us, when we did get the enemy in an unfavourable situation, completely to destroy him. In technical matters we were also busy. Skilled artificers and armourers were constantly engaged with the factory engineers in the manufacture of suitable apparatus for blowing up the railways. Some of these appliances fired according as they were set, either at once, or after a certain number of wheels had passed over them. With the latter arrangement we hoped to destroy the engines, even if the English tried to protect them by pushing one or two trucks filled with sand in front of them. There was abundance of dynamite to be had on the plantations, but the demolition charges captured at Tanga were much more effective.

We occasionally got German newspapers, but we had had no private mails for a long time. On the 12th February, 1915, I was sitting at dinner in the Railway Station at New Moshi, when I got a letter from Germany. It was from my sister, who wrote to say she had already repeatedly informed me of the death of my brother, who had been killed on the Western Front at Libramont on the 22nd August, 1914.

In April, 1915, we were surprised by the news of the arrival of a store-ship. When entering Mansa Bay, north of Tanga, she was chased and fired at by an English cruiser, and her captain had to run her aground. Although during the ensuing weeks we salved almost the whole of the valuable cargo, we found that unfortunately the cartridges had suffered severely from the sea-water. The powder and caps deteriorated more and more, and so the number of miss-fires increased.

There was nothing for it but to break up the whole of the ammunition, clean the powder, and replace some of the caps by new ones. Luckily there were caps in the Colony, though of a different pattern; but for months all the *Askari* and carriers we could lay hands on were employed at Moshi from morning till night making ammunition. The serviceable cartridges we had left were kept exclusively for the machine-guns; of the remade ammunition, that which gave about 20 *per cent,* of miss-fires was kept for action, while that giving a higher percentage was used for practice.

The arrival of the store-ship aroused tremendous enthusiasm, since it proved that communication between ourselves and home still existed. All of us listened with eagerness to the stories of the Captain, Lieutenant Christiansen, when he arrived at my Headquarters at New Moshi after his wound was healed. The terrific fighting at home, the spirit of self-sacrifice and boundless enterprise which inspired the deeds of the German troops, awakened a response in our hearts. Many who had been despondent now took courage once more, since they learned that what appears impossible can be achieved if effort is sustained by determination.

Another means of raising the spirit of the force was by promotion. Generally speaking, I could only make promotions to non-commissioned rank, and within the commissioned ranks; but the grant of a commission, which would in many cases have been well-deserved, was beyond my power. Each case was very carefully considered, so as to determine whether really good work had been done. In this way unmerited promotions, which ruin the spirit of the troops, were avoided. On the whole, however, we had to cultivate the moral factors less by rewards than by other means. Decorations for war service were practically unknown among us. It was not personal ambition to which we appealed; we sought to arouse and maintain a real sense of duty dictated by patriotism, and an ever-growing feeling of comradeship. Perhaps it was the very fact that this lasting and pure motive remained unsoiled by any other purpose that inspired Europeans and *Askari* with that endurance and energy which the Protective Force manifested until the end.

In the Kilima Njaro country the English were not inactive. From Oldorobo Mountain, seven and a half miles east of Taveta, which was held by a German detached post under an officer, an attack by two Indian Companies was reported by telephone one morning. Thereupon Captain Koehl and the Austrian Lieutenant Freiherr von Unterrichter at once marched off from Taveta; the two companies had become immobilized on the steep slopes of the mountain, and our people attacked them on both flanks with such vigour that they fled, leaving about twenty dead behind, while one machine-gun and 70,000 rounds fell into our hands.

Other hostile expeditions were undertaken along the Tsavo River to the north-east side of Kilima Njaro; they were based on Mzima Camp on the Tsavo, which was strongly fortified and held by several companies. The patrol encounters that took place north-east of Kilima Njaro all ended in our favour; even the young *Askari* of the Rombo Detachment, which had a strength of sixty and was named after the mission on the Eastern Kilima Njaro, had unbounded faith in their commander, Lieutenant-Colonel von Bock, who was over sixty years old. I remember a wounded man who came from him to New Moshi, with a report for me, and refused to be attended to so as to lose no time in getting back to his commanding officer.

In several fights, when the enemy occasionally amounted to two companies, these young troops were victorious, and it is a significant fact that among the English all manner of tales were current about these actions. The British commander-in-chief sent me a written complaint, saying that a German woman was taking part in them, and perpetrating inhuman cruelties, an idea which was, of course, without any foundation, and merely served to show the degree of nerves with which the enemy authorities had become afflicted.

Notwithstanding the great amount of booty taken at Tanga, it was evident that, as the war seemed likely to be prolonged, the stocks in the Colony would become exhausted. The natives at New Moshi began all of a sudden to wear silk : this was by no means a sign of special extravagance: the stocks of cotton clothing in the Indian shops were simply coming to an end. We had seriously to think of starting manufactures ourselves, in order to convert the abundant raw material into finished products.

A curious existence now developed, reminding one of the industry of the Swiss family Robinson. Cotton fields existed in plenty. Popular books were hunted up, giving information about the forgotten arts of hand spinning and weaving; white and black women took to spinning by hand; at the missions and in private workshops spinning-wheels and looms were built. In this manner, in a short time, the first useful piece of cotton cloth was produced. After various trials, the most suitable dye was obtained from the root of a tree called *Ndaa*, which imparted a brownish-yellow colour, very inconspicuous both in the grass and in the bush, and therefore specially suitable for uniforms.

The rubber gathered by the planters was vulcanized with sulphur, and we succeeded in producing efficient tyres for motors and bicycles. At Morogoro a few planters successfully produced a motor-fuel from *cocos*, known as *trebol*, which was like *benzol*, and was employed in the automobiles. As in former times, candles were made out of tallow and wax, both by private persons and by the troops, and also soap. Then again, the numerous factories on the plantations in the northern territories and on the Tanganyika Railway were adapted to produce various means of subsistence.

A particularly important item was the provision of footwear. The raw material was obtained from the plentiful skins of cattle and game; tanning materials from the mangroves on the coast. In peace time the missions had already made good boots; their activity was now further developed, while the troops also established tanneries and shoemakers' shops on a larger scale. It is true some little time elapsed before the authorities complied with the urgent and inevitable demands of the troops in an adequate manner, and, in particular, before they placed at our disposal the buffalo-hides necessary for making sole-leather. So the old historic fight for the cow-hide revived again, *mutatis mutandis*, in East Africa.

The first boots made in any quantity were turned out at Tanga. Although at first their shape needed improving, they at any rate protected the feet of our white and black troops when marching and patrolling in the thorn bush of the *Pori*. For the thorns that fall to the ground bore into the feet again and again. All the small beginnings of food-stuff production that had already existed on the plantations in time of peace were galvanized into more extensive activity by the war, and by the need of subsisting large masses. On several farms in the Kilima Njaro country butter and excellent cheese were produced in great quantities, and the slaughter-houses round about Wilhelmstal could hardly keep up with the demands for sausages and other smoked meats.

It was to be anticipated that quinine, which was so important for the health of the Europeans, would soon become exhausted, and that our requirements could not be met by capture alone. So it was a matter of great importance that we succeeded in producing good quinine tablets at the Amani Biological Institute in Usambara out of bark obtained in the North.

The provision of proper communications for ox-wagons and motors involved the construction of permanent bridges. Engineer Rentell, who had been called to the colours, built an arched bridge of stone and concrete, with a heavy pier, over the Kikafu torrent, west of New Moshi. During the rains, particularly in April, no wooden structure would have withstood the masses of water coming down the steep river-bed, which was nearly 70 feet deep.

These examples will suffice to show the stimulating influence of the war and its requirements on the economic life of the Colony.

The organization of the Force was also constantly improved. By transferring Europeans from the Rifle Companies, when they were numerous, to the *Askari* Companies, the losses of Europeans in the latter were made good; *Askari* were enrolled in the European Companies. In this way the Field and Rifle Companies became more similar in their composition, which during the course of 1915 became identical. At Muansa, Kigoma, Bismarckburg, Lindi, Langenburg, and elsewhere, small bodies of troops had been formed under various designations, of the existence of which in most cases Headquarters only became aware after a considerable time. These units were also gradually expanded into companies; in this way, during 1915, the number of Field Companies gradually rose to 30, that of the Rifle Companies to 10, and that of other units of company strength to about 20.

The maximum total attained was thus about 60 companies. Owing to the limited number of suitable Europeans and of reliable *Askari* N.C.O.'s, it was not advisable still further to increase the number of companies: it would only have meant the creation of units without cohesion. In order, however, to increase the number of combatants the establishment of the companies was raised from 160 to 200, and the companies were allowed to enrol supernumerary *Askari*. To some extent the companies trained their own recruits; but the great bulk of *Askari* reinforcements came from the Recruit Depots established in the populous districts of Tabora, Muansa and the Northern Railway, which also provided for local security and order. But owing to the great number of newly-raised companies the depots could not furnish enough men to bring them all up to their establishment of 200. The maximum strength attained by the end of 1915 was 2,998 Europeans and 11,300 *Askari*, including Naval personnel, administrative staffs, hospitals and field postal service.

How necessary were all these military preparations was proved by the news received at the end of June, 1915, that General Botha was coming to the East African theatre from South Africa with 15,000 Boers. That this information was highly probably correct had to be assumed from the outset. The scanty wireless messages and other communications about events in the outside world were yet enough to indicate that our affairs in South-West Africa were going badly, and that the British troops employed there would probably become available for other purposes in the immediate future.

CHAPTER 8

Awaiting the Great Offensive

At first, it is true, the anticipated intervention of the South Africans did not seem to be materializing; the English were evidently trying to subdue us with their own forces, without their assistance. In July, 1915, they attacked the Colony at several points. East of Lake Victoria large bodies of Masai, organized and led by Englishmen, and said to number many thousands, invaded the country of the German Wassukuma, which was rich in cattle. However, in the matter of cattle-lifting the Wassukuma stood no joking; they gave our weak detachments every assistance, defeated the Masai, recaptured the stolen cattle, and, as a proof that they had "spoken the truth," laid out the heads of ninety-six Masai in front of our police station.

Against the main body of our force in the Kilima Njaro country the enemy advanced in considerable strength. In order, on the one hand, to ensure effective protection of the Usambara Railway, and the rich plantations through which it passes, and, on the other, to shorten the distance the patrols had to go to reach the Uganda Railway, a detachment of three companies had been pushed out from Taveta to Mbuyuni, a long day's march east of Taveta. Another day's march to the east was the well-fortified and strongly-held English camp of Makatan, on the main road leading from Moshi, by Taveta, Mbuyuni, Makatan, and Bura, to Voi, on the Uganda Railway. Vague rumours had led us to surmise that an attack on a fairly large scale in the direction of Kilima Njaro was to be expected from about Voi.

On the 14th July a hostile brigade, under General Malleson, appeared in the desert of Makatan, which is generally covered with fairly open thorn-bush. The fire of a field battery, which opened on the trenches of our *Askari*, was fairly ineffective, but the enemy's superiority of seven to one was so considerable that our position became critical. Hostile European horsemen got round the left wing of our own; however, our line was held by the 10th Field Company, which had distinguished itself in the fighting near Longido Mountain, under Lieutenant Steinhäuser, of the *Landwehr*, and it is a credit to this officer, who was unfortunately killed later, that he held on, although our mounted troops fell back past his flank. Just at the critical moment, Lieutenant von Lewinsky, who was also killed later, immediately marched off to the scene of action, arrived with a patrol, and took this dangerous flank attack in rear.

The English troops, consisting of natives, mixed with Europeans and Indians, had very gallantly attacked our front, over ground affording very little cover. The failure of the English flank attack, however, set the seal on their defeat. At New Moshi Station I was kept accurately informed of the progress of the action, and thus, although at a distance, I shared in all the excitement from the unfavourable period at the beginning until complete success was assured.

This success, together with the considerable booty, still further increased the spirit of adventure among both Europeans and *Askari*. The experience and skill that had by now been acquired enabled us henceforth to prosecute our plan of sending out a continuous succession of fighting and demolition patrols. I do not think I exaggerate in assuming that at least twenty English railway trains were destroyed, or, at least, considerably damaged. Picked up photographs and our own observation confirmed the supposition that a railway was actually being built from Voi to Makatan, which, being so easily accessible to us, and so important, formed a glorious objective for our patrols.

The construction of this military line proved that an attack with large forces was in preparation, and that it was to be directed on this particular part of the Kilima Njaro country. The anticipated intervention of the South Africans was therefore imminent. It was important to encourage the enemy in this intention, in order that the South Africans should really come, and that in the greatest strength possible, and thus be diverted from other and more important theatres of war. With the greatest energy, therefore, we continued our enterprises against the Uganda Railway, which, owing to the circumstances, had still to be mainly carried out by patrols, and could only exceptionally be undertaken by a force as large as a company.

Closer acquaintance with the desert country between the Uganda Railway and the Anglo-German border had revealed the fact, that of the various mountain groups rising abruptly out of the plain, the

Kasigao was well watered and moderately populous. Being only from twelve to twenty miles from the Uganda Railway, Kasigao Mountain was bound to afford a favourably situated base for patrol work. The patrol of Lieut. Freiherr Grote had already made a surprise attack on the small Anglo-Indian camp situated half-way up its slopes.

The riflemen of Grote's patrol had worked round the camp, which was surrounded by a stone wall, and fired into it with effect from the dominating part of the mountain. Very soon the white flag appeared, and an English officer and some thirty Indians surrendered. A part of the enemy had succeeded in getting away to the mountain and fired on the patrol as it marched off. It was then we suffered our only casualties, consisting of a few wounded, among whom was a German corporal of the Medical Corps. We had also, on one occasion, surprised the enemy's post on Kasigao Mountain by the fire of a 2.4-inch gun.

Towards the end of 1915, the enemy having in the meantime shifted his camp on Kasigao Mountain, we attacked him once more. During the night a German fighting patrol, under Lieutenant von Ruckteschell, had ascended the mountain in nine hours, and arrived rather exhausted near the enemy's work. A second patrol, under Lieutenant Freiherr Grote, which was co-operating with Ruckteschell's, had been somewhat delayed by the sickness and exhaustion of its commander. Lieutenant von Ruckteschell sent a reliable old coloured N.C.O. to the enemy to demand surrender. He observed that our *Askari* was cordially welcomed by the enemy; he had found a number of good friends among the English *Askari*. But, in spite of all friendliness, the enemy refused to surrender.

Our situation was critical, in consequence of exhaustion and want of food. If anything was to be done at all, it must be done at once. Fortunately, the enemy in their entrenchments did not withstand our machine-gun fire and the assault which immediately followed it; they were destroyed, and a large number of them were killed in their flight by falling from the steep cliffs. The booty included abundant supplies, also clothing and valuable camp equipment.

The feeling of comradeship which our *Askari* had for us Germans, and which was tremendously developed by the numerous expeditions undertaken together, led on this occasion to a curious incident. After climbing Kasigao Mountain by night, among rocks and thorn-bushes, an *Askari* noticed that Lieutenant von Ruckteschell was bleeding from a scratch on his face. He at once took his sock, which he had probably not changed for six days, and wiped the "*Bwana* Lieutenant's" face with it, anticipating the somewhat surprised question with the remark: "That is a custom of war; one only does it to one's friends."

In order to study the situation on the spot and to push on the attacks on Kasigao, I had gone by rail to Same, thence by car to Sonya Mission, and then either by cycle or on foot in the direction of the mountain to the German border, where a company was encamped at a water-hole. From there we had fair communication to Kasigao by heliograph, and we were thus enabled to make good the success we had gained there. Troops were at once pushed up, so that until the arrival of the South Africans the mountain was held by several companies. It was, indeed, decidedly difficult to keep them supplied; for although the German frontier territory west of Kasigao was fertile, it could not permanently support a force which with carriers amounted to about one thousand.

I then drove in the car round the South Pare Mountains, on a road that had been made in time of peace. The construction of this road had been dropped on account of expense, and for years the heaps of metal had been lying unused at the roadside. The culverts—consisting of pipes passing under the road—were to a great extent in good order. But little work was needed to make this road suitable for supply by lorry. Supplies were sent from near Buiko on the Northern Railway by lorry to Sonya, and thence to Kasigao by carriers. The telephone line was already under construction as far as the frontier, and was completed in a few days' time. From then on patrols pushing out from Kasigao had several encounters with detachments of the enemy, and did some damage to the Uganda Railway. But the ruggedness of the country and the dense thorn-bush made movement so difficult that by the time the South Africans arrived, we had not derived full benefit from Kasigao as a base for patrols.

However, the continual menace to the railway had, at any rate, obliged the enemy to take extensive measures for its protection. Wide clearings had been made along it, of which the outer edges had been closed by thick *zarebas* (abatis of thorns). Every couple of miles there were strong block-houses, or entrenchments with obstacles, from which the line was constantly patrolled. Mobile supports, of the strength of a company or more, were held in readiness, so that, whenever the railway was reported to be in danger, they could at once go off by special train. In addition, protective detachments were pushed out in our direction, who tried to cut off our patrols on their way back on receiving reports from spies or from observation posts on the high ground.

We also identified English camps on the high ground south-east of Kasigao, as far as the coast, and also in the settled country along the coast. They also received attention from our patrols and raiders. Our constant endeavour was to injure the enemy, to force him to adopt protective measures, and thus to contain his forces here, in the district of the Uganda Railway.

While thus establishing points of support for our fighting patrols from the coast to Mbuyuni (on the Taveta-Voi road), we worked in the same sense further north. The enemy's camp at Mzima, on the upper Tsavo River, and its communications, which followed that river, were frequently the objective of our expeditions, even of fairly large detachments. On one occasion Captain Augar, with the 13th Company, was surprised south-west of Mzima Camp in thick bush by three European companies of the newly-arrived 2nd Rhodesian Regiment. The enemy attacked from several directions, but being still inexperienced in bush fighting, failed to secure concerted action. So our *Askari* Company was able first to overthrow one part of the enemy's forces, and then by quickness and resolution to defeat the other, which had appeared behind it.

Further north, also, there was some fighting in the bush which went in our favour; we worked with whole companies and inflicted painful losses on the enemy, who was often in greater force. North of the Engare Len the 3rd Field Company from Lindi worked with special energy, and sent its fighting patrols out as far as the Uganda Railway. The mere fact that we were now able to make raids with forces amounting to a company and more in the midst of a desert devoid of supplies, and in many places waterless, shows the enormous progress the force had made in this type of guerrilla warfare. The European had learned that a great many things that are very desirable when travelling in the Tropics simply have to be dispensed with on patrol in war, and that one can at a pinch get on for a time with only a single carrier-load.

The patrols also had to avoid camping in such a way as to betray themselves, and as far as possible to carry food ready prepared. But if food had to be cooked, this was particularly dangerous in the evening or morning; the leader had to select a concealed spot, and invariably shift his camp after cooking before going to rest. Complete hygienic protection was incompatible with the conditions of patrol duty. A number of cases of malaria invariably occurred among the members of a patrol after its return. But as, in spite of the continual damage done to the enemy, patrol duty only required comparatively few men, only a part of the companies had to be kept in the front line. After a few weeks each company was withdrawn to rest camps in healthy regions, European and *Askari* were able to recover from their tremendous exertions, and their training and discipline could be restored.

Towards the end of 1915 the shortage of water at Mbuyuni Camp had become so serious, and supply so difficult, that only a post was left there, the detachment itself being withdrawn to the westward to the vicinity of Oldorobo Mountain. Meanwhile, the enemy's camp at Makatan grew steadily larger. A frequent train service was maintained to it, and one could clearly see a big clearing being made to the west for the prolongation of the railway. Our fighting patrols had, indeed, many opportunities of inflicting losses on the enemy while at work, or protecting his working parties, but the line continued to make progress towards the west.

It was necessary to consider the possibility of the country through which the Northern Railway passed soon falling into the hands of the enemy. Steps had, therefore, to be taken to safeguard the military stores in that district in time. Where railways were available this was, of course, not difficult; but the further transport by land needed much preparation. The bulk of our stocks of ammunition, clothing and medical stores was at New Moshi and Mombo. It was evident that we would be unable to carry away the factories, or parts of them, by land; they must, therefore, be made use of and kept working for as long as possible where they were. Assuming the enemy would attack from the north, our evacuation would obviously be towards the south, and not only the preparations, but the movement itself, must be started without loss of time—that is, as early as August, 1915.

The Commandant of the Line, Lieutenant Kroeber, retired, therefore, in an able manner, collected light-railway material from the plantations, and built a line from Mombo to Handeni, at the rate of about two kilometres (one and a quarter miles) per day. The trucks were also brought from the plantations, and after mature consideration, man draught was decided on in preference to locomotives.

Thus our stores were moved from the north by rail, complete, and in time, to Handeni. From there to Kimamba, on the Central Railway, we principally used carriers, except for a few wagons. It was, after all, necessary not to hurry the movement unduly, for, in spite of all the visible preparations for a hostile attack on the Kilima Njaro country,

I still thought it possible that the main force of the enemy, or at least a considerable proportion of it, would not operate there, but in the Bagamoyo-Dar-es-Salaam area.

At the end of 1915 the enemy was pushing his rail-head further and further westward, and Major Kraut, who was opposing him, reinforced his position on Oldorobo Mountain with three companies and two light guns. This mountain rises from the flat thorn desert near the main road, seven and a half miles east of Taveta, and dominates the country for a great distance all round. Entrenchments and numerous dummy works had been made, part being cut out of the rock, and formed an almost impregnable fort. The disadvantage of the position was the complete lack of water. A planter who had been called to the Colours, Lieutenant Matuschka, of the Reserve, was an expert water finder; at Taveta he had discovered excellent wells; but on Oldorobo no water was found, although at the points he indicated we dug down more than one hundred feet.

Water had therefore to be taken from Taveta on small donkey-carts to Oldorobo, where it was collected in barrels. This carriage of water was an extraordinary strain on our transport. Strangely enough, it did not occur to the enemy to interfere with it, and thus render Oldorobo Mountain untenable. Instead of that, basing himself on his railway, he pushed up to within about three miles of the mountain, where he established strongly fortified camps. We had been unable to prevent this, as, owing to difficulties of water and transport, larger forces could only move away from Taveta for short periods. The enemy obtained his water supply by means of a long pipe-line, which came from the springs in the Bura Mountains. The destruction of the enemy's reservoir by patrols under Lieutenant von S'Antenecai, of the Reserve, only caused him temporary inconvenience.

At this time, also, the first hostile aeroplanes appeared, and bombed our positions on Oldorobo Mountain, and at Taveta and later even New Moshi. On the 27th January one of these airmen, while on his way back from Oldorobo, was successfully fired on and brought down by our advanced infantry. The English had told the natives that this aeroplane was a new "*Munga*" (God); but now that this new *Munga* had been brought down and captured by us, it rather increased our prestige than otherwise.

CHAPTER 9

The Subsidiary Theatres of War

While employing the bulk of the Protective Force in the regions on the Northern Railway we could not afford entirely to denude the remainder of the Colony. In the interior it was essential to remain undisputed master of the natives, in order, if necessary, to enforce the growing demands for carriers, agriculture, supplies, and all manner of work. Accordingly, the 12th Company remained at Mahenge, and the 2nd at Iringa. In addition to their other duties both of them acted as large depots, serving to fill vacancies at the front, and providing the machinery for raising new units.

The commanders of detachments on the frontiers, who were far away from Headquarters and beyond the reach of the telegraph, rightly endeavoured to anticipate the enemy and to attack him in his own territory. Owing to the lack of communications on our side this fighting resolved itself into a series of local operations, which were quite independent of each other. It was different with the enemy, who clearly endeavoured to establish a proper relationship between his main operations and the subsidiary enterprises at other points on the frontier.

In October, 1914, before the fighting at Tanga, Captain Zimmer reported from Kigoma that there were about 2,000 men on the Belgian frontier; and Captain Braunschweig sent word from Muansa that at Kisumu on Lake Victoria there were also strong hostile forces, about two companies at Kisii, and more troops at Karungu. According to independent native reports, Indian troops landed at Mombasa in October and were then transported towards Voi. In the Bukoba District English troops crossed the Kagera, and the sub-station at Umbulu reported that the enemy was invading the Ssonyo country. Obviously these movements were preparatory to the operations which were to

79

be co-ordinated with the great attack on Tanga in November, 1914.

The means of intercommunication in the Colony were not sufficiently developed to enable us rapidly to concentrate our main force, first against one and then against another of these hostile detachments deploying along the frontier. We had, therefore, to adhere to the fundamental idea of our plan, of vigorously attacking the enemy opposed to us in the area of the Northern Railway and on the Uganda Railway, and of thus indirectly relieving the other points where operations were in progress. Of necessity, however, these subsidiary points had occasionally to be reinforced.

Thus, in September, 1914, Captains Falkenstein and Aumann, with portions of the 2nd Company, had moved from Iringa and Ubena into the Langenburg District. In March, 1915, the 26th Field Company was pushed up from Dar-es-Salaam *via* Tabora to Muansa. In April, 1915, hostile concentration in the Mara Triangle (east of Lake Victoria) and at Bismarckburg caused us to waste much time in moving troops up from Dar-es-Salaam *via* Muansa to the Mara Triangle, and *via* Kigoma to Bismarckburg. The latter move was particularly delayed on Lake Tanganyika owing to the slow progress being made on the steamer *Götzen*, which was building at Kigoma.

At first, the enemy's attacks were principally directed against the coast.

At the commencement of the war our light cruiser *Königsberg* had left the harbour of Dar-es-Salaam and had, on the 29th September, surprised and destroyed the English cruiser *Pegasus* at Zanzibar. Then several large enemy cruisers had arrived and industriously looked for the *Königsberg*. On the 19th October, at Lindi, a *pinnace* steamed up to the steamer *Praesident*, of the East African Line, which was concealed in the Lukuledi River. The local Defence Force raised at Lindi, and the Reinforcement Company, were at the moment away under Captain Augar, to repel a landing expected at Mikindani, so that nothing could be undertaken against the *pinnace*.

It was not till the 29th July, 1915, that several whalers went up the Lukuledi and blew up the *Praesident*.

After successful cruises in the Indian Ocean the *Königsberg* had concealed herself in the Rufiji River, but her whereabouts had become known to the enemy. The mouth of the river forms an intricate delta, the view being obstructed by the dense bush with which the islands are overgrown. The various river-mouths were defended by the "Delta" Detachment, under Lieutenant-Commander Schoenfeld;

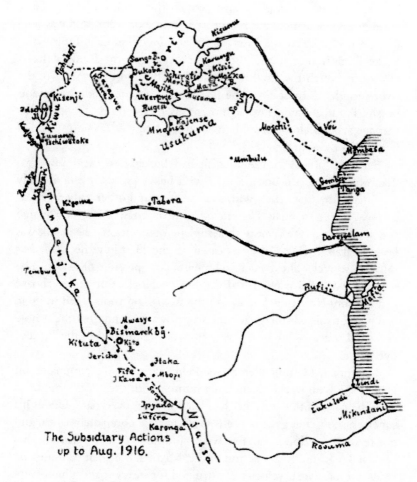

The Subsidiary Actions
up to Aug. 1916.

Fig. VI. Subsidiary Actions up to August, 1916.

this detachment consisted of Naval ratings, European reservists, and *Askari*, and its strength was about 150 rifles, a few light guns, and a few machine guns. The enemy made many attempts to enter the river-mouths with light craft, but was invariably repulsed with severe loss. The *Adjutant*, a small steamer which the English had taken as a good prize, and armed, was recaptured on one occasion, and was used thenceforward by us as an auxiliary man-of-war on Lake Tanganyika. Some English aircraft had also come to grief in the Rufiji delta. A blockship, which the English had sunk in the most northerly of the river-mouths, did not close the fairway. The frequent bombardments by ships' guns, which he had no means of opposing, Lieut.-Commander Schoenfeld defeated by the skilful design of his positions, and by shifting them in time.

Early in July, 1915, the English had brought to the Rufiji two shallow-draught gun-boats, armed with heavy guns. On the 6th July they made the first attack with four cruisers and other armed vessels, and two river gun-boats. The enemy bombarded the *Königsberg*, which was at anchor in the river with aeroplane observation. The attack was beaten off, but when it was repeated on the 11th July, the *Königsberg* suffered severely. The gun-detachments were put out of action. The severely wounded captain had the breech-blocks thrown overboard and the ship blown up. The loss of the *Königsberg*, though sad in itself, had at least this advantage for the campaign on land, that the whole crew and the valuable stores were now at the disposal of the Protective Force.

Lieutenant-Commander Schoenfeld, who was in command on land at the Rufiji delta, at once set himself with great forethought to raise the parts of the guns that had been thrown overboard. Under his supervision the ten guns of the *Königsberg* were completely salved and got ready for action again; five were mounted at Dar-es-Salaam, two each at Tanga and Kigoma, and one at Muansa. For their transport he made use of several vehicles constructed for heavy loads which were found on a neighbouring plantation. In their concealed positions on land these guns rendered excellent service, and as far as I know not one of them was damaged on this service, although they were often bombarded by the enemy's vessels.

On the 26th September, by night, the steamer *Wami* was taken out of the Rufiji to Dar-es-Salaam.

At the end of August several boats came to Lindi from Mozambique with men belonging to the steamer *Ziethen*, in order to join the

Force.

On the 10th January, 1915, about 300 Indian and black troops with machine guns landed on the island of Mafia. Our police detachment, three Europeans, fifteen *Askari*, and eleven recruits, opposed them bravely for six hours, but surrendered when their commander, Lieutenant Schiller of the Reserve, was severely wounded, who had been maintaining a well-aimed fire on the enemy from a mango tree. The English held Mafia with a few hundred men, and also established posts of observation on the smaller islands in the vicinity.

It was apparently from here that the work of rousing the natives against us was undertaken. On the night of the 29th-30th July, 1915, we captured a *dhow* at Kisija carrying propaganda papers.

The events at Dar-es-Salaam, where, on the 22nd October, the captain of an English cruiser declined to be bound by any agreement, have already been discussed.

On the outbreak of hostilities an aeroplane, which had been sent to Dar-es-Salaam for the Exhibition, was taken into use, but was destroyed by an accident at Dar-es-Salaam on the 15th November, when Lieutenant Henneberger lost his life.

At Tanga things had been quiet since the big battle of November, 1914. On the 13th March, 1915, a ship went ashore on a reef, but got off again on the spring-tide. We at once began salving 200 tons of coal which had been thrown overboard.

Several rows of mines which had been made on the spot, and could be fired from the shore, proved ineffective, and it was found later that they had become unserviceable.

On the 15th August, 1915, the *Hyacinth* and four guard-boats appeared off Tanga. Our two 2.4-inch guns were quickly moved from their rest-camp at Gombezi to Tanga, and with one light gun from Tanga, took an effective part on the 19th August, when the *Hyacinth* reappeared with two gun-boats and six whalers, destroyed the steamer *Markgraf* and bombarded Tanga. One gun-boat was hit twice, the whalers, of which one steamed away with a list,[1] four times.

Bombardments of the coast towns were constantly taking place. On the 20th March a man-of-war bombarded Lindi, when its demand for the surrender of the troops posted there was refused. Similarly, the country south of Pangani was bombarded on the 1st April, the island of Kwale on the 12th, and the Rufiji delta on the night of the 23rd-24th.

1. *Seitenschlag.*

For some months past hostile patrols had been visiting the Ssonyo country, between Kilima Njaro and Lake Victoria, and the natives seemed inclined to become truculent. As a result of their treachery, Sergeant-Major Bast, who was sent there with a patrol, was ambushed on the 17th November, 1914, and lost his life with five *Askari*. The District Commissioner of Arusha, Lieutenant Kaempfe of the Reserve, who had been called up, undertook a punitive expedition which reduced the Ssonyo people to submission.

It was not until July, 1915, that any further patrol encounters took place in this country; in one of them twenty-two hostile armed natives were killed. At the end of September and early October, 1915, Lieutenant Buechsel's mounted patrol spent several weeks in Ssonyo and in the English territory without meeting the enemy, as an English post, which had evidently been warned, had made off.

On Lake Victoria the 7th Company at Bukoba and the 14th Company at Muansa could communicate with each other by wireless. The command of the Lake was undisputedly in the hands of the English, as they had on it at least seven large steamers. But in spite of this our small steamer *Muansa* and other smaller vessels were able to maintain great freedom of movement. While the Resident at Bukoba, Major von Stuemer, protected the frontier with his police and with auxiliaries furnished by friendly sultans, Captain Bock von Wülfingen had marched with the main body of the 7th Company from Bukoba to Muansa. From here he marched early in September, 1914, with a detachment composed of parts of the 7th and 14th Companies, Wassakuma recruits, and auxiliaries, along the eastern shore of Lake Victoria to the north, in the direction of the Uganda Railway.

On the 12th September he drove back a hostile detachment at Kisii, beyond the border, but on hearing of the approach of other forces of the enemy he withdrew again to the south. After that the frontier east of Lake Victoria was only defended by weak detachments.

Warfare near Lake Victoria was for us very difficult; there was always the danger that the enemy might land at Muansa, or some other place on the south shore, seize Usukuma and threaten Tabora, the historic capital of the country. If, however, our troops remained near Muansa, the country round Bukoba, and therefore also Ruanda, would be in danger. The best results in this area were to be expected from active operations under a united command. But the execution of this idea was not quite easy either, for Major von Stuemer, who was the most obvious officer to be entrusted with it, was tied by his work as

Resident to the Bukoba District, while that of Muansa was the more important of the two.

At the end of October, 1914, an attempt to take back part of the troops in boats from Muansa to Bukoba had been frustrated by the appearance of armed English ships at the former place. Apparently the enemy had deciphered our wireless messages and taken steps accordingly. On the 31st October a force of 570 rifles, 2 guns and 4 machine guns, left Muansa for the relief of Bukoba on board the steamer *Muansa*, 2 tugs and 10 *dhows*, but was scattered the same morning by hostile steamers which suddenly appeared; they were, however, collected again at Muansa without loss soon afterwards. On the same day the English tried to land at Kayense, north of Muansa, but were prevented; a few days later, the English steamer *Sybil* was found on shore at Mayita and destroyed.

On the 20th November, in a twelve-hours' action, Stuemer's detachment repulsed the English troops who had penetrated into German territory, north of Bukoba, and defeated them again, on the 5th December, at Kifumbiro, after they had crossed the Kagera River. On the 5th December, the English bombarded Shirarti from the lake, without success, and Bukoba on the 6th.

Minor encounters between patrols constantly took place east and west of Lake Victoria. On the 8th January the enemy attempted a more ambitious operation; he bombarded Shirarti from the Lake with six guns and with machine guns, and landed two companies of Indians as well as a considerable number of mounted Europeans. Lieutenant von Haxthausen, who had only 22 rifles, gave way before this superior force after fighting 3½ hours. The enemy's strength was increased during the next few days to 300 Europeans and 700 Indians. On the 17th January, von Haxthausen defeated 70 Europeans and 150 *Askari* with 2 machine guns on the frontier, and on the 30th January the enemy left Shirarti and embarked for Karungu. I believe this withdrawal was a result of the severe defeat sustained by the enemy at Jassini on the 18th. He considered it desirable to re-concentrate his forces nearer the Uganda Railway, where they would be more readily available.

On the west side of the lake, Captain von Bock surprised a hostile post of 40 men north of Kifumbiro and drove it off with a loss of 17 killed.

On the 6th March, 1915, English vessels had attacked the steamer *Muansa* in Rugesi Passage. *Muansa* had sprung a leak and went ashore close to the land. The enemy attempted to tow her off, but was prevented by our fire, so that we were able, the next day, to salve the steamer and get her away to Muansa, where she was repaired. The difficulty of moving troops by water between Muansa and Bukoba rendered the continuation of the single command unworkable; the officers commanding the two Districts were therefore placed directly under Headquarters.

The English attempted to land at Mori Bay on the 4th March, at Ukerewe on the 7th, and at Musoma on the 9th; all these attempts were defeated by our posts. At the same time, several patrol encounters occurred near Shirarti, in which the commander, Lieutenant Recke, was killed, and our patrols were dispersed. On the 9th March, Lieutenant von Haxthausen, with 100 Europeans and *Askari*, defeated an enemy many times his superior at Maika Mountain; the enemy withdrew after having 17 whites and a considerable number of *Askari* killed. On our side, one European and 10 *Askari* were killed, 2 Europeans and 25 *Askari* wounded, while one wounded European was taken prisoner. Besides the 26th Field Company already mentioned, Muansa was reinforced by 100 *Askari* from Bukoba District, who arrived on the 6th April.

Early in April a few places on the eastern shore were again bombarded from the Lake; at the same time some Masai made an invasion east of the lake, killed a missionary and several natives, and looted cattle. In the middle of April, Captain Braunschweig left Muansa with 110 Europeans, 430 *Askari*, 2 machine guns, and 2 guns, for the Mara Triangle, and reinforced Lieutenant von Haxthausen. Over 500 rifles remained at Muansa.

On the 4th May, in Mara Bay, an English steamer was hit three times by a '73 pattern field-gun, which apparently prevented a landing. On the 12th May 300 men landed at Mayita; but they steamed off again on the 18th June, towing the wreck of the *Sybil* with them. By the 20th May the enemy, who had 900 men there, had also evacuated the Mara Triangle, and entrenched himself on several mountains beyond the frontier. Bombardments of the shore took place frequently at that time.

Since early December, 1914, Major von Stuemer had held a very extended position on the Kagera. Gradually the enemy, who was estimated at about 300 men, became more active. He seemed to be collecting material for crossing the Kagera, and his ships appeared more frequently in Sango Bay.

On the night of the 4th-5th June, on the Shirarti frontier, Becker's post of 10 men was surrounded by 10 Europeans and 50 Indians of the 98 th Regiment. An armed steamer also took part. But the enemy was beaten, losing 2 Europeans and 5 *Askari* killed.

I may here mention that the enemy's armed scouts used poisoned arrows on the Shirarti frontier also.

On the 21st June the English, with a force of 800 Europeans 400 *Askari*, 300 Indians, 3 guns and 8 machine guns, and supported by the fire of the armed steamers, attacked Bukoba. Our garrison of little more than 200 rifles evacuated the place after two days of fighting. The enemy plundered it, destroyed the wireless tower, and left again on the 24th towards Kissumu. He had suffered severely, admitting 10 Europeans killed and 22 wounded. The Germans had, however, observed that a steamer had left with about 150 dead and wounded on board. On our side 2 Europeans, 5 *Askari*, and 7 auxiliaries had been killed, 4 Europeans and 30 coloured men wounded, and we also lost the gun.

Of the events of the ensuing period it may be remarked that Bukoba was bombarded without result on the 18th July. In Mpororo a great chief went over to the English.

On the 12th September one of the *Königsberg's* four-inch guns arrived at Muansa, where we had in process of time raised five new companies among the Wassukuma people.

It seemed as though the enemy were rather holding back at Bukoba, and moving troops from there to Kissenyi. On the 20th October the English attacked with some one hundred rifles, machine guns, a gun, and a trench mortar, but were repulsed, apparently with heavy casualties. Hostile attacks on the lower Kagera on the 4th and 5th December were also unsuccessful. Several detachments of the enemy invaded the Karagwe country. The command at Bukoba was taken over by Captain Gudovius, hitherto District Commissioner in Tangarei, who marched off from Tabora on the 21st December, and was followed by the newly-raised 7th Reserve Company as a reinforcement for Bukoba.

In Ruanda the energetic measures adopted by the President, Captain Wintgens, produced good results. On the 24th September he surprised the island of Ijvi in Lake Kivu, and captured the Belgian post stationed there, and its steel boat. Another steel boat had been captured by Lieutenant Wunderlich, of the Navy, who had moved to Lake Kivu with some men of the *Moewe*, where he had requisitioned a motor-boat. On the 4th October, Wintgens, with his Police *Askari*, some auxiliaries, and a few men of the *Moewe*, drove back several companies of Belgians north of Kissenyi, inflicting heavy casualties on them. After some minor engagements, Captain Wintgens then inflicted a partial defeat on the superior Belgian force of seventeen hundred men and six guns, north of Kissenyi, on the 20th and 30th November, and again on the 2nd December, 1914. Near Lake Tshahafi he drove out an English post. One English- man and twenty *Askari* were killed; we had two *Askari* killed and one European severely wounded.

After that, in February, 1915, several minor actions were fought near Kissenyi and on the frontier. On the 28th May, Lieutenant Lang, commanding the small garrison of Kissenyi, beat off the Belgians, who had seven hundred men and two machine guns. The enemy sustained heavy losses; we had one European killed.

In June, 1915, it was said that over two thousand Belgian *Askari*, with nine guns, and five hundred English *Askari* were concentrated near Lake Kivu, the fact that the Belgian commander-in-chief, Tombeur, went to Lake Kivu makes this information appear probable. On the 21st June the Belgians attacked Kissenyi with nine hundred men, two machine guns and two guns, but were repulsed. On the 5th July they again attacked the place by night with four hundred men, and suffered severe losses. On the 3rd August Kissenyi was ineffectively bombarded by artillery and machine guns. In consequence of the crushing superiority of the enemy, the 26th Field Company was transferred from Muansa to Kissenyi.

Immediately after the arrival of this company at Kissenyi, on the 31st August, Captain Wintgens defeated the Belgian outposts, of whom ten *Askari* were killed. On September 2nd he took by storm a position held by one hundred and fifty *Askari*, with three guns and one machine gun. During the next few weeks minor actions were fought every day. On the 3rd October an attack on Kissenyi by two hundred and fifty *Askari* with a machine gun was repulsed, and fourteen casualties were observed among the enemy. After that, possibly in consequence of the action at Luwungi on the 27th September, considerable forces of the enemy were discovered to have marched off for the south.

On the 22nd October another Belgian detached post of three hundred *Askari*, with two guns and two machine guns, was surprised, when the enemy had ten *Askari* killed. On the 26th November the Ruanda Detachment, with one platoon of the 7th Company, which had arrived from Bukoba, in all three hundred and twenty rifles, four machine guns and one 1.45-inch gun, drove the enemy, numbering two hundred, out of a fortified position, when he lost two Europeans and seventy *Askari* killed, five *Askari* prisoners, and many wounded. We had one European and three *Askari* killed, four Europeans, five *Askari* and one auxiliary wounded. On the 21st December the enemy once more attacked Kissenyi with one thousand *Askari*, two machine guns and eight guns, including four modern 2.75-inch howitzers. He left behind twenty-one dead *Askari*, three were captured, wounded, and many wounded were carried away. Our force of three hundred and fifty rifles, four machine guns and two guns, had three *Askari* killed, one European and one *Askari* severely wounded.

On the 12th January, 1916, Captain Wintgens surprised a Belgian column north of Kissenyi, killing eleven Belgian *Askari*. On the 27th January Captain Klinghardt, with three companies, beat off an attack on the Kissenyi position made by two thousand Belgian *Askari* with hand grenades and twelve guns, inflicting severe casualties on them.

In the Russissi country there were also numerous engagements. Successful minor actions between German patrols and Congo troops had taken place on the 10th and 13th October, 1914, at Changugu, on the 21st and 22nd at Chiwitoke, and on the 24th at Kajagga.

On the 12th January, 1915, Captain Schimmer attacked a Belgian camp at Luwungi, but the intended surprise was unsuccessful. Captain Zimmer and three *Askari* were killed and five wounded.

Then, on the 16th, 17th and 20th March small patrol skirmishes took place, and on the 20th May a Belgian post was surprised. There was thus incessant fighting, which continued in June and July. In August the enemy seemed to be increasing his forces in that region. The command on the Russissi was now taken over by Captain Schulz; the forces we had there now consisted of four field companies, part of the crew of the *Moewe*, and the Urundi Detachment, which about equalled one company. There were also two light guns there. On the 27th September Captain Schulz attacked Luwungi, when we were able to establish that the enemy lost fifty-four *Askari* killed, and we also counted seventy-one *Askari* hit. So the enemy's losses amounted to about two hundred, as confirmed by native reports received later. We had four Europeans and twenty *Askari* killed, nine Europeans and thirty-four *Askari* wounded.

Owing to the nature of the country and the relative strengths, we were unable to achieve a decisive success on the Russissi. Only the Urundi Detachment and one field company were, therefore, left there; two companies left on the 18th and 19th December, 1915, to join Captain Wintgens in Ruanda; three others moved to the Central Railway.

On the 19th October the enemy met the 14th Reserve Company, and although outnumbering it by two to one, lost twenty *Askari*, while we had three *Askari* killed and twelve wounded. Although the Belgian main camp, which reliable natives reported to contain two thousand *Askari*, was so near, it was possible to reduce the troops on the Russissi in favour of other districts, since on both sides the conditions seemed unfavourable for an offensive. The Urundi Detachment and the 14th Reserve Company remained on the Russissi under Major von Langenn.

On Lake Tanganyika, at the beginning of the war, Captain Zimmer had collected about one hundred men of the *Moewe*, and in Usambara, about one hundred *Askari*; in addition, he had a few Europeans who were called up in Kigoma, also some one hundred *Askari* belonging to the posts in Urundi and from Ruanda (Wintgens)—all told, about four hundred rifles.

On the 22nd August, 1914, Lieutenant Horn, of the *Moewe*, commanding the small armed steamer *Hedwig von Wissmann*, fought a successful action against the Belgian steamer *Delcommune*. The captain of the *Moewe*, Lieutenant-Commander Zimmer, had gone to Kigoma with his crew, after destroying his ship, which had been blown up in August, 1914. The steamer *Kingani*, which had also been transported to the same place by rail from Dar-es-Salaam, and several smaller craft on Lake Tanganyika, were then armed and put in commission by Lieutenant-Commander Zimmer. He also mounted a 3.5-inch naval gun on a raft and bombarded a number of Belgian stations on the shore. He strongly fortified Kigoma itself, and developed it into a base for naval warfare on Lake Tanganyika.

On the 20th November, 1914, the Bismarckburg Detachment (half company), co-operating with the small armed steamers *Hedwig von Wissmann* and *Kingani*, drove off a Belgian company in the bay west of Bismarckburg, captured four .43-inch machine guns and over ninety miles of telegraph wire, which was used to continue the line Kilossa-Iringa up to New Langenburg, a work which was, from a military point of view, extremely urgent.

Early in October attempts were made to complete the destruction of the Belgian steamer *Delcommune*, which was lying at Baraka, on the Congo shore, but without success. After bombarding her once more on the 23rd October, Captain Zimmer looked upon her as permanently out of action. On the 27th February, 1915, the crew of the *Hedwig von Wissmann* surprised a Belgian post at Tombwe, and captured its machine gun. One Belgian officer and ten *Askari* were killed, one severely wounded Belgian officer and one Englishman were captured. We had one *Askari* killed, one European mortally wounded, one *Askari* severely wounded.

In March, 1915, the Belgians made arrests on a large scale in Ubwari, the inhabitants of which had shown themselves friendly to us, and hanged a number of people.

According to wireless messages which we took in, several Belgian whale-boats were got ready on Lake Tanganyika during June, and work was being carried on on a new Belgian steamer, the *Baron Dhanis*. On our side the steamer *Goetzen* was completed on the 9th June, 1915, and taken over by the Force. She rendered good service in effecting movements of troops on Lake Tanganyika.

The Police at Bismarckburg, under Lieutenant Haun of the Reserve, the capable administrator of the Baziots, had joined the Protective Force. Several skirmishes took place in hostile territory, and in this district also the enemy was, on the whole, kept successfully at a distance.

It was not till early in February, 1915, that several hundred hostile *Askari* invaded Abercorn, and some of them penetrated to near Mwasge Mission, but then retired.

Then, in the middle of March, Lieutenant Haun's force was surprised in camp at Mount Kito by an Anglo-Belgian detachment. The commander was severely wounded and taken prisoner, and several *Askari* were killed. Lieutenant Aumann, with a force subsequently formed into a company, was detached from Captain Falkenstein, and covered the German border in the neighbourhood of Mbozi, where, in February, 1915, detachments several hundred strong had frequently invaded German territory; at the end of March an unknown number of Europeans were reported in Karonga, while at Fife and other places on the frontier there were some eight hundred men.

So the enemy appeared to be preparing to attack. He was patrolling as far as the country near Itaka, and early in April it was reported that Kituta, at the southern end of Lake Tanganyika, had been entrenched by the Belgians. Major von Langenn, who, after recovering from his severe wound—he had lost an eye—was working on the Russissi River, was entrusted with the conduct of operations in

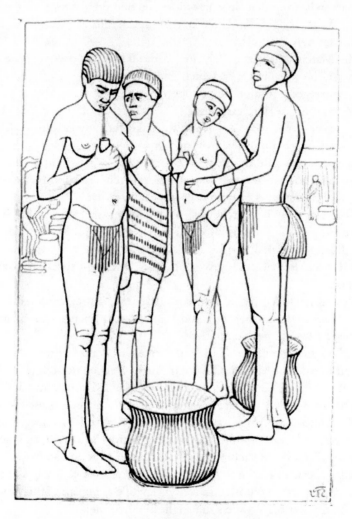

NATIVE WOMEN.
DRAWN BY GENERAL VON LETTOW-VORBECK'S ADJUTANT.

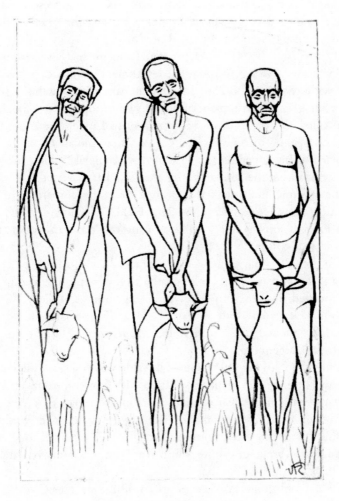

NATIVES BRINGING FOOD.
DRAWN GENERAL VON LETTOW-VORBECK'S ADJUTANT.

the well-known Bismarckburg-Langenburg country. Besides the 5th Field Company, which he had formerly commanded, and which was stationed at Ipyana and in the Mbozi country, he was also given the Bismarckburg Detachment, strength about one company, and three companies which were brought up from Dar-es-Salaam and Kigoma. During their passage to Bismarckburg on the lake successful actions were fought east of that place by our patrols against hostile raiding parties of fifty to two hundred and fifty men.

By the 7th May, 1915, Major von Langenn had assembled four companies at Mwasge; a Belgian detachment stationed in front of him withdrew. On the 23rd May Lieutenant von Delschitz's patrol drove off a Belgian company, of which two Europeans and six *Askari* were killed. On the 24th orders were sent to Langenn to move with three companies to New Langenburg to meet the attack which was reported to be impending in that quarter. General Wahle took over the command in the Bismarckburg area. The latter arrived at Kigoma on the 6th June, and collected at Bismarckburg the Bismarckburg Detachment, now re-formed as the 29th Field Company, as well as the 24th Field Company and a half-company of Europeans brought up from Dar-es-Salaam.

On the 28th June General Wahle attacked Jericho Farm with two and a half companies, but broke off the engagement on realizing that this fortified position could not be taken without artillery. We had three Europeans and four *Askari* killed, two Europeans and twenty-two *Askari* wounded. General Wahle was reinforced by two companies from Langenburg.

Since the 25th July, 1915, General Wahle was besieging the enemy, who was strongly entrenched at Jericho, with four companies and two 1873-pattern guns. Relief expeditions from Abercorn were defeated, but the siege was raised on the 2nd August, as no effect could be produced with the guns available. General Wahle returned to Dar-es-Salaam with three companies. The 29th Company remained at Jericho, the two guns at Kigoma.

Or the 19th June the *Goetzen* towed off the steamer *Cecil Rhodes,* which was lying beached at Kituta, and sank her.

During September and October there were continual skirmishes between patrols on the border near Bismarckburg; Belgian reinforcements again invaded the country about Abercorn. On the 3rd December it was observed that the defences of Jericho had been abandoned and dismantled. A new fort, north-east of Abercorn, was bombarded by Lieutenant Franken on the 6th December with one hundred rifles and one machine gun; the enemy appeared to sustain some casualties.

The English Naval Expedition, the approach of which, by Bukoma and Elizabethville, had long been under observation, had reached the Lukuga Railway on the 22nd October, 1919. We picked up leaflets which stated that a surprise was being prepared for the Germans on Lake Tanganyika; this made me think that we might now have to deal with specially-built small craft which might possibly be equipped with torpedoes. We had, therefore, to meet a very serious menace to our command of Lake Tanganyika, which might prove decisive to our whole campaign. The simultaneous transfer of hostile troops towards Lake Kivu and Abercorn proved that an offensive by land was to be co-ordinated with the expedition. In order to defeat the enemy if possible while his concentration was still in progress, Captain Schulz attacked the Belgians at Luwungi on the 27th September, inflicting heavy loss.

On the night of the 28th October the steamer *Kingani* surprised a Belgian working-party, who were constructing a telegraph line, and captured some stores. In the mouth of the Lukuga river a railway train was observed on the move. At last, the Kingani did not return from a reconnaissance to the mouth of the Lukuga, and, according to a Belgian wireless message of the 31st December, she had been lost, four Europeans and eight natives were said to have been killed, the remainder to have been captured. Evidently, the favourable opportunity for interfering with the enemy's preparations for gaining command of the Lake had passed.

Then, on the 9th February, 1916, another of our armed steamers was captured by the enemy.

On Lake Nyassa the German steamer *Hermann von Wissmann*, whose captain did not know that war had broken out, was surprised and taken by the English Government steamer *Gwendolen* on the 13th August, 1914.

On the 9th September, 1914, Captain von Langenn, with his 5th Field Company, which was stationed at Massoko, near New Langenburg, had attacked the English station of Karongo. In the action with the English, who were holding a fortified position, Captain von Langenn himself was severely wounded. The two company officers were also severely wounded and taken prisoners. The German non-commissioned officers and the *Askari* fought very gallantly, but were obliged to recognize that they could do nothing against the enemy's entrenchments, and, therefore, broke off the hopeless engagement. Over twenty *Askari* had been killed, several machine guns and light guns had been lost.

Reinforcements from the 2nd Company at once arrived from Iringa and Ubena, and several hundred Wahehe auxiliaries were raised. Gradually it turned out that the enemy had also suffered severely. He avoided expeditions on a large scale against the Langenburg District, and so this fertile country, which was so necessary to us as a source of supply, remained in our possession for eighteen months.

Later on our company at Langenburg moved its main body nearer the border to Ipyana Mission. On the 2nd November an affair of outposts occurred on the Lufira River, and the steamer *Gwendolen* on Lake Nyassa was hit several times by our artillery.

Early in December, 1914, some fighting between patrols took place north of Karongo, on the Ssongwe River. Lieutenant Dr. Gothein, of the Medical Corps, who had been returned to us from captivity by the English in May, 1915, told us that in the first action at Karongo, on the 9th September, 1914, the enemy had had six Europeans and fifty *Askari* killed, and seven Europeans and more than fifty *Askari* severely wounded. The English spies were very active, especially through the agency of the "*Vali,*" the native administrative official, on the Ssongwe.

In May, 1915, we were able to effect several successful surprises on the frontier. The rains were late, so that we could consider the southern part of Langenburg District as safe from attack until the end of June.

In June, 1915, when Major von Langenn had arrived with his reinforcements, there were, contrary to our expectations, no considerable actions. We made use of the time to dismantle a telegraph line in English territory, and to put it up again in our own, in the direction of Ubena. In August, the rumours of an intended attack by the enemy were again falsified. It was not till the 8th October that considerable hostile forces of Europeans and *Askari* arrived at Fife. On this border also there were numerous little skirmishes. Towards the end of the year the arrival of fresh reinforcements at Ikawa was also established. In that region, on the 23rd December, 1915, Captain Aumann repulsed a force of about 60 Europeans with 2 machine guns, who were attempting a surprise.

On the shores of Lake Nyassa there were only insignificant encounters.

On the 30th May the English landed 30 Europeans, 200 *Askari* 2 guns and 2 machine guns at Sphinx Harbour. We had there 13 rifles and one machine gun, who inflicted on them, apparently, over 20 casualties, whereupon, after destroying the wreck of the *Hermann von Wissmann*, they retired.

PART 2

THE CONCENTRIC ATTACK BY SUPERIOR FORCES
(From the arrival of the South African troops to the loss of the Colony)

CHAPTER 1

The Enemy's Attack at Oldorobo Mountain

East of Oldorobo the enemy now frequently showed considerable bodies of troops, amounting to 1,000 or more men, who deployed in the direction of the mountain at great distances, but did not approach it closely. These movements, therefore, were exercises, by which the young European troops from South Africa were to be trained to move and fight in the bush.

Early in February the enemy advanced against Oldorobo from the east with several regiments. For us it was desirable that he should take so firm a hold there that he could not get away again, so that we could defeat him by means of a counter-attack with Captain Schulz' Detachment, encamped at Taveta. Other German detachments, of several companies each, were stationed west of Taveta on the road to New Moshi, and on that to Kaho, at New Steglitz Plantation.

On the 12th February again, European troops, estimated at several regiments, advanced to within 300 yards of Oldorobo. Headquarters at New Moshi, which was in constant telephonic communication with Major Kraut, considered that the favourable opportunity had now presented itself, and ordered fire to be opened. The effect of our machine-guns, and our two light guns, had been reported to be good, when Headquarters left New Moshi by car for the field of battle. Schulz' Detachment was ordered to march from Taveta along the rear of Kraut's Detachment, covered from the fire of the enemy's heavy artillery, and to make a decisive attack on the enemy's right, or northern, wing.

The troops at New Steglitz advanced to Taveta, where some fantastic reports came in about hostile armoured cars, which were alleged to be moving through the thorn-bush desert. The imagination of the natives, to whom these armoured cars were something altogether new and surprising, had made them see ghosts. On arriving on Oldorobo, Headquarters was informed by telephone that the enemy, who had attacked our strongly entrenched front, had been repulsed with heavy losses, and that Schulz' Detachment was fully deployed and advancing against his right flank.

The numerous English howitzer shells which fell in our position on Oldorobo did hardly any damage, although they were very well placed. In contrast to the great expenditure of ammunition by the hostile artillery, our light guns had to restrict themselves to taking advantage of specially favourable targets, not only because ammunition was scarce, but also because we had no shrapnel. The enemy retreated through the bush in disorder. We buried more than 60 Europeans. According to prisoners' statements and captured papers, three regiments of the 2nd South African Infantry Brigade had been in action.

According to the documents it appeared that in recruiting the men the prospect of acquiring farms and plantations had been used as a bait. The sudden illness of the British General Smith-Dorrien, who was already on his way out to take over command in East Africa, may not have been altogether inconvenient to the English (*Smith-Dorrien* by Horace Smith-Dorrien also published by Leonaur). The transfer of the command to a South African, General Smuts, reacted favourably on recruiting in South Africa. The training of these newly raised formations was slight, and the conduct of the Europeans, many of whom were very young, proved that many had never yet taken part in a serious action. After the action of Oldorobo, however, we observed that the enemy sought very thoroughly to make good the deficiencies in his training.

In spite of pursuit by Schulz' Detachment, and repeated fire opened on collections of hostile troops, the enemy, owing to the difficult and close nature of the country, made good his escape to his fortified camps.

It was interesting to find, in several diaries we picked up, notes to the effect that strict orders had been given to take no prisoners. As a matter of fact the enemy had taken none, but it seemed advisable nevertheless to address an inquiry to the British Commander, in order that we might regulate our conduct towards the English prisoners accordingly. There is no reason to doubt Brigadier-General Malleson's statement that no such order was given; but this case, and several later instances, show what nonsense is to be found in private diaries. It was quite wrong on the part of the enemy if he accepted the German notes which fell into his hands as true, without detailed investigation.

At this time also the hostile troops on Longido Mountain had been considerably reinforced. This mountain had been evacuated by the enemy, probably owing to difficulties of supply, but had latterly been reoccupied. The rock is covered with dense vegetation, and our patrols had several times ascended it and examined the enemy's camps at close quarters. It is at any time difficult correctly to estimate the strength of troops, but in bush country, where more than a few men are never to be seen at a time, and where the view is constantly changing, it is impossible. The reports of the natives were too inaccurate. On the whole, however, we could but conclude from the general situation, and from the increased quantity of supplies which were being brought to Longido from the north, by ox wagon, without interruption, that the enemy was being considerably reinforced.

His raids into the Kilima Njaro country had been repulsed with slaughter. When a squadron of Indian lancers moved south, between Kilima Njaro and Meru Mountain, it was at once vigorously attacked by one of our mounted patrols under Lieutenant Freiherr von Lyncker. Our *Askari* had come to understand the great value of saddle-horses in our operations, and charged the enemy, who was mounted, with the cry: "*Wahindi, kameta frasi!*" ("They are Indians, catch the horses!") The Indians were so surprised by the rapidity of our people that they fled in confusion, leaving some of their horses behind. Among others the gallant European commander had been left dead on the field; he had not been able to prevent his men from losing their heads.

I should like to remark generally that during this first period of the war the conduct of the British regular officers was invariably chivalrous, and that the respect they paid us was fully reciprocated. But our *Askari* also earned the respect of the enemy by their bravery in action and their humane conduct. On the 10th March the English Lieutenant Barrett was severely wounded and fell into our hands; owing to false accounts he thought his last moment had come, and was surprised when our *Askari*, who had no European with them, tied him up as well as they could and carried him to a doctor. In his astonishment he remarked: "Why, your *Askari* are gentlemen."

How greatly the English soldiers had been misled I learned on the 12th February from a young South African captured on Oldorobo,

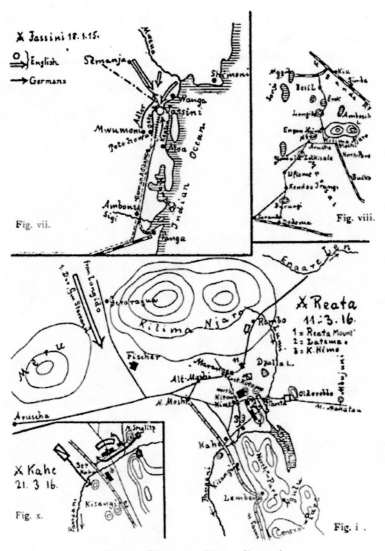

FIG. VII. BATTLE OF VASIN (JASSINI).
FIG. VIII. KILIMA NJARO AND MASAI DESERT
FIG. IX. BATTLE OF REATA
FIG. X. BATTLE OF KAHE.

who asked whether he was going to be shot. Of course we laughed at him. No doubt, in a long war, cases of brutality and inhumanity do occur. But that happens on both sides, and one should not generalize from isolated cases, and exploit them for the purpose of unworthy agitation, as has been done by the English Press.

Chapter 2

Action at Reata

At that time we noticed the first parties of hostile spies, and captured some of them. They were "*Shensi*" (innocent-looking natives), who, as a proof of having really reached the objective of their mission, had to bring back certain objects, such as parts of the permanent way of the Usambara Railway. The general review of the situation showed that the enemy was making a detailed reconnaissance of the Usambara Railway and the approaches to it. A glance at the map shows that a simultaneous advance by the enemy from Oldorobo and Longido towards New Moshi was bound to entail the loss of the Kilima Njaro country, which was of value to us from the point of view of maintenance.

If, however, we wanted to retire before a superior enemy on our main line of communication, we should be obliged to move our main forces along the Usambara Railway, thus making almost an acute angle with the direction of an attack coming from Oldorobo. The danger of being cut off by the enemy from this, our principal line of communication, was for us very great. Should the enemy advance north of Lake Jipe, he would be cramped by Kilima Njaro and by the steep group of the North Pare Mountains. It is obvious that in that case his advance directly on Kahe would be the most inconvenient for us, and if successful, would cut the Usambara Railway, our line of communications. But it would be even more serious for us if the enemy should pass south of Lake Jipe, and press forward by the valley leading between the North and Middle Pare, to the Northern Railway, south of Lembeni. Finally, he could reach the railway by way of the valley at Same, between the Middle and South Pare.

In his advance on Lembeni and Same the enemy would be able to make a road suitable for motor traffic with rapidity, and in places without preparation, across the open plain, and to base his operations upon it.

The small forces we had in the Kilima Njaro country—about 4,000 rifles—rendered it impossible to divide them in order to render ourselves secure against all these possibilities. Even for purely defensive reasons we must keep our forces concentrated and maintain close touch with the enemy, in order to hold him fast where we were, and thus keep his movements under observation. It was from the outset very doubtful whether we could in succession defeat the two main hostile groups, whose advance towards the Kilima Njaro country was to be expected from Longido and Makatau, and which were each considerably stronger than ourselves.

There was no prospect of doing so unless our troops could be moved with lightning rapidity, first against one of the enemy's forces and then, just as quickly, against the other. The necessary preparations were made, and after personal reconnaissance, a number of cross-country tracks in the rugged forest country north of the great road which leads from New Moshi to the west were decided upon. As it happened, no considerable use was made of these tracks. It would not do to be afraid of trying anything ninety-nine times, if there was a chance of succeeding at the hundredth. In following this principle we did not do badly.

The enemy's activity increased, and he displayed good training in numerous minor encounters. He had also raised a number of new *Askari* formations, largely recruited among the intelligent tribes of the Wyassa country. Being only sparsely covered with bush, and therefore very open, the desert country lying to the north-west of Kilima Njaro did not favour sudden offensive operations by us; for this purpose the dense bush district between Kilima Njaro and Meru Mountain itself, which the enemy, coming from Longido, would probably have to traverse, was more promising. Here we concentrated a detachment of some 1,000 rifles, composed of five selected *Askari* Companies. But, owing to the limited range of vision, this detachment did not succeed in forcing a decisive engagement on any of the numerous hostile columns which pushed down to the south in the beginning of March.

The enemy, also, had great difficulty in finding his way; and we only learned from an Indian despatch-rider, who brought a report to us instead of to his own people, that the 1st East African Division, under General Stewart, was in this district. As these encounters took place in the neighbourhood of Gararagua, and south-west of that place, it was too far away for our reserves at New Steglitz and Himo to intervene. (It is about two marches from Gararagua to New Moshi.) Before the chance of doing so arrived the enemy also advanced from the east. The direction taken by the enemy's airmen showed his evident interest in the country one or two hours north of Taveta. One was bound to hit on the idea that the enemy encamped east of Oldorobo did not intend to get his head broken a second time on that mountain, but meant to work round the position by the north, and so reach the Lumi River, one hour north of Taveta.

On the 8th March observers on Oldorobo noticed huge clouds of dust moving from the enemy's camp in that direction. Numerous motors were also seen. From East Kitovo, a mountain four miles west of Taveta, Headquarters also observed these movements. Our fighting patrols, who were able to fire with effect on the hostile columns, and to take a few prisoners, established with certainty that the enemy's main force was approaching at this point, and that General Smuts was present.

On the afternoon of the 8th March Headquarters observed strong hostile columns near Lake Dsalla, who advanced from there in a widely extended line of skirmishers for some distance towards East Kitovo. On this occasion, and on many others, our want of artillery obliged us to look on quietly while the enemy executed unskilful movements at no great distance from our front. But it was evident that this enveloping movement of the enemy rendered the Oldorobo position, to which we owed many successful engagements during the course of the war, untenable. I therefore decided to deploy the troops for a fresh stand on the mountains which close the gap between the North Pare Mountains and Kilima Njaro to the westward of Taveta. Kraut's Detachment was ordered by telephone to take up a position on the Resta-Latema Mountains, on the road leading from Taveta to New Steglitz.

North-west of Latema Mountain, on the road from Taveta to Himo, Schulz's Detachment occupied the mountains of North Kitovo, and covered the move of Kraut's Detachment. These movements were executed by night, without being interfered with by the enemy. On our extreme left wing, on the south-eastern slopes of Kilima Njaro, Captain Stemmermann's Company blocked the road leading from Rombo Mission to Himo and New Moshi. Rombo Mission was occupied by the enemy. Some of the natives made no attempt to conceal the fact that they now adhered to the English. This lends colour to the supposition that English espionage and propaganda among the natives had for a long time been going on in this district, and that the light-signals which had often been seen on the eastern slopes of Kilima Njaro had some connection with it.

The mountain position taken up by us was very favourable as regards ground, but suffered from the great disadvantage that our few thousand *Askari* were far too few really to fill up the front, which was some twelve miles in extent. Only a few points in the front line could be occupied; the bulk of the force was kept at my disposal at Himo, to be brought into action according to how the situation might develop. It was a time of great tension. Before us was the greatly superior enemy; behind us, advancing to the south from Londigo, another superior opponent, while our communications, which also formed our line of retreat, were threatened by the enemy in the very unpleasant manner already described.

But, in view of the ground, which we knew, and the apparently not too skilful tactical leading on the part of the enemy, I did not think it impossible to give at least one of his detachments a thorough beating. The positions on the line Reata-North Kitovo were therefore to be prepared for a stubborn defence. From Tanga, one of the *Königsberg's* guns mounted there was brought up by rail. The reader will rightly ask why this had not been done long before. But the gun had no wheels, and fired from a fixed pivot, so that it was very immobile. It is therefore comprehensible that we delayed bringing it into action until there could be no doubt as to the precise spot where it would be wanted.

The situation now developed so rapidly that the gun could not be used against Taveta. It was therefore mounted near the railway at Kahe, on the south bank of the Pangani River, from which position it did excellent service later in the actions at Kahe.

On the 10th March the enemy reconnoitred along our whole front. Mounted detachments of about 50 men rode up, dismounted, and then advanced in a widely extended line, leading their horses, until they were fired on. This was their object. The fire disclosed our positions, although imperfectly. This method of reconnaissance gave us the opportunity for scoring local successes, which cost the enemy a certain number of men, and brought us in some score of horses. From North Kitovo Mountain we could plainly see how portions of our firing line, taking advantage of favourable situations, rapidly advanced and fired upon the enemy's reconnoitring parties from several directions. To me the force employed by the enemy in these enterprises appeared too large to be explained by the mere intention of reconnaissance; they looked to me more like serious but somewhat abortive attacks.

It was not yet possible to form a clear idea of the direction from which the enemy's main attack would come. The tactical difficulties of enveloping our left (north) wing were far less, but this operation would prevent him from exerting effective pressure on our communications. The direction from Taveta through Reata towards Kahe would be the worst for us, but entailed for the enemy a difficult frontal attack on the fortified heights of Reata and Latema, which promised but little success even if made in greatly superior strength. I, therefore, thought it advisable to move Captain Koehl with two companies so close up in rear of Major Kraut's Detachment, which was on the high ground between Reata and Latema, that we could intervene rapidly without waiting for orders.

For the moment, telephonic communication with our detachments was secure. But it was to be anticipated that it would become at least very difficult, so soon as any detachment moved away from the existing lines. There was no material available for rapidly laying a cable that could follow moving troops. We were also deficient of light wireless apparatus, by means of which later on the English successfully controlled the movements of their columns in the bush.

On the 11th March another aeroplane appeared over New Moshi and dropped a few bombs. I was just talking to an old Boer about the fight on the 12th February, and saying that the English were incurring a grave responsibility in ruthlessly exposing so many young men, who were quite ignorant of the Tropics, to the dangers of our climate and of tropical warfare. Major Kraut reported from Reata that strong hostile forces were moving up towards his positions from the direction of Taveta. Soon after, a powerful attack was made by several thousand men on the three companies holding our position. Our three light guns could, of course, not engage in a duel with the heavy artillery, and, as at Oldorobo, had to restrict themselves to employing their few shells against the denser masses of the enemy at favourable moments.

Knowing the difficulties of the ground, I thought the attack had little prospect of success, but the two companies of Captain Koehl held in readiness behind Major Kraut's Detachment were, nevertheless, sent in to attack. Captain Koehl, who had originally intended to attack the enemy in flank, which would have suited the situation and proved decisive, was obliged to recognize that in the unknown and dense bush this was impossible. The time and place, and, therefore, the effectiveness of this attack, would have become matters of pure chance. He, therefore, quite rightly marched up to the immediate support of Major Kraut. From what I could observe for myself from North Kitovo, and according to the reports that came in, it appeared that the enemy wanted to keep us occupied in front from Reata to Kitovo, while his decisive movement was being made round our left wing. In the first instance large bodies of horsemen were moving in that direction who appeared and disappeared again among the heights and gullies of the south-east slopes of Kilima Njaro.

The 11th Company, under Captain Stemmermann, which was on the slopes above these horsemen, prevented them from reaching the summit. During the course of the afternoon the leading horsemen had worked their way through the dense banana-plantations to near Marangu. They appeared to be very exhausted. Some of them were seen to be eating the unripe bananas.

During the afternoon it became evident that the enemy was making a strong frontal attack against Kraut's Detachment on Reata and Latema Mountain. But the telephonic reports were favourable : the enemy was obviously suffering heavy casualties; hundreds of stretchers were being employed in getting away the wounded. By evening all the enemy's attacks on our front had been repulsed with heavy losses. In the darkness Captain Koehl's two companies had pursued with energy and opened machine-gun fire on the enemy when he tried to make a stand. In the evening I had gone to Himo, and about 11 p.m. I was engaged in issuing orders for an attack to be made early on the 12th on the enemy's horsemen, whose presence had been established at Marangu.

Just then Lieutenant Sternheim, commanding the guns with Kraut's Detachment, telephoned that the enemy had attacked once more in the night and had penetrated into the Reata position in great force. This report made it appear probable that this strong, hostile force would now press forward from Reata in the direction of Kahe, and cut us off from our communications. To accept this risk, and still carry out the attack on the enemy at Marangu, appeared to be too dangerous. I therefore ordered the troops at Kitovo and Himo to fall back during the night to the Reata-Kahe road. As a covering force Stemmermann's Company was for the time being to remain at Himo.

This march was bound to entail the unpleasant consequence that, at the very best, all communication between Headquarters and the various units would cease. Anyone who has experienced these night marches knows also how easily some parts of the force may become entirely detached and cannot be reached for ever and a day. Fortunately I had at least some knowledge of the ground, as we moved across country to the new road, while we heard continuous heavy firing going on on Reata and Latema Mountains. A few stragglers who had lost their way in the bush came towards us; when we said we were Germans they did not believe us, and disappeared again.

On the new road we found the dressing station. Here, too, the reports of the numerous wounded were so contradictory and obscure that one could only gather the impression of very heavy fighting in the bush at close quarters, but failed to learn anything of its various phases or results. By and by we got through on the telephone to Major Kraut, who, with part of his detachment, was on the Kahe-Taveta road, on the south-west slope of Reata Mountain. On the heights the fire had gradually died down, and his patrols had found no more trace of the enemy on Reata Mountain. Early in the morning of the 12th Major Kraut found some of his detachment again in their old positions on the hills: the enemy had fallen back to Taveta.

When I arrived at Reata Mountain at six in the morning the great quantity of booty was being collected. Very great confusion had occurred in the close-quarter fighting by night. English dead, who were lying in the bush far in rear of the front of Kraut's Detachment, proved that certain detachments of the enemy had got behind our line. Individual snipers, hidden away among the rocks, maintained a well-aimed fire, and could not be dislodged. It was, however, clear that the enemy had been repulsed with heavy casualties. Both our own wounded and those of the enemy were got away without a hitch, and so were the prisoners. With the detachments that were moving from the vicinity of Himo through the dense bush to the Kahe-Reata road we had no communication, and could expect to have none for several hours more.

In this situation it was regrettable that I had ordered the troops forming our left wing, who had been posted between Kitovo and Himo, to withdraw to the Kahe-Reata road. After giving up the high ground held by our left wing the Reata position would in time become untenable, the more so as it had no supply of water, which had to be brought up from a place an hour's march further back. It was impossible to turn back the units of the left wing to reoccupy the

Himo-Kitovo area as we were at the moment completely out of touch with them, and, as has been mentioned, there was no expectation of regaining it for hours to come. I decided to evacuate the Reata position, and after the battlefield was cleared I returned with the line that was nearest to the enemy to the water south-west of Reata Mountain. In the course of the day the other detachments reached the Kahe-Reata road at different points further to the rear and encamped.

Headquarters moved to New Steglitz Plantation. The buildings are situated halfway between Kahe and Reata, on a slight elevation affording a distant view over the forest, which is particularly dense along the Kahe-Reata road. On the way I met Captain Schoenfeld, who reported that he had mounted his 4-inch gun out of the *Königsberg* near Kahe village on the south bank of the Pangani. After our withdrawal the enemy occupied Reata Mountain and for a while fired into the blue with light guns and rifles.

During the next few days we observed the advance of strong hostile forces from the direction of Taveta to Himo, and the pitching of large camps at that place. Against the Little Himo, a mountain in front of our line which we were not holding, the enemy developed a powerful attack from the east, across a perfectly open plain, which, after a long and heavy bombardment of the empty hill, ended in its capture. Unfortunately, we were unable to move our troops sufficiently rapidly to come down upon this attack out of the thick bush. From the Little Himo the enemy frequently bombarded the Plantation building of New Steglitz with light artillery.

Some weeks before, after a successful buffalo-hunt, I had enjoyed a hospitable hour in the few rooms of this building. The native who had guided us on that occasion had deserted to the English. Now it provided decidedly cramped accommodation for Headquarters and the telephone exchange. I myself was lucky enough to find a fairly comfortable shake-down on the sofa, with the cloth off the dining-table. Telephone messages and reports came in day and night without ceasing; but they did not prevent us from making the material side of our existence tolerably comfortable.

We had a roof over our heads, and the use of a kitchen equipped in European style, and carried on our combined mess as previously at New Moshi. The circumstances peculiar to East Africa make it necessary for the European to maintain a number of servants which to home ideas seems excessive. Even now, on active service, nearly everyone had two "Boys" who took charge of the cooking utensils and provisions we carried with us, cooked excellently, baked bread, washed, and generally provided us in the bush with a good proportion of the comforts which in Europe are only to be found in dwelling houses. Even in the heart of the bush I restricted these alleviations as little as possible, out of consideration for the strength, health and spirit of the Europeans. If, in spite of this, Headquarters often preferred to occupy buildings, this was done less for the sake of comfort than in order to facilitate the unavoidable work of writing and drawing.

While we were at New Steglitz we received the surprising news that a second store-ship had reached the Colony, with arms, ammunition including several thousand rounds for the 4-inch *Königsberg* guns, which were now employed on land and other warlike stores. The ship had run into Ssudi Bay, at the extreme south of our coast, and had immediately begun to discharge her cargo. In spite of the great distance, and the exclusive use of carriers, the whole of it was made available for the troops. This achievement was indeed surprising, in view of the large number of hostile ships that were blockading and searching our coast-line, and which were aware of the arrival of the store-ship.

But she probably surprised the English also, for after discharging her cargo, she put to sea again, and disappeared, much to the astonishment of the enemy. Chaff between the Navy and the Army is not unknown even in England, and if the latter is reproached for not having been able to finish us off, the former may be silenced with the justifiable retort that it should not have allowed us to obtain such great supplies of arms and ammunition. The bulk of the stores was transported by land to the Central Railway, and was stored along, or near it, at the disposal of Headquarters. Owing to our lack of suitable artillery it was particularly advantageous that we were quickly able to bring up the four field-howitzers and two mountain guns which had come in the ship.

The store-ship had also brought out decorations for war service: one Iron Cross of the First Class for the captain of the *Königsberg*, and enough of the Second Class to enable half her company to have one each. For the Protective Force there were an Iron Cross of the First Class, and one of the Second Class, which were for me, and a number of decorations for the *Askari*. As regards the Europeans, we only heard in September, 1916, by wireless that the decorations recommended by Headquarters had been approved.

CHAPTER 3

Retreat Before Overwhelming Hostile Pressure

In our rear, Major Fischer, who with five companies had been employed between Kilima Njaro and Meru, had evaded the enemy's superior forces by moving on New Moshi, and had been ordered up to Kahe. Captain Rothert, who had been acting under his orders with his company and the Arusha Detachment (strength about one company), had been energetically pursued by the enemy, and had made his way by Arusha towards Kondoa-Irangi. We could only expect to get into touch with him by the wire which had been put up from Dodome, by Kondoa-Irangi to Umbulu, and that only after a considerable time. By abandoning New Moshi we, of necessity, left the road Taveta-New Moshi-Arusha open to the enemy. The latter was thus also enabled to penetrate into the interior of the Colony with his troops from Taveta by Arusha and Kondoa-Irangi, and to act there against our communication at an extremely dangerous point.

From our troops concentrated in the neighbourhood of Kahe and New Steglitz he had not much to fear during this operation. Although we had brought up all our companies from Tanga, leaving there only the troops absolutely indispensable for security, all we could do with our four thousand rifles was to let the enemy run up against us on suitable ground, and, possibly, to take advantage of any mistakes he might make by skilful and rapid action; but the odds against us being seven to one we could attempt no more. From an attack on an enemy superior not only in numbers, but also in equipment, and holding fortified positions into the bargain, I could not possibly hope for success. I could not, therefore, accede to the requests of my company commanders that we should attack, but this expression of a bold soldierly spirit gave me strength and hope in the serious situation in which we were placed.

Minor enterprises, undertaken against the enemy's camps by patrols and small detachments, produced no results of consequence; but they may have helped to make the enemy's main force take some notice of us instead of simply marching on past us. He certainly did push on to the west from Himo, and heavy clouds of dust were seen moving to New Moshi and further on to the west. But a large part of the enemy coming from Himo turned in our direction. For the commander such situations are extraordinarily trying; he is not master of the situation, and must, of necessity, renounce the initiative. Only the most careful reconnaissance may perhaps reveal some weakness of the opponent, and in order to utilize this weakness and regain the initiative, not a moment must be lost. Fortunately, however, the enemy did expose weak points of which we were able to take at least partial advantage.

Owing to the dense bush and high forest in which our camps were hidden, aerial reconnaissance can hardly have been any use to the enemy. The bombs dropped by the enemy caused only a few casualties at Kahe, and did not interfere with us in getting away our stores through that place. In order to draw our fire, the well-known English horsemen appeared once more north-west of New Steglitz in a widely-extended skirmishing line. In front of them, hidden in the bush, were our companies, ready to take hold immediately larger bodies should appear. A counter-attack of this description was made late in the afternoon on the 15th March, and with fair success. In order to become thoroughly acquainted with the ground, European patrols were constantly moving about, and I also made use of every available minute. Through the bush we cut and marked tracks. By this means we could clearly indicate any point to which a detachment was required to go.

On the main road leading from Himo to Kahe a strong hostile force had also appeared and pushed close up to the front of Stemmermann's Detachment, which occupied a fortified position on this road at Kahe, facing north. With considerable skill patrols worked close up to the detachment, and so concealed the movements of the enemy. When I arrived there in the afternoon of the 20th March, it was not at all clear what was really going on in front. It was quite possible that the enemy was merely making a demonstration in order to attack at some other, more dangerous, spot.

Such a manoeuvre would have been very menacing to us, as the close nature of the bush country would prevent us from detecting it until very late, probably too late. I decided to drive the enemy's screen back on his position proper. Earlier in the day it had been given out that the companies were to move off to their former positions at one a.m.; the machine guns were left in our entrenchments so as not to lose them, and as a measure of protection. It was bright moonlight when the leading company was fired on, apparently by a hostile outpost, or patrol, which moved off.

After that we encountered several patrols, but then, about three miles north of our own trenches, we came upon a stronger opponent with machine guns. The very severe action which now developed proved that we had come up against the enemy's main position; to assault it seemed hopeless. Leaving patrols out, I withdrew step by step. Our casualties were not inconsiderable, and unfortunately included three company commanders, who were difficult to replace; of the three, Lieutenant von Stosch and Freiherr Grote died of their wounds a few days later, while Captain Augar only became fit for duty again after a long time and when provided with an artificial foot.

Our withdrawal, which the enemy probably took to be involuntary, apparently led him to believe that he would be able to rout us next day by a vigorous attack. The attacks made by powerful hostile forces on the front of Stemmermann's Detachment at Kahe on the 21st March were unsuccessful; the enemy, composed mainly of South African infantry, was beaten off with heavy loss. Our four-inch *Königsberg* gun, directed from elevated sites affording a good view, fired on the approaching enemy, apparently with good effect. It may be assumed that part of their severe casualties, which the English stated to have amounted on this day to several hundred among the South African Europeans alone, were caused by this gun. The enemy realized that he could not advance over the field of fire extending for five hundred yards in front of our trenches with any hope of success, and endeavoured to envelop our right flank.

But having previously reconnoitred and determined tracks, we were also well prepared to execute a counter-attack, and in the afternoon Schulz's Detachment effectively struck at the enemy's flank. The last part of Schulz's advance had, indeed, been very arduous owing to the thick bush. The *Askari* could only work through it step by step, when they suddenly heard the enemy's machine guns at work only a few paces in front of them.

Unfortunately, however, this counter-attack was not completed owing to the events which occurred in the meantime on our left.

The activity displayed by patrols during the preceding days, and the clouds of dust, had shown that strong detachments of the enemy's horse, coming from near New Moshi and keeping to westward of the Kahe-New Moshi railway, were trying to work round our front, which faced north, and of which the left wing was at Kahe Station. The continuation of this movement would have brought them on to the railway in our rear, and cut us from our communications while we were engaged with a superior opponent with our front to the north. I had, therefore, posted a strong reserve of eight companies in readiness at Kahe Station.

But as I thought it necessary during the action to remain at Kahe village, near Stemmermann's Detachment, I was unable to exercise rapid and direct control over the reserves at Kahe. The dense vegetation prevented any distant observation. The control of the reserve at Kahe had to be left to the initiative of the commander on the spot and his subordinates. The latter had observed that hostile troops had advanced through the bush and occupied a hill south-west of Kahe Railway Station. One company had, on its own initiative, attacked this force, but the advance had broken down under shrapnel fire. Thereupon our four-inch gun opened fire on these light guns and drove them off.

Late in the afternoon I received an urgent message that strong forces of the enemy were advancing in our rear towards the railway at Kissangire, and that the event we feared had actually occurred. I was, therefore, compelled to issue orders for an immediate withdrawal towards Kissangire. The enemy could not yet have reached there in strength, and I hoped to defeat him there by rapidly throwing all my forces against him. Thus it happened that Captain Schulz's well-directed counter-attack could not be carried through, or produce its full effect. The transfer by night of our force across the Pangani, which was close behind us, and over which we had previously made a number of bridges and crossings, was effected smoothly and without interference. Even on the following day the patrols we had left behind found its north bank clear of the enemy.

Our good four-inch gun, which we could not take away owing to its lack of mobility, was blown up. After midnight, that is, quite early on the 22nd March, I arrived at Kissangire Station, and discovered to my very great astonishment that all the reports about strong hostile forces moving on that place were erroneous, and that our withdrawal had therefore been unnecessary. This incident afforded me a remarkably striking proof of the extraordinary difficulty of observing the movements of troops in thick bush, and of the great care every commander must exercise in estimating the value of such reports. But it also demonstrates how difficult it is for any commander to combine his own powers of reasoning and his judgment of the situation with the constantly conflicting reports, both of *Askari* and Europeans, in order to base his decision on a foundation that even approximately resembles the reality. In the African bush it is particularly important, whenever possible, to supplement the reports one receives by personal observation.

However, our withdrawal could not now be altered, and the most important thing was to re-group our forces. In this operation the decisive factor was water-supply. This, and the necessity for distribution in depth, caused me to leave only a detachment of a few companies on the high ground at Kissangire, from where it observed the seven and a half miles of waterless thorn desert extending to the Pangani. To the east of this detachment at Kissangire, under Major von Boehmken, was Otto's detachment, pushed up on to the North Pare Mountains in order to close the passes leading over them. Major Kraut took up a position on Ngulu Pass, between the North Pare and Middle Pare ranges. The main body of the force settled down in several fortified camps in the fertile Lembeni country. In spite of the various withdrawals we had recently carried out, the spirit of the troops was good, and the *Askaris* were imbued with a justifiable pride in their achievements against an enemy so greatly superior. Only a very few individuals deserted, and they were almost without exception men whose cattle was in the territory now occupied by the enemy, and who were therefore afraid of losing their property.

Almost the entire German civil population had left the Kilima Njaro country; most of them had moved to Usambara into the Wilhelmstal district. The Arusha country had also been evacuated, and the farmers had moved off by ox-wagon by Kondoa-Irangi to Dodoma. The numerous Greeks had for the most part remained on their coffee-plantations on Kilima Njaro, and the Boers of British nationality had stayed in their cattle farms, which extended from the north-west slopes of Kilima Njaro northwards round Meru Mountain and along the western slopes of the latter to the vicinity of Arusha.

At Lembeni the regular course of existence had not been interrupted; supply trains rolled right up to the station; the companies which were not in the front line worked diligently at their training, and Headquarters continued its work in the railway station buildings of Lembeni just as it had done previously at Moshi. Airmen appeared and dropped bombs, just as before.

The country was carefully prepared to meet various possible battle conditions, passages were cut through the dense rhinoceros bush, and a field of fire cleared where necessary. Personal reconnaissance took up much of my time, and often led me to the companies encamped in the thick bush and on the dominating heights. The troops had already developed to a tolerable degree in adaptability, and in the art of making the material side of their existence as comfortable as possible. I remember with pleasure the occasions when, in a comfortably arranged grass hut, I was offered a cup of coffee with beautiful rich milk, prepared from the ground-down kernel of a ripe cocoa-nut. The North Pare Mountains also were frequently the goal of my expeditions.

Up there I found a rich and well-watered area of primeval forest, through which it was hardly possible to penetrate off the roads. The water-supply of the country proved to be far more plentiful than the results of former surveys had led us to expect; in this respect also it was shown how the necessities of war cause the resources of a country to be opened up, and utilized to an extent greatly exceeding previous estimates. The natives of North Pare are, like those of Kilima Njaro, masters in the art of irrigating their fields by means of the water coming down from the mountains.

On the 4th April, one of my reconnaissances took me to Otto's Detachment on the Pare Mountains. From the north-west corner one had a clear view of the enemy's camp, lying down below at Kahe Station. The obvious idea of bombarding it with one of our long-range guns—in the meantime we had brought to Lembeni one 4-inch *Königsberg* gun on wheels, and one 3.5-inch gun mounted on a '73 pattern carriage could—unfortunately not be carried out. With rather too much zeal the troops had thoroughly destroyed the permanent way of the line between Lembeni and Kahe. With the means at our disposal it could not be made sufficiently fit for traffic to enable us to move one of our guns up and down on it with rapidity. All our observations and reports agreed that the enemy, who had formerly often sent patrols and even stronger forces to the south of Jipe Lake, no longer displayed any interest in that district. He had in any case moved his principal forces towards Kahe and also beyond New Moshi westward towards Arusha.

After passing a cold night on the damp height at North Pare I descended to Lembeni on the 5th April. Here I found a report that on the previous day Captain Rothert, who was encamped with the 28th Company beside the Lolkisale, a high mountain in the Masai desert, two days' march south-west of Arusha, had been attacked by superior forces. The heliograph communication with Lolkisale from the south-west had then been interrupted. It was not till later that the following facts became known. Several mounted companies of the enemy, coming across the desert from Arusha, had attacked the 28th Company, who were in position on the mountain, from several directions.

As our people were in possession of the water they could well sustain the fight against the enemy, who had none. On the second day of the action the situation became critical for the enemy, because of this very absence of water. Unfortunately, however, after Captain Rothert was severely wounded, this circumstance was not properly appreciated on our side. The situation was thought to be so hopeless that the company surrendered with its machine guns and ammunition. On this occasion also some of the *Askari* gave evidence of sound military education by refusing to join in the surrender. They, together with the wounded, rejoined our forces near Ufiome, without being interfered with by the enemy. There they met a new rifle company and the Arusha Detachment, of which the former had arrived from the Central Railway, the latter from the direction of Arusha.

The road to Kondoa-Irangi and the interior of the Colony was now hardly closed to the enemy coming from Arusha. There were three companies in the neighbourhood of Lake Kivu, in the north-west corner of the Colony, under Captain Klinghardt, retired, who had done so well in the actions at Kissenyi; they were moved by march route and on Tanganyika steamer to Kigoma, and from there by rail to Saranda. From there again they marched up towards Kondoa-Irangi. Captain Klinghardt was also given command of the troops already north of Kondoa-Irangi (about two companies) and of another company that came by rail from Dar-es-Salaam.

These movements would take a long time. Consequently, the good and well-tried 13th Company, whose peace-station had been Kondoa-Irangi, was at once brought by rail to near Buiko, whence it marched through the Masai desert to Kondoa-Irangi. The march through this water-less and little-known country had to be undertaken before the completion of the reconnaissances, which were in progress; and to do so with what was, according to African ideas, the large force of one company with carriers, in the dry season, and before the heavy rains had set in, involved some risk.

But this risk had to be run; for the force facing us at Kahe, after its reconnoitring parties had been several times repulsed, was showing no signs of advancing against us. At the time, therefore, the enemy was evidently directing his principal effort towards Kondoa-Irangi. As, for the reasons already set forth, it appeared unsound for us to attack from Lembeni towards Kahe, I decided merely to occupy the enemy station in the Kilima Njaro country, and to direct my main force against the hostile group which had meanwhile pushed forward to near Kondoa-Irangi. The execution of this project was not quite easy; much time was needed to cover the distance of 125 miles from the detraining stations on the Northern Railway to the Central Railway on foot, and at any moment a change in the situation might render it necessary for Headquarters immediately to make fresh dispositions.

All the troops must therefore be kept within reach. The various detachments could not, as on the march from the Central to the Northern Railway, be set in motion on different and widely-separated roads. The march of our fifteen field and two mounted companies had to be made on one road. The Force was thus confronted with an entirely novel and difficult task. There was no time to lose. The detachments of Captain von Kornatzky, Captain Otto, Lieutenant-Colonel von Bock and Captain Stemmermann, each of four or three companies, were moved by rail at intervals of one day, from Lembeni to Mombo and Korogwe. Thence they marched on to Kimamba (station west of Morogoro) to the Central Railway. Manifold difficulties arose. Hard and fast destinations could not be laid down for the detachments for each day, more especially because heavy rains set in which in places so softened the black soil that the troops could literally hardly get along.

Thus it happened that one detachment made quite short marches, and the one behind got jammed on top of it. This, however, was very inconvenient, and interfered both with the regular service of supply on the line of communication, and with the transport of the company baggage, in which the relay-carriers belonging to the line of communication had to be called in to assist. The companies now began, according to ancient African custom, to help themselves, seized the line of communication carriers, regardless of other orders, and simply kept them. As the whole service on the communications depended upon the regular working of the relay-carriers, it also became seriously dislocated.

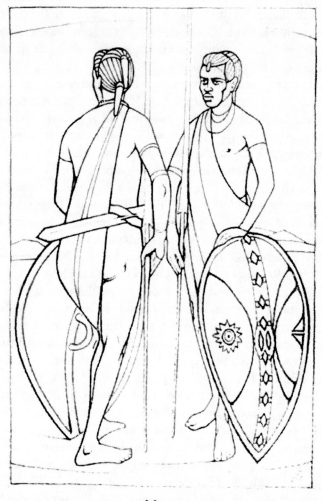

MASAI.
DRAWN BY GENERAL VON LETTOW-VORBEEK'S ADJUTANT.

EUROPEAN DINNER–TIME
DRAWN BY GENERAL VON LETTOW-VORBECK'S ADJUTANT.

The Enemy's Advance in the Area of the Northern Railway

After the trains had left Lembeni I handed over the command of all the troops on the Northern Railway to Major Kraut. An independent administrative service was also organized for them. Our railway journey to Korogwe proved to us once more how closely the German population of the Northern Territories were knit to the Force, and how they appreciated its work. At every station the people had assembled, sometimes from great distances; every one of them knew that our departure from the Northern Territories was final, and that they would fall into the enemy's hands. In spite of this, their spirit was gallant. A large part of the few remaining European provisions was brought to us. The widow of the former Line-Commandant Kroeber, who had recently been buried at Buiko, insisted on offering us the last bottles of the stock in her cellar.

Major Kraut and Captain Schoenfeld accompanied me to Buiko, from where we were able to view several portions of the ground which I thought might become of importance in our future operations. These gentlemen remained there in order to make more detailed personal reconnaissances. From Korogwe our cars rapidly took us to Handeni, the head of the light railway that had been laid from Mombo. On the way we caught up our mounted companies, and the exclamation of the Civil Administrator of Handeni: "Why, that's the notorious poacher of Booyen," showed me once more that there were among our mounted troops men accustomed to danger and sport, on whom I could rely in the troubles that were to come. Handeni was the first collecting station for the stores withdrawn from the north; Major von Stuemer, who had left his former post at Bukoba in order to take charge of this line of communication, which was for the moment the most important one, complained not a little of the way in which the troops marching through had interfered with the further dispatch of the stores.

At Handeni, the seat of the Civil Administration, where the supply routes from Morogoro, Korogwe and Kondoa-Irangi met at the railhead of the Mombo-Handeni line, the war had called into being a European settlement that had almost the appearance of a town. Lieutenant Horn, of the Navy, had built cottages in the Norwegian style, which were quite charming to look at, although at the moment the rain was rather against them. The interiors, consisting for the most part of three rooms, were comfortably arranged for the accommodation of Europeans. What was unpleasant was the enormous number of rats, which often ran about on one when trying to sleep at night. Captain von Kaltenborn, who had arrived in the second store-ship which put into Ssudi Bay, reported himself to me here, and was able to supplement the home news he had already transmitted in writing by verbal accounts.

Proceeding the next day by car, we caught up a number of our detachments on the march, and were able to remove at least some of the various causes of friction between them. Telephonic communication was rarely possible on account of earths caused by the heavy rain, and breakages caused by columns of carriers, wagons and giraffes. It was all the more important for me to traverse this area of breakdowns, which cut me off from the troops and prevented my receiving reports as quickly as possible. But that became increasingly difficult.

The rain came down harder and harder, and the roads became deeper and deeper. At first there were only a few bad places, and twenty or more carriers managed to get us through them by pulling and pushing. The *niempara* (headmen of carriers) went ahead, dancing and singing. The whole crowd joined in with "*Amsigo*," and "*Kabubi, kabubi*," and to the rhythm of these chants the work went on cheerily, and at first easily enough. But on passing through Tulieni we found that the rains had so swollen an otherwise quite shallow river, that during the morning its torrential waters had completely carried away the wagon bridge.

We felled one of the big trees on the bank, but it was not tall enough for its branches to form a firm holdfast on the far side. It was three feet thick, but was carried away like a match. The adjutant, Lieutenant Mueller, tried to swim across, but was also swept away, and landed again on the near bank. Now Captain Tafel tried, who

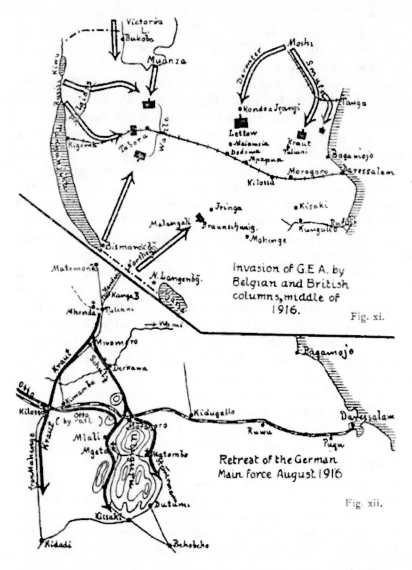

Invasion of G.E.A. by
Belgian and British
columns, middle of
1916.

Fig. xi.

Retreat of the German
Main force August 1916

Fig. xii.

FIG. XI. INVASION OF GERMAN EAST AFRICA BY BELGIAN AND BRITISH
COLUMNS, MIDDLE OF 1916.
FIG. XII. RETREAT OF GERMAN MAIN FORCE, AUGUST, 1916.

had recovered from his severe wound, and was now in charge of the operations section at Headquarters. He reached the far side, and a few natives who were good swimmers also succeeded in doing so. But we could not manage to get a line across by swimming, and so there we were, Captain Tafel without any clothes on the far side, and we on this one. The prospect of having to wait for the river to fall was not enticing, for I could not afford to waste one minute in reaching the head of the marching troops.

At last, late in the afternoon, a native said he knew of a ford a little lower down. Even there it was not altogether a simple matter to wade across, and took at least three-quarters of an hour; we had to follow our guide carefully by a very devious route, and work cautiously on from one shallow to the next. The water reached our shoulders, and the current was so strong that we needed all our strength to avoid falling. At last, in the dark, and with our clothes thoroughly wet, we reached the far side, where we were met by three mules and an escort of *Askari* sent back by a detachment which we had luckily been able to reach by telephone.

We continued our journey the whole night through in pouring rain, and had several times to ride for hours at a time with the water up to our saddles, or to wade with it up to our necks; but at last, still in the night, we reached the great bridge over the Wami, which had been put up during the war. That, too, was almost entirely carried away, but part was left, so that we were able to clamber across and reach the light railway leading to Kimamba Station. This line, like that from Mombo to Handeni, had been constructed during the war and was worked by man-power. In their endeavour to do the job really well, the good people took several curves rather too fast, and the trucks, with everything on them—including us—repeatedly flew off into the ditch alongside, or beyond it.

At any rate, we had had enough and to spare of this journey by water by the time we arrived in the early morning at Kimamba. Vice-Sergeant-Major[1] Rehfeld, who was stationed there and had been called to the Colours, received us most kindly. As there was a clothing depot at Kimamba, we were, at any rate, able to obtain *Askari* clothing to change into. When the remainder of Headquarters would turn up with our kits it was, of course, impossible to say.

---

1. We have no corresponding rank. He is a reservist who has served as a "One-year Volunteer," but has not yet done enough reserve training to qualify as an officer in the Reserve.

After discussing the situation with the Governor, who had come to Kimamba for the purpose, I went next day to Dodoma. On the Central Railway, quick working under war conditions, which in the north had become everyone's second nature, had hardly been heard of. Captain von Kornatzky's detachment, which had arrived at Dodoma shortly before us, had some difficulty in obtaining supplies, although Dodoma was on the railway, and could be supplied quickly. I got in touch by telephone with Captain Klinghardt, who had occupied the heights of Burungi, one day's march south of Kondoa-Irangi, and on the next morning, with a few officers of Headquarters, I rode off to see him.

The road lay through uninhabited bush-desert; it had been made during the war, its trace was governed by the need for easy construction, and it touched settlements but seldom. The Ugogo country is distinguished for its great wealth of cattle. The inhabitants belong to the nomad tribes, who copy the customs of the Masai, and are, therefore, often called Masai-apes. We met many ox-wagons in which German and Boer farmers, with their families, were driving from the country around Meru Mountain to Kondoa. It was a scene, so well known in South-West Africa, of comfortable "trekking," in these vehicles so eminently suited to the conditions of the *veld*.

The supply service of Klinghardt's Detachment was not yet in working order; we camped that night in the first of the small posts on the line of communication. It was evident that the work of transport and supply would have to be greatly increased if it was to maintain the large number of troops now being pushed forward in the direction of Kondoa-Irangi. There was another difficulty: up to date the various Field *Intendants* had not been physically equal to the enormous demands which the whole field of the work of maintenance made upon the head of the service. Captain Schmid, of the *Landwehr*, had very soon been succeeded by Captain Feilke, of the *Landwehr*, he again by Captain Freiherr von Ledebur, of the Reserve, and this officer by Captain Richter, retired, an elderly gentleman.

The latter, unfortunately, had just now, at the commencement of an important fresh operation, reached the limit of his strength. Major Stuemer, retired, who had been working on the line of communication at Handeni, had been obliged to take over his duties, but had not yet had time to become thoroughly at home in them.

By the evening of the following day we had completed our journey of four marches, and reached Captain Klinghardt at the Burungi

Mountains. The detachments coming from the country of the Northern Railway were following on behind us, and some days were bound to elapse before they would all have arrived; so we had the opportunity of making extensive reconnaissances. Here we had the great good fortune to make the acquaintance of a perfectly new and excellent map. The District Commissioner of Kondoa-Irangi had, when leaving his district, given it with other things to a *yumbe* (chief), who lived on the Burungi Mountains, to take care of. It was in his possession that we found this valuable property, the secrecy of which had thus remained intact.

Patrols of mounted English Europeans often came near our positions, and it was known that stronger mounted forces were behind them. But where they were was not known. Some reports stated that they were in Kondoa-Irangi; others said south of that place, and others again placed them on the road leading from Kondoa-Irangi to Saranda. An important factor was that there were considerable native plantations at Burungi, so that supplies were plentiful. It was, therefore, not necessary to wait until the transport of supplies from Dodoma was in full swing. The troops were more independent of the line of communication than hitherto, and could draw the bulk of their subsistence from the country. As soon as the rear detachments had closed up the advance on Kondoa was started. South of that place we met only fairly strong mounted protective detachments, who were quickly driven back, and at the beginning of May, without any serious fighting, we obtained possession of the great heights which lie four miles in front of Kondoa village.

We had brought with us two naval guns, one 3.5-inch and one 4-inch, on travelling carriages, and at once got them into action. From our dominating position they bombarded, apparently with good effect, the enemy's camps south of Kondoa. The tents were at once struck. We could see the enemy hard at work entrenching his positions, and his vehicles hurrying away towards Kondoa. Several patrol encounters went in our favour, and small hostile posts, that had been left out in various places, were quickly driven in.

From the south—that is, from behind us—we saw a mounted patrol riding towards our positions. As our mounted patrols were also out, I thought at first that they were Germans. But soon the regular carriage of their carbines in the buckets proved that they were English. They evidently had no idea of our presence. They were allowed to approach quite close, and at the short range they lost about half their number. From what we had hitherto observed, it seemed probable that the enemy in our front was evacuating his positions. On the 9th May, 1916, I decided, if this expectation proved correct, immediately to take possession of the low hills now held by the enemy. The conditions did not favour an attack, as our advance was sure to be observed, and a surprise assault was out of the question.

But without surprise the attempt to capture the occupied position by assault had no hope of success; the enemy was sufficiently entrenched on the small hills, and the latter completely commanded the ground over which the attack would have to be pushed home, and which could only be traversed slowly owing to the low thorn-bush and the numerous rocks.

I was with the companies that were following the advanced patrols; the latter reported, shortly before dark, that the hills were unoccupied. So our companies proceeded, and the commanders ordered up the baggage in order to settle down for the night. I myself went to the Headquarters Camp, which had remained on the big hills a little further back. I tried to relieve my great exhaustion with a cup of coffee and a little rum; but, knowing that I had no more orders to issue, I soon fell fast asleep. Next to my sleeping place was the 3.5-inch gun. Towards eleven p.m. I was awakened by remarks made by Lieutenant Wunderlich, of the Navy, who was in command of the gun; he could not make out the frequent flashes he saw in the direction of the enemy.

Neither, at first, was I quite certain about them. But soon there could be no doubt that these flashes, which became more and more frequent, were caused by rifles and machine guns. When the wind shifted the sound of the fighting became clearly audible. Contrary to all our expectations, therefore, a stiff fight was taking place in our front, but owing to the great distance, and the bushy and rocky country that would have to be traversed, I did not think I could engage the reserves I still had in hand with any prospect of success. It would take hours to obtain even the very roughest idea of the situation, and the moon would be up for barely an hour more. For well or ill, therefore, I had to leave the fight in front to take its course.

Our companies had, indeed, found the high ground, which had been examined by the patrols, to be clear of the enemy; but immediately in rear of it was another rise, and on this was the enemy, in an entrenched position, which our companies ran up against. In the close country and the darkness no general survey of the situation was possible, and connection between the various units was lost. Our *Askari* established themselves in front of the enemy, and Captain Lincke, who had assumed command after Lieutenant-Colonel von Bock had been severely wounded and Captain von Kornatzky had been killed, came to the conclusion that, although he could remain where he was, he would, after daybreak, be obliged to abandon all hope of being able to move, on account of the dominating fire of the enemy.

As, therefore, no success appeared attainable, he cautiously broke off the action while it was still dark, and fell back on the position he had started from. The enemy, consisting mainly of the 11th South African Infantry Regiment, had fought well, and had repeatedly brought effective machine-gun fire to bear on our companies. Considering the small number of rifles that actually took part in the fight about four hundred—our casualties, amounting to about fifty killed and wounded, must be considered heavy.

During the following days we also proceeded to take possession of the high hills lying further to the eastward, and drove off the mounted detachments working in the foreground, inflicting quite unpleasant casualties on them. It happened several times that out of parties of about twenty men, none, or only a few, got away, and in the foreground also a whole series of encounters ended in our favour. The heights held by us afforded an extensive view, and with good glasses we several times observed columns of hostile troops and wagons approaching Kondoa from the north, and then turning east and disappearing into the mountains. Our patrols, whom we sent far away to the enemy's rear, reported considerable bodies marching from about Arusha in the direction of Kondoa-Irangi.

The English had at once taken over the civil administration at Kondoa, and had cleverly ordered the *yumbi* (chiefs) to come to that place and given them instructions. Among other things, they imposed on them the duty of reporting the movements of German troops. It was, therefore, often advantageous for our patrols to pretend to be English while in enemy country. The differences in uniform were not great, and the prolonged period of active service had further diminished them; uniform coats were often not worn at all, but only blouse-like shirts, and the little cloth badges which the English wore on their sun-helmets were not conspicuous. The difference in armament had often disappeared, as some of the Germans carried English rifles.

On the whole, the enemy in Kondoa did not seem to be in great strength as yet; but, even if successful, our attack would have to be made over open ground against defences which with our few guns we could not sufficiently neutralize. The certainty of suffering considerable and irreplaceable losses decided me to refrain from a general attack, and instead to damage the enemy by continuing the minor enterprises, which had hitherto proved so advantageous.

Our artillery—the two mountain guns and two field howitzers, which had come out in the second store-ship, had also arrived—fired upon such favourable targets as presented themselves. The buildings of Kondoa-Irangi, where General van Deventer had arrived, were also fired at occasionally by our four-inch gun. To the west of our main force, on the Saranda-Kondoa-Irangi road, our newly-raised 2nd Rifle Company had had several successful engagements with portions of the 4th South African Horse, and had gradually forced them back to the neighbourhood of Kondoa-Irangi.

The enemy now grew continually stronger. Early in June he also shelled us at long range, about thirteen thousand yards, with heavy guns of about four-inch and five-inch calibre. His observation and fire-control were worthy of all respect; anyhow, on the 13th June his shell soon fell with great accuracy in our Headquarters camp. I stopped my work which I had commenced under cover of a grass roof, and took cover a little to one side behind a slab of rock. No sooner had the orderly officer, Lieutenant Boell, also reached the spot, than a shell burst close above us, wounded Lieutenant Boell severely in the thigh, and myself and a few other Europeans slightly. Otherwise the fire of the enemy's artillery did us hardly any material damage, but it was a nuisance, all the same, to have his heavy shell pitching into our camp every now and then.

We dispensed with the heavy work which the provision of good protection against fire would have entailed, as the whole strength of our people was required for patrols and outposts, and for collecting supplies. As far as the eye could reach, the whole country was covered by native cultivation. The principal crop—which formed the main supply of the troops—was *mtema*, a kind of millet, which was just ripening. Most of the natives had run away; the supplies from Dodoma had been unable to keep up with us, and so our subsistence depended almost entirely on the stuff which the foraging-parties of the companies were able to bring in. In the hot sun the sheaves quickly dried on the rocks.

All the companies were busy making flour, either by grinding the threshed grain between stones, or by stamping it into meal with poles in vessels of hard wood, called *kinos*. The Europeans at that time could still get wheat flour, which came up on the line of communication. The bread we made before Kondoa out of a mixture of wheat flour and native flour was of really excellent quality. Besides *mtema* and other grains there were also sugar-cane, *muhogo* (a plant with a pleasant-tasting, edible root), yams, various kinds of peas, and other native produce, besides sufficient cattle. In this extremely rich Kondoa country the troops could obtain a variety of food in abundance.

The enemy's extension from Kondoa to the east drew our attention also to this hitherto little-known country. Captain Schulz was sent there with several companies, and found it to be an extraordinarily difficult and densely-wooded mountain district, interspersed with settlements of great fertility. A whole series of actions, in which one or more of our companies were engaged, and which resulted in severe loss to the enemy, now took place in this district. A strong hostile force tried to penetrate between the companies of Schulz' s Detachment and ourselves, probably with the intention of cutting off the detachment. But this attempt failed completely. Our troops pressed forward against this force from both sides and repulsed it.

The old *effendi* (native officer), Yuma Mursal, acted with great skill on this occasion; he lay in ambush at a water-place, and fired at the English, who came there for water, with good effect; according to his observation, six of them were killed. During this period of fighting at Kondoa-Irangi the enemy's battle casualties gradually mounted up to a considerable figure. If we add to them his losses by sickness, due to the youth of his white troops, who were not used to the Tropics, and were extraordinarily careless about precautions against tropical diseases, the total losses incurred by him during the Kondoa-Irangi period can hardly have been less than one thousand Europeans.

CHAPTER 5

Between the Northern and Central Railways

I ask the reader to imagine himself in the position of a commander, with insufficient means, exposed to attack by superior numbers, who has continually to ask himself: What must I do in order to retain freedom of movement and hope?

At the end of June, 1916, events in the other theatres of war began to exercise a decisive influence on our operations at Kondoa. The Belgians pushed in from near Lake Kivu and from Russisi, the English from the Kagera, west of Lake Victoria, and, since the middle of July, from Muansa also, and all these forces were converging on Tabora. Our troops stationed in the north-west were all combined under the command of General Wahle, who was at Tabora; and he gradually drew in his detachments from the frontiers towards that place.

Owing to the difficulties of communication Headquarters had but meagre information of these events. Hostile detachments were also pressing in from the south-west, from the country between Lakes Tanganyika and Nyassa. Before them, our company righting in the neighbourhood of Bisrnarckburg fell back slowly in a north-easterly direction towards Tabora. The two companies left behind to secure the Langenburg district gradually retreated on Iringa, followed by General Northey, whose division was equipped with all the appliances of modern warfare.

On the Northern Railway, Major Kraut's patrols, who started out from his fortified position at Lembeni, had occasionally scored pleasing successes. Several aeroplanes were brought down, or came to grief, the passengers being captured and the machines destroyed. When the heavy rains had ceased, the enemy commenced his advance from Kahe along the Northern Railway, as well as east of it through the Pare Mountains, and west of it along the Pangani. Hundreds of automobiles and large numbers of mounted troops were observed. In order to avoid the danger of being cut off by the greatly superior enemy, Major Kraut withdrew his main body by rail to Buiko, leaving small detachments in contact with the enemy. In this vicinity, as well as near Mombo, a few actions took place, in some of which our companies drove through the enemy, who tried to block the line, and fired on him from the train.

Being in superior force, the enemy was always able, with little trouble, to execute outflanking movements with fresh troops, but their effectiveness was greatly reduced by the difficulty of the country. It seemed, therefore, as though the enemy frequently departed from this idea and adopted a sort of tactics of attrition instead. Today he would attack with one portion of his force, then let that rest, and put in another the next day, and a different portion again on the third. In spite of all his obvious urging, and his favourable conditions of supply, his advance was fairly slow. Major Kraut's troops never got into a really difficult situation; on the contrary, they were often able to catch the enemy under fire unawares, and to gain partial successes, which occasionally caused him very considerable losses, such as Captain Freiherr von Bodecker's rear-guard action near Handeni.

In view of this concentric advance from all directions, the question arose, what should be done with the main body of the Protective Force now before Kondoa? For an attack the situation was altogether too unfavourable. The problem, therefore, was, what should be the general direction of our retreat? I decided on the Mahenge country. By moving there we should avoid being surrounded, it was fertile, and suitable for guerrilla warfare. From there also it would be possible to withdraw further to the south and to continue the war for a long time to come.

Another important consideration was the safeguarding of our stores deposited along the Central Railway, particularly in the vicinity of Morogoro. These were greatly endangered by the rapid advance of General Smuts, who was opposing Major Kraut, and had penetrated far to the south beyond Handeni. Although it was to be assumed that General Smuts would be delayed by the continually increasing length of his communications, he seemed to me to be the most dangerous and important of our opponents. I therefore decided to leave in front of the Kondoa force only a detachment at Burungi, under Captain

Klinghardt, but to march my main body back to Dodoma, proceed thence by rail to Morogoro, and move up in support of Major Kraut.

It turned out afterwards that the English were informed of this movement down to the smallest details, and that, for instance, they knew all about a railway accident that happened to one company during its progress. When our companies arrived at Morogoro and the Europeans there saw the splendid bearing of the *Askari* they lost the last traces of their depression; every man and woman had comprehended that our situation was indeed difficult, but also that there was nothing for it but to go on fighting, and that our Force was, from its whole quality and nature, capable of carrying on for a long time to come.

Early in July I reached Major Kraut, who was holding a fortified position on Kanga Mountain, north-east of Tuliani. I had expected the *Askari* to be depressed by their retreat, but found them in excellent spirits and full of confidence. In front of their position they had cleared the foreground for 50 to 100 yards and were fully convinced that they could beat off an attack. I employed the time that elapsed before the arrival of the other detachments in reconnaissance, and soon formed a mental picture of the passes which led across the difficult rock and forest country westward of our line of communication.

Owing to the remarkably dense bush an attempt to send a strong detachment round the enemy's camp to attack it in rear was unsuccessful. But the enemy did sustain casualties through numerous minor enterprises by our patrols, who fired at his transport columns and the automobiles working behind his front. In this way also a Staff car was once effectively fired on. The enemy's patrols were also active and several of his distant patrols had got behind us. One of them, commanded by Lieutenant Wienholt, betrayed its presence by surprising a column of our carriers and burning the loads. Among other things these contained a quantity of trousers which had come out in the store-ship and were anxiously expected.

Wienholt, therefore, aroused painful interest on the part of everyone. His patrol was discovered in camp in the dense bush and surprised. He himself got away, and trusting to the fact that it is not easy to find anyone in the African bush, wanted to work his way alone through our lines and back to the English. Our well-tried men, zan Rongew, Nieuwenhudgu and Trappel, who had effected the clever capture of the horses near Longido Mountain, succeeded in tracking and capturing him. On my return from a reconnaissance I met Wienholt in our camp at Tuliani enjoying a cheery meal with his captors. We could none of us help honestly admiring the excellent work of his patrol, whose route was accurately marked on the map that was captured in his possession. Wienholt was then taken to a prisoners' camp in the interior, from which he escaped some months later while bathing.

In 1917 he did excellent work on patrol round Kilwa and Livale, and also later on, in 1918, in Portuguese East Africa. I was greatly interested in his description of an attack by a leopard which, with great boldness, killed his companion in camp. I presume he has by now given friends and acquaintances the benefit of his vivid account, of which he unfortunately lost the original later on in a patrol encounter.

Weeks now passed, during which the English annoyed us mainly by bombs from aircraft. They had evidently found out the exact site of our Headquarter camp at Tuliani. I remember one day when four aeroplanes, against which we could do nothing, circled over our camp for hours and dropped bombs. But we had learned to make ourselves invisible, and only the European employed in the telephone hut was so badly hurt that he lost his hand. An adjoining hut full of valuable documents was set alight by an incendiary bomb.

My cars were then still working, and from Tuliani I was often able quickly to reach Kraut's Detachment in front by the good line-of-communication road. Lieutenant-Commander Schoenfeld had there made excellent arrangements for directing the fire of the 4-inch and 3.5-inch naval guns. From his observation posts on the heights of Kanga Mountain one had a good view of the English camps. Some weak German detachments had not followed Major Kraut from Usambara towards Tuliani, but had escaped along the Usambara Railway towards Tanga. There, and also near Korogwe, they had minor encounters with the enemy and gradually fell back towards the south, on the east side of Kraut's Detachment. They were followed by more considerable portions of the enemy.

Gradually the force at Tuliani became liable to be circumvented on the east, and to lose its communication with the Morogoro country, which was so important for the supply of stores, ammunition and food. At the same time General van Deventer, whose force had been augmented to a division, advanced from Kondoa to the south, and Captain Klinghardt retired before him, first to the south, and then towards Mpapua.

The closeness and difficulty of the country caused Captain Klinghardt to still further subdivide his already small force (five companies) in order to watch and block important passes. The enemy followed with a large number of automobiles, and occasionally one of them was successfully blown up by mines sunk in the roads. Owing to the unavoidable dissemination of Captain Klinghardt's troops, and the difficulty of maintaining touch between them, one part often could not know what was happening to its neighbours. A large German mounted patrol was attempting to connect up from the east with a detachment believed to be at Meiameia, on the road from Dodoma to Kondoa-Irangi.

All unconsciously it rode straight into a hostile camp and was captured almost without exception. The retirement of our troops from Kondoa, who had not merely to escape, but also to inflict damage on the enemy, was a very difficult manoeuvre; the right moment to fall back, to halt again, to advance for a sudden counter-stroke, and then break off again quickly, and in sufficient time, is difficult to gauge. Reliable reports were lacking. Owing to the scarcity of means of communication the difficulties attending the retirement of several columns through unknown country grew infinitely great. The influence of the commander was often eliminated, and too much had to be left to chance.

On the 31st July, 1916, the enemy reached the Central Railway at Dodoma. Captain Klinghardt slipped off to the east along the railway. In the actions which took place west of Mpapua several favourable opportunities were not recognized, and neighbouring detachments, whose assistance had been relied on, did not arrive in tune. Such things easily give rise to a feeling of insecurity among the troops and weaken confidence and enterprise. The difficulties were accentuated in this case by the fact that Captain Klinghardt was taken ill with typhoid and became a casualty just at the critical moment. Captain Otto was sent from Tuliani to replace him, and succeeded in once more collecting the scattered parties and in establishing united control.

The 2nd Rifle Company also, which had been obliged to retire on Saranda by the Kondoa-Saranda road, and with which all touch had been lost, made a great circuit on the south side of the railway and rejoined Otto's Detachment. Owing to the numerical superiority of the enemy, in the actions which now took place, Otto's Detachment frequently found itself exposed to an attack on its front while being enveloped on both flanks. The enemy did not always succeed in timing these movements correctly.

Thus, at Mpapua, the frontal attack got too close to our line and suffered severely; and the flank attack, even when directed on the rear of our positions, produced no decisive effect. The short range of visibility always enabled us either to avoid the danger, or, if the opportunity was favourable, to attack the troops outflanking us in detail. In any event, these outflanking tactics of the enemy, when followed, as in this case, in extraordinarily thick bush, and among numerous rocks, demanded great exertions and used up his strength.

Every day Captain Otto fell back only a couple of miles further to the east, and in these operations the railway enabled him to change the position of his big gun at will. When Otto's Detachment approached Kilossa it became necessary to move the main body at Tuliani also. Headquarters and a part of the force moved to Morogoro, Major Kraut, with several companies and a 4-inch gun, to Kilossa. At Tuliani Captain Schulz took command.

I now considered that columns pressing on from the north would soon reach the country west of Bagamoyo, and that at this place also troops would be landed. In order to reconnoitre personally, I travelled to Ruwa Station and thence by bicycle over the sandy, undulating road to Bagamoyo. One day's march south of Bagamoyo I came on the camp of two Europeans: it was District Commissioner Michels, who wanted to remove his threatened District Headquarters from Bagamoyo towards the interior. The inhabitants were confiding and were living as in peace. So far the universal war had passed them by without a trace. As time pressed I had to turn back and Herr Michels' fast Muscat donkey carried me back to Ruwa in a few hours.

On the next day, from Kidugallo, I reconnoitred the supply depots established there and further to the north by cycle and then returned to Morogoro. Other reconnaissances, mostly also by cycle, took me to the mountains lying to westward in the direction of Kilossa, and along the roads leading round the Uluguru Mountains on the west and east. The passes leading from Morogoro up the northern slopes of the gigantic Uluguru group, and down again on the south side towards Kissaki, had to be examined on foot. Owing to the pressure exerted by General van Deventer on Kilossa, and the danger that Captain Schulz might also be circumvented at Tuliani, it was imperative not to miss the right moment for withdrawing Captain Schulz to Morogoro. But in order to retain the power of delivering counter-strokes we had to hold on to the Tuliani area as long as possible.

Captain Stemmermann's Detachment, which had been pushed out

a short day's march due north of Tuliani, was attacked at Maomondo by a strong force of Europeans and Indians. The enemy was very skilful. A machine gun of the 6th Company, placed on a rocky slope, was seized by a few Indians, who had crept up to it from the front unobserved, and thrown down the steep slope, so that it could not be found again. The enemy, who had penetrated our lines, was thrown out again with heavy loss by a counter-attack by the 21st Company.

At close quarters the English Major Buller, a son of the well-known General of the South African War days, put a bullet through the hat of the Company Commander, Lieutenant von Ruckteschell, but was then severely wounded by the latter. Major Buller was got away to the German hospital at Dar-es-Salaam and nursed back to health by the wife of his opponent, who was working there as a nurse. During the actions at Maternondo English horsemen had worked round farther to the west, and suddenly appeared in one of the mountain passes leading from the west to Tuliani. In the dense bush the 2nd Mounted Brigade, which had come from South Africa under General Brits, apparently sustained heavy casualties.

With the consent of Headquarters, Captain Schulz now withdrew to Derkawa, which is situated in dense bush on the Wami River, on the road from Tuliani to Morogoro. Here he occupied a fortified position on the south bank, where he was attacked on the 13th August by the enemy pursuing from Tuliani, with a force of at least one brigade of infantry, and General Brits' Mounted Brigade, while simultaneously another brigade, which had marched up the right bank of the Wami, attacked him from the east. During the action continuous telephonic communication was maintained with Captain Schulz from Morogoro. The enemy's losses were estimated at several hundred, and were afterwards confirmed by the English.

The attacks were beaten off, but in the dense bush it was so difficult to obtain a clear idea of the situation that it did not seem possible to achieve a decisive success. Captain Schulz was chary of putting in the one formed company he had left. I approved his intention of falling back to Morogoro at the end of the action, as the general situation made it desirable for me to concentrate my forces. After Major Kraut's arrival at Kilossa I also brought Captain Otto in to Morogoro, with part of his companies. Major Kraut had passed behind Otto's Detachment through Kilossa and after some engagements at that place, he took up a position immediately to the south of it, on the road to Mahenge. Even after the enemy had moved into Kilossa telephonic communication with Kraut's Detachment had continued to work for a few hours through the enemy.

From that time on direct communication with Major Kraut was interrupted. Signalling by helio did not work, and the wires which led from Kissaki, and later from the Rufiji, to Mahenge, and thence to Major Kraut, were not yet completed—in some cases not even begun. With General Wahle at Tabora we had also had no communication since the second half of July, that is, for over a month. Bagamoyo had fallen into the enemy's hands; and every day we expected to hear of the fall of Dar-es-Salaam and to lose touch with that place.

CHAPTER 6

Continuous Fighting Near the Rufiji

In order to oppose the troops of General Northey, who were advancing from the direction of New Langenburg, Captain Braunschweig had been dispatched from Dodoma at the end of June. He had taken up reinforcements from Kondoa and Dar-es-Salaam to the two German *Askari* companies that had slipped away from the New Langenburg country, and had concentrated his own troops, totalling five companies and one field howitzer, at Malangali. At that place his force had fought a brave action with a superior force of the enemy, but had been obliged to fall back towards Mahenge.

As the converging hostile columns were now approaching each other in the direction of Morogoro, it became necessary to consider our future plan of operations. The enemy expected us to stand and fight a final decisive engagement near Morogoro, on the northern slopes of the Uluguru Mountains. To me, this idea was never altogether intelligible. Being so very much the weaker party, it was surely madness to await at this place the junction of the hostile columns, of which each one individually was already superior to us in numbers, and then to fight with our back to the steep and rocky mountains, of which the passes were easy to close, and which deprived us of all freedom of movement in our rear.

I thought it sounder so to conduct our operations that we should only have to deal with a part of the enemy. Knowing that the enemy, and General Brits in particular, had a liking for wide turning movements, I felt sure that one column would move off from Dakawa, where large hostile camps had been identified, or from Kilossa, in order to reach our rear by working round the west side of the Uluguru Mountains. This possibility was so obvious that I cycled out every day to the mountains west of Morogoro, so as to get the reports from the patrols in good time, and to supplement them by personal observation of the clouds of smoke and dust.

The latter soon put it beyond doubt that a strong column was moving from near Dakawa towards the railway between Morogoro and Kilossa. Patrols identified enemy troops that had crossed the railway and were marching further south. The observers on the mountains reported the clouds of dust to be moving towards Mlali.

As I meant to let this movement run its full course and then attack the isolated detachment with the whole of my forces, I waited until I thought it was near Mlali. On the evening of the 23rd August, Captain Otto, who was encamped at Morogoro, was ordered to march off for Mlali during the night with three companies. He arrived there early on the 24th, just as English horsemen had taken possession of the depot. When I reached Otto's Detachment the fight was in full swing. The country was, however, unsuitable for short decisive strokes, owing to the many steep hills which impeded movement. The other troops at Morogoro, except Captain Stemmermann's Detachment, were ordered up by telephone.

I myself went back again to Morogoro to talk things over. Stemmermann's Detachment, to which, on account of the roads, the 4-inch *Königsberg* gun and the howitzer battery were attached, was ordered to fall back along the eastern slopes of the Uluguru Mountains, and to delay the enemy there. The passes over the mountains themselves were closed by weak patrols. When I arrived once more at Mlali in the afternoon, the fight was still undecided. At several points the enemy had been driven back, and several people thought they had seen him suffer considerably. But by nightfall we had got so entangled in the mountains, and every movement had become so difficult and took so much time, that we halted. We found the night very cold, lying out on the hills without the carriers' loads. Luckily, however, this fertile region had so far hardly suffered at all from the war, and a fowl roasted on a spit soon appeased our hunger.

The next morning numerous explosions in the German depots, which had been surprised by the enemy, indicated that he had moved off and had destroyed the 4-inch shells stored there. We surmised that he was moving south-west, which eventually turned out to be the case. The enemy was probably making a turning movement so as to reach Kissaki before us. At the wealthy Administration Office at that place, 600 tons of food supplies and the military stores removed from Morogoro had been collected. Wild rumours exaggerated the actual facts, and stated that strong forces had already reached the roads leading to Kissaki before us.

Although the wagon road stopped at Mlali, and the remainder of the route to Kissaki consisted only of paths broken by many ravines and obstacles, the possibility that the enemy might make a rapid march on Kissaki had to be taken very seriously, and we had no tune to waste. In the evening we were most hospitably entertained by the Father at Mgeta Mission. The buildings are charmingly situated in the deep ravine of the Mgeta River, which in this part comes down very swiftly. The many lights on the slope of the hill made one think one was approaching some small watering-place in Germany. A few European women from Morogoro were also staying there, and bade farewell to the Force for the last time. With the exception of a few nurses all women had to stay behind.

The removal of our loads was carried out fairly satisfactorily. The Force profited by the fact that owing to the insistence of the energetic Captain Feilke, about a thousand native labourers, who had until a few days previously been working in the forestry department at Morogoro, were placed at its disposal. But the carrier question was beginning to be difficult. The natives saw that we were evacuating the country; a number of them, who had promised to come, stayed away, to the despair of the sensible Chiefs, who would gladly have helped us. As only small parties of the enemy appeared in the country round Mgeta, it began to seem probable that his principal forces were making a turning movement. Leaving a rear-guard behind, which only followed us slowly, our main body was, during the ensuing days, moved nearer to Kissaki.

One night an *Askari* appeared at my bedside, bearing himself in a smart military manner: it was the Effendi Yuma Mursal, of the 4th Field Company, who had been left behind sick at Morogoro. He reported that a force of the enemy, as strong as that at Kahe had been, had marched round the west side of the Uluguru Mountains from Morogoro, and that a number of German *Askari* had found the recent fighting too much for them. They had deserted, and were now plundering the plantations south-west of Morogoro.

A telephone line was laid from Kissaki to us, by means of which Captain Tafel kept us continually informed; up to date no enemy had been seen at Kissaki. But to the west of us, patrols reported the enemy to be marching to the south. I therefore moved to Kissaki, and had to destroy some of our stores, which were collected in small depots along our route. Unfortunately, in carrying this out, an efficient Ordnance N.C.O. was accidentally killed, as had happened before on a similar occasion at Morogoro. At Kissaki, several days passed before we came seriously into collision with the enemy. It was not advisable to occupy the *boma* (fort) itself; it consisted of a group of buildings surrounded by a massive high wall, and was situated in the middle of a completely cleared bit of country.

The enemy could, therefore, only capture it by a costly attack; but he had no need to assault it at all; by means of artillery and bombs from aircraft, he could have made it intolerable for us to remain in the cramped *boma*, and we ourselves should then have been forced to make a sortie over the open and to endure the fire which the enemy would have been able to pour into us in perfect security. Our defences were, therefore, placed a long way outside the *boma*, covered from the view of aircraft, and so arranged that they could be occupied and evacuated unobserved.

It was not until I arrived at Kissaki myself that I obtained a proper idea of the abundance of stores and supplies available there. I learned that, contrary to my belief, practically nothing was stored further south at Behobeho or at Kungulio, on the Rufiji. At Kissaki there were large stocks, but notwithstanding the dense native population, it was impossible to get them away. The numerous inhabitants, to whom the war and the many *Askari* were something quite new, lost their heads and ran away into the bush. The Civil Administration, which enjoyed the complete confidence of the people, proved powerless against the overwhelming influences now bursting in upon them. Even presents of clothing, which were ordinarily so highly valued, failed to hold them. It seemed as if all the evil spirits had conspired together to deprive us of transport.

Our column of several hundred pack-donkeys had been driven over the mountains from Morogoro. It arrived at Kissaki late and completely exhausted. Our ox-wagons, which had to go round the east side of the Uluguru Mountains on account of the state of the roads, seemed to be never going to arrive. The head of the Communications Service could not find any other means of carrying away the stocks which were essential to us for continuing the war. And yet it was obvious that we must continue to fall back further south, towards the Rufiji, before the superior numbers of the enemy.

One circumstance that brightened the gloom was that our great herds of cattle, which had been grazing east of Mpapua, had been brought away in good time. Several thousand head, mostly beautiful cattle, arrived at Kissaki, and would have formed a most welcome mobile reserve of supplies. But, unfortunately, our pleasure at this was diminished by the frequent occurrence of the tsetse fly at some places; if the animals got stung by them they lost condition badly, and mostly died after a few weeks.

The bulk of the cattle was, therefore, driven on into the healthy districts on the Rufiji. As for the rest, we simply worked with energy at getting away the stores to Behobeho and on to Kungulio, using the carriers belonging to the troops, all the people we could raise in the district, and our few wagons. In order to effect this, we had to gain time, and Captain Stemmermann, who was marching round the Uluguru Mountains by the eastern road, could only be allowed to fall back quite slowly before the hostile division which was pushing after him with all its might.

I waited at Kissaki with the main body, in order to be able quickly to recognize and make use of any favourable opportunity. As was to be expected, the enemy had, owing to our withdrawal to Kissaki, abandoned his concentration on Morogoro; he had sent a few detachments direct over the Uluguru Mountains, but his other columns had separated and followed us, extending far to the east and west. The hope of being able to defeat one or more of these columns separately was fulfilled beyond expectation. West of the Uluguru Mountains General Brits had divided his division into brigade columns (two mounted and one infantry), which had difficulty in keeping touch. Soon large hostile camps were discovered a day's march west of Kissaki, and on the 7th September, 1916, Captain Otto's Detachment, which was encamped at a plantation near Kissaki, was attacked by a large force of European horse, and by native and white infantry.

It turned out later that this force consisted of General Enslin's Mounted Brigade, and of portions of the infantry brigade of General Brits's Division. The turning movement which the enemy was making round the left wing of Otto's Detachment was allowed to continue until the outflanking detachment had got right round in rear of Captain Otto, near the Boma of Kissaki. Evidently the enemy did not expect German reserves to be posted under cover still further back. These reserves were now loosed upon him. The gallant nth Field Company, under Lieutenant Volkwein of the Reserve, worked through the dense bush close up to the outflanking enemy, and immediately attacked with the bayonet, cheering. With that the enemy's beautiful plans completely collapsed; our further advance simply rolled him up, and he was completely defeated. The almost impenetrable bush made it impossible vigorously to push the enemy, or to undertake a pursuit on a large scale; but the bulk of his troops was broken up, and the small fragments were scattered in the bush in hopeless confusion.

The led-horses and horse-holders were captured, and about fifteen Europeans taken prisoner. Even the next day an English soldier arrived from quite another direction; he had lost himself with his led-horses in the dense bush and had no idea where to go. The man had plenty of humour; he threw his rifle and ammunition across a small stream and said: "It's just luck; I might have taken the right road or the wrong one. I had the bad luck to take the wrong one. That's my fault."

Tafel's Detachment, which was encamped north of Kissaki, on the road we had come by, had only partially joined in the fight on the evening of the 7th. I had kept it back, as I thought that, simultaneously with the attack on the 7th from the west, another one would be made from the north along the road. And General Brits undoubtedly did hold this perfectly sound intention; but the execution failed. General Nussy's Mounted Brigade, without having any idea of the action of the 7th, marched along towards Tafel's Detachment from the north on the 8th. It was just as thoroughly beaten as its friends had been the day before. In the dense bush it was, on the 8th, even more difficult to survey the fighting, and a considerable number of prisoners taken by the 1st Company managed to escape.

In the two days we took some thirty European prisoners, and some of them were sent back to the enemy, on taking an oath not to fight again in this war against the Germans or their allies. The humanity of this step, which was, under tropical conditions, in the best interest of the prisoners themselves, was not recognized by the English. They suspected spying, seized the German envoy who brought back the prisoners, sent him far into the bush with his eyes bound, and then let him go where good luck might take him. It was a wonder that the man, who was exhausted by prolonged wandering about, found his way back.

This shows how difficult the English made it for us to avoid unnecessary severity towards the enemy. At the same time, the English private soldiers had faith in the treatment we meted out to our prisoners. While the battlefield was being cleared, in which both English and German medical officers took part, wounded Englishmen begged to be treated by the German doctor. And later on, also, wounded men remarked that they would hardly have been cured if they had been treated by English medical personnel.

It was my opinion that these satisfactory successes at Kissaki had not brought us a final decision against the troops of General Brits, and I still believe that in the dense bush and the rugged country an energetic pursuit, which alone would have secured the desired result, was impossible of execution. My attention was all the more drawn towards the force pursuing Stemmermann's Detachment, as it had already come within two days' march north-east of Kissaki. During the last few days the situation there had not been favourable; the broken ground had in several instances caused our already weak forces to be disseminated. Some portions had been ambushed, the troops were very fatigued, and several people were suffering badly from nerves.

On the 9th September Stemmermann's Detachment approached the village of Dutumi, which was known to me from previous reconnaissance. I thought the enemy would press on on the following day, and considered the opportunity favourable for achieving a success at Dutumi by rapidly moving my main body there from Kissaki. In the evening we marched away from Kissaki by the fine broad road, and reached Dutumi that night. Captain Otto remained at Kissaki with five companies. On arrival I decided to make use of the factor of surprise, and to make an enveloping attack in the early morning on the enemy's left wing, which was identified close in front of Stemmermann's Detachment. I knew that this wing was in the plain, while, looking from our side, the enemy's centre and right stretched away to the left up the foothills of the Uluguru Mountains. It was because of these foot-hills that the chances of attack were less favourable on our left.

Early on the 9th September, Schulz's Detachment attacked from our right. Rifle and machine-gun fire soon started, and the enemy's light artillery also opened fire; but the thick high elephant grass, with which the plain was covered, made it impossible to form a clear idea of things. I thought the attack was going well, and proceeded to the left in order to get a view of the situation. The heights there were also densely overgrown. It was very fatiguing to get along and difficult to find anybody. I was clambering about, fairly exhausted in the heat of a tropical noon, when I luckily heard the sound of tin pots, and found I was right in concluding that some European was just having lunch. It was Captain Goering, who had taken up his post in the bush on a height which afforded a good view.

Here, towards three p.m., I received the unwelcome news that the attack by Schulz's Detachment on our right had not attained its object. It had been simply impossible to get at the enemy through the dense elephant grass. If, therefore, any decisive action was to be taken on that day at all, it could only be done on our left. Even here, owing to the difficult country, success was not very probable. The advancing companies got into a very intersected mountain tract, in which they shot at the enemy, and were shot at by him without any result, and at dusk returned to their original positions. During the following days the enemy directed his attacks mainly against our left, and was frequently driven back by counter-strokes. But, on the whole, it was evident that success was only possible if the enemy proved very unskilful.

On the other hand, our communications, which from now on no longer ran to Kissaki, but towards Behobeho in the south-east, were in a great degree threatened by the enemy. I therefore abandoned Dutumi, and withdrew the main body an hour's march to the south, across the Mgeta River, where the Force occupied an extensive fortified camp, which it continued to hold for months.

By this move the rich fields of Dutumi were unfortunately given up. In the poor country of Kiderengwa we had to depend mainly on supplies from the rear, which were sent up from the Rufiji. Unfortunately the fatigues of this transport work, combined with sickness caused by tsetse, very soon led to the almost complete loss of our pack-donkeys. From Kiderengwa our fighting patrols attacked the enemy's communications, which ran to the north-east from Dutumi, as well as the Dutumi-Kissaki road, which soon became alive with enemy detachments and transport.

Various observations now concurred in disclosing remarkable movements on the part of the enemy. Both east and west of the Uluguru Mountains movements of troops in such strength were seen to be taking place towards Morogoro, that the natives said: "*Wana hama*" ("They are moving elsewhere"). A large number of the South African Europeans, of whom, by the way, many had come to the end of their strength, were sent home. Other observations disclosed a movement of troops towards the east. Generally speaking, a period of rest ensued, which was only interrupted by minor expeditions of patrols and occasional artillery bombardments.

General Smuts realized that his blow had failed. He sent me a letter calling upon me to surrender, by which he showed that, as far as force was concerned, he had reached the end of his resources.

CHAPTER 7

Hostile Attacks in the South-East of the Colony

Meanwhile, the situation at Kilwa began to demand increased attention. We had there only weak detachments for protecting the coast, which consisted mainly of young, newly-enlisted *Askari*, and had been organized as a company. This company was not sufficient, and there was a danger that the enemy might march from Kilwa to the Rufiji, or to Livale, and get in our rear. No doubt the enemy had some such intention, and something had to be done to prevent it. Major von Boemken, with three companies, had already marched off from the battlefield of Dutumi for Kunguliu on the Rufiji, proceeding thence to Utete by route march and on the stern-wheeler *Tomondo*. The *Tomondo* was the only shallow-draught steamer on the Rufiji, and carried most of the supplies, which came from the lower Rufiji to Kunguliu, whence they were carried to the troops at Kiderengwa by donkeys and carriers.

It now required a certain amount of discussion before the civil authorities would place the Tomondo at my disposal for carrying the necessary troops. At Kilwa the situation did not develop altogether satisfactorily. It is true that a few minor engagements were more or less in our favour, but, as so often happened during the war, we did not manage to secure united control of our forces. Among other things, the enemy succeeded in destroying a supply depot west of Kilwa, which was too near the coast. The enemy cleverly incited the natives to rebellion, and they rendered him valuable service as spies. Several German reconnoitring detachments were ambushed and suffered severely. The District Commissioner of Kilwa was taken prisoner. The awkwardness of the already difficult situation at Kilwa was increased by the fact that the District Commissioner's *Askari* were not placed under the orders of the military commander.

At the same time, the pressure of hostile forces was felt from the direction of Dar-es-Salaam, in the north, towards the lower Rufiji. Our weak detachments, which had fallen back from Dar-es-Salaam in a southerly direction towards the Rufiji, and consisted principally of a young company of *Askari* and part of the ship's company of the *Königsberg*, were not enough to protect the rich sources of subsistence in the lower Rufiji country. But at the time this country was what the Force depended on, for the middle Rufiji country was but sparsely settled, and could not maintain both troops and carriers for any length of time.

In view of this necessitous situation, we had at once started to grow maize in the fertile lowlands of Logeloge and Mpanganya, but the harvest could not be expected before March, 1917. We were, therefore, threatened by a great danger when several companies of Indians attacked our advanced officers' post in the Boma of Kissengire. The enemy, who assaulted the steep walls without sufficient preparatory fire, was driven off with considerable loss. Unfortunately, the German commander, Lieutenant Baldamus, of the Reserve, who exposed himself too freely to the enemy projectiles, was killed. But his resolute and gallant defence secured us in the possession of the seat of administration at Kissengire until the arrival of adequate reinforcements; it is, therefore, due to this officer that we retained control of the rich supply area of the lower Rufiji for months to come.

It has already been mentioned that a pause in the operations had occurred at Kiderengwa; an attack on the enemy, who was entrenched in a strong position, promised no success. Headquarters accordingly left only eight companies, under Captain Tafel, in the Kissaki-Kiderengwa area (and this force was reduced later), moving with the bulk of the troops to the lower Rufiji. The road to Kunguliu led past large lakes, which, like the Rufiji, were full of hippopotami. Owing to the general demand for fat, hippopotamus shooting became a question of existence.

One has to watch until the animal's head is clearly visible, so as to hit in a spot that will cause instantaneous death. The animal then sinks, and comes up again after a little time when it can be drawn to the bank by means of a rope, quickly made of bark. There it is cut up, and the expert knows exactly where to find the white, appetizing fat. The quantity varies: a well-fed beast provides over two bucketfuls. But one has to learn, not only how to prepare the fat, but also how to kill immediately with the first shot. Some foolish people had been reckless, and in many places the dead bodies of wounded animals were to be seen, which quickly decompose and become unfit for food. The elephant also was now regarded in a new light; ordinarily the elephant hunter gauges the length and weight of the tusk before firing; now the pressing question was: how much fat will the beast supply? For elephant fat is very good, and possibly tastes even better than that of the hippo.

At Kunguliu the herds of cattle we had brought along were driven into the river, and swam across. Up till then the troops had crossed by ferry, on which Herr Kühlwein, the former traffic manager of our lost Northern Railway, now contented himself with the more modest post of "Traffic Manager, Kunguliu Ferry." When we arrived, a bridge, three hundred and thirty yards long, had been completed, which was also capable of taking vehicles. On the south bank we went into camp near Niakisiku Plantation, belonging to Lieutenant Bleeck, of the Reserve, who had been called up. The Europeans' houses had been fitted up as hospitals, and were fully occupied. At Logeloge we found the Headquarters of the Line of Communication, where a large number of roomy grass huts had been put up for the troops.

The plantation itself, belonging to a company, comprised extensive *sisal* fields. Food also was cultivated in plenty. The country being free of tsetse, supported a large amount of cattle, and the survivors of our pack-donkeys had been brought there from the tsetse country north of the Rufiji. Here the families of the Europeans still lived in their solidly-built houses, and were thankful that the course of the operations had enabled them to continue their home and business life undisturbed for more than two years.

At Logeloge, and at the agricultural experimental establishment of Mpanganya, which we reached next day, other Europeans of the neighbourhood had also collected, and, where the existing buildings failed to accommodate them, had built themselves houses with poles and cane, or grass. Here an unpleasant symptom also made its appearance. While the troops at the front were animated by the best spirit and great enterprise, things behind the front were not always the same. The people who understood least of the business always knew everything better, and fostered a certain amount of discontent. That kind of thing is catching, and in the long run undermines right feeling.

Fortunately, however, many of the troops behind the front had

ASKARI. A halt.

Drawn by General von Lettow-Vorbeck's Adjutant.

THE BANYAN TREE.
DRAWN BY GENERAL VON LETTOW-VORBECK'S ADJUTANT.

enough soldierly pride to shut up the grousers pretty bluntly on occasion. In one of the hospitals there someone was becoming rather too free with his destructive criticism, and a wounded man answered: "I tell you what, the Commandant is the brain of the Force, but you're its backside!" This unvarnished epithet was so apt, that it at once turned the laugh on the side of the speaker, and polished away the spot of tarnish that threatened to spread.

The question now was, whether we should first turn to the north against the force at Kissengire, or against the one at Kilwa. The latter had not, as Major von Boemken had feared, moved on towards Li vale, but, possibly influenced by the movements of our troops, had turned towards the north. It thus worked into the Kibata country, which, though rich, was very mountainous, and difficult for manoeuvre, and as long as it remained there I did not think it would be very dangerous. I considered it sufficient merely to prevent it from pushing further towards the Rufiji, for which a weak force of five companies, under Major Schulz, was enough. Major von Boemken, who was anxious about Livale, had, with two companies and a 4-inch gun, made his way into the neighbourhood of Mpotora, a chance circumstance, from which, as will be seen, we later reaped great benefit.

I had, therefore, a free hand to move on towards Kissengire. That was important, and enabled us to secure the rich supply country north of the lower Rufiji, and to get away the valuable stocks from thence to the middle Rufiji. Whether there would be an opportunity of obtaining a success in the field it was not possible to tell; but I thought that the enemy, since he had pushed troops from the Uluguru Mountains in an easterly direction to the neighbourhood of Kissengire, would exert some pressure from the north.

So it was quite possible that we might find a favourable opportunity for a fight. We crossed the Rufiji at Utete in boats, and in a few days reached Makima, one day's march south of Kissengire. By that time a sufficient garrison of two companies had been assembled at Kissengire, where it was actively employed in strengthening the position. A little to the north, at Maneromango, was a strong force of the enemy, and a European patrol, which had started out from Kiderengwa, reported that hostile troops had been moved from the west towards the Maneromango-Kissengire area.

A few days after leaving Kiderengwa this patrol had got into a waterless country in terrible heat, and the various members had lost each other in the dense bush. They made their presence known by firing,

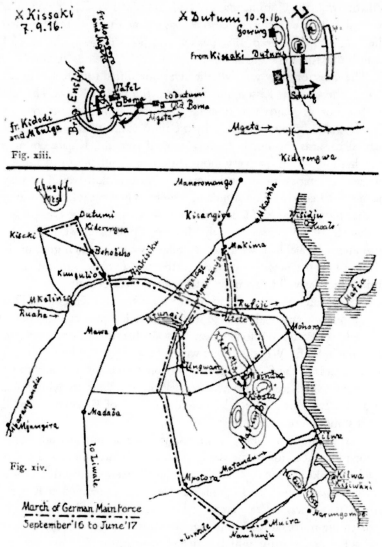

FIG. XIII. BATTLES OF KISSAKI AND DUTUMI.
FIG. XIV. MARCH OF GERMAN MAIN FORCE,
SEPTEMBER, 1916, TO JUNE, 1917.

and had no choice but to surrender to the English. Only the determined patrol-leader had managed to escape to a native village, where the inhabitants greeted him with apparent friendliness and brought him eggs. As he bent down to take them, they fell upon him, and handed him over to a patrol of English *Askari* concealed close by. An *Askari* with a mule, who behaved rather arrogantly, was to escort the German back. On the way the German, during conversation, drew his attention to faults in his bridle, and succeeded in seizing the mule and riding off on it with all speed. In the struggle which took place, he had seized the *Askari's* rifle and shot him with it.

To the east of Kissengire our patrols also pushed on to the north, and quite a number of minor engagements took place in the bush, in which the enemy at times suffered very severely. Further to the east, on the coast near Kissiju, other hostile detachments were also roaming about, and a small English man-of-war was there too. One morning Captain von Lieberman, with the 11th Company, surprised this opponent, and our *Askari* went for him with a will, cheering. The man-of-war was also fired upon with the field gun, and apparently several hits were obtained. After driving the enemy out of Kissiju, Captain von Lieberman returned. We also operated against the enemy's communications, and small fights occurred almost daily.

The closely-settled country is of simply fabulous fertility. Besides abundant flour, both Europeans and *Askari* had mangos, paw paws, *mustapheles*, cocoa-nuts, and other tropical fruits. We were surprised to see the large rice-fields, which were here close to the south side of Dar-es-Salaam, seeing that in peacetime most of the rice had come from India. Of cattle there was but little, but the companies began to send out shooting parties into the prairie, which was full of game, and extended especially on the western side of our positions. That there must be game in the vicinity was proved by the presence of numerous lions. Frequently a family of five lions wandered through our camp at night, and occasionally killed animals in it.

While Headquarters was at Makima in October, a report came in which caused me to suppose that the landing of strong enemy forces at Kilwa, and the appearance of hostile detachments which, coming from the west towards Livale, had arrived on the Mbaranganda River, formed part of a big converging movement by the enemy against Livale. Strong forces of Portuguese had crossed the Rovuma, invaded the highlands of Makonde, and established themselves in the district of Nevala. The captain of the *Königsberg*, Captain Looff, had, after the evacuation of Dar-es-Salaam, proceeded by land, first to the *Königs-berg's* old area on the Rufiji, and then to Lindi.

He had now taken over command in the south. With the three newly-raised companies of *Askari*, the only troops available there at the moment, he had entrenched himself in front of the strong positions of the enemy who had landed at Lindi, covered the removal of the cargo of the store-ship from Ssudi to the north, and inflicted damage on the Portuguese, who had shown themselves on the lower Rovuma, by means of minor expeditions. His force was, however, rather too weak to enable him to turn against the Portuguese, who were advancing in his rear about Nevala, with any prospect of a rapid and decisive success.

It was, therefore, very convenient that, as already mentioned, two companies and the 4-inch *Königsberg* gun of von Boemken's Detachment happened to be at Mpotora. To command this detachment, Captain Rothe, of the Reserve, was sent from the Rufiji, as he could in the circumstances be spared from his duties as Principal Postmaster (*Oberpostdirektor*), and had, at his urgent request, been placed at the unrestricted disposal of the Protective Force. In a few days he arrived from Niakisiku by cycle, took over his detachment, and led it towards Nevala. Captain Looff took command of the whole force, the Portuguese were thoroughly well hammered by the *Königsberg* gun, and their positions were captured by assault.

We took a really very considerable amount of booty, including four mountain guns, a number of machine guns, several hundred rifles, much ammunition, several automobiles, supplies, and all kinds of equipment. During the following weeks we continually found quantities of buried stores and ammunition. The very secret places were particularly well stocked. The Portuguese were driven completely out of German territory, and pursued for some distance into their own country. But consideration of the general situation prevented me from carrying on the pursuit to the uttermost. Rothe's Detachment was brought back to Mpotora, in order to keep an eye on the enemy at Kilwa, who grew continually stronger.

Even before this movement was executed, I considered it necessary to transfer strong forces from the neighbourhood of Kissengire towards Kibata. No opportunity had presented itself of fighting a decisive successful battle north of the lower Rufiji; as I had expected, I was obliged to proceed to a prolonged operation in the mountains of Kibata, which offered but little prospect of leading to a decision.

The transfer of the troops towards Kibata took place at the end of November, 1916. On the way we encamped at Utete, where roomy hospitals had been established in the building of the Civil Government, and where an officers' mess had been established on a *baraza* (an airy veranda). The place was situated on dominating heights, and had been strongly fortified with trenches and abatis, and commanded the lower-lying and very extensive native town.

Almost all night one heard the deep grunting of the hippo, and one impudent lion, having failed in his attack on a native, tried to kill another man in our camp. Fortunately his quarry was taken from him at the last moment by a European, who hurried to the spot, and several natives. Continuing, we reached the Moboro-Kibata road. Captain Schulz, who had with his detachment occupied a strong position two hours north of Kibata, was drawing his supplies from the country round Moboro. Several depots on this road were filled from the fertile country immediately surrounding them. In addition, Captain Schulz sent out parties to buy supplies in the districts near his camp, in which the whole wealth of the country is revealed.

From a mountain near Mbindia, the camp of Schulz's Detachment, one could see a broad forest track passing over the heights. This was the road for a 4-inch *Königsberg* gun, which was being brought up to its position before Kibata by Lieut.-Commander Apel. Chanting in rhythm, hundreds of natives dragged the heavy load up and down the steep slopes, over which a suitable track had been surveyed and cut through the thick bush. Shortly after its arrival at Mbindia, the gun had been placed in position on a mountain saddle from which, later on, the bombardment was successfully carried out.

One of the 4-inch howitzers was also got into position further forward in a valley, so as to fire over the high ground in front and reach the enemy's camps. Detailed reconnaissances had disclosed the possibility of moving our infantry, concealed by the dense bush, into some high ground which commanded the country north of Kibata. The weak hostile force holding this high ground was surprised by an attack from the rear and quickly driven off. Then another height was attacked, situated at a water-hole immediately to the north of the solid European buildings. We could soon see our *Askari* climbing up it, and establishing themselves on it about eighty yards in front of a hostile position.

By this time the deployment of our artillery was completed; besides the 4-inch *Königsberg* gun and the field-howitzer the two mountain guns had been brought into action, in line with our infantry. We had delayed opening fire on the buildings, where we saw numbers of men and animals walking about on the bare hill-top, until everything was ready. One company which had got round the enemy's rear, and established itself on his main line of communication, running from Kibata to Kilwa, observed that the heavy shells falling near the *boma* (fort) caused a frightful panic. Heaps of the enemy's *Askari* ran away as fast as they could, across the front of the company which was lying in concealment.

But unfortunately the company allowed itself to be deterred from taking advantage of this favourable opportunity. It hoped that the scattered parties of *Askari* would soon be followed by larger bodies, and did not want to give away the chance of a surprise prematurely. But the expected large bodies did not come, and thus, as unfortunately happened often, a good opportunity was lost through waiting for a better. The infantry attack on the above-mentioned heights immediately north of Kibata had involved the loss of several very efficient Europeans. Sergeant-Major Mirow was killed, Vice-Sergeant-Major Jitzmann was shot in the leg and sustained a severe and very painful injury to the nerve of his leg. He had previously often distinguished himself by his untiring and successful raids on the Uganda Railway. Through prolonged detention in hospital he was now lost to the Service, and fell into the enemy's hands before he was recovered.

It was very difficult to find one's way in the extraordinarily rugged mountains of Kibata. A number of reconnoitring expeditions were sent out and after a few days we felt more or less at home. It was possible to obtain a good view of Kibata and of the enemy's communications, and we ascertained that he was reinforcing his troops more and more. As a matter of fact he employed at Kibata the main body of the division landed at Kilwa. Our observations and the peculiarities of the ground led us to expect that the enemy intended to work from Kibata round our right, or western, flank, and thus force us to evacuate the heights commanding Kibata and its water-supply from the north.

A direct attack by the 120th Baluchis had been defeated with great loss to the enemy. During the opening days of December we observed at first weak, and then stronger detachments, which pushed forward from hill to hill towards our right flank, and whose advanced parties soon reached a commanding mountain, known to the English as Gold Coast Hill. Our counter-stroke against this force was at first favoured by ravines and forests, and our *Askari* surprised even us when they became visible close in front of the enemy's positions. Our guns were ready to fire, but unluckily the first shell pitched among our own men, and the infantry attack, which could only succeed by rapidity and surprise, failed. However, the fire of our two mountain guns at under 1,800 yards, and of our howitzers, which were further back, caused quite considerable casualties among the Gold Coast Regiment. The enemy was on a narrow hog's-back, the steep slopes of which were for the most part bare. He could, therefore, hardly withdraw, and in the hard ground entrenching took a long time. We then surrounded the hill with infantry, and poured a converging fire on the good targets presented to us. It became impossible for the enemy to hold this highly important position any longer. After it was evacuated we found a large number of graves, each for many bodies, and at this point the enemy must have lost not less than 150 killed.

The advance of the Gold Coast Regiment had nevertheless been of advantage to the enemy. My force being so weak—we had, all told, about nine companies—I had withdrawn one of the two companies stationed in the immediate vicinity of Kibata in order to employ it against Gold Coast Hill. After I had returned to camp that night I heard the sound of a number of small detonations emanating from the one company left alone to face the enemy. It was only after some time that we recognized this as a grenade attack, a manoeuvre then unknown to us. Several companies of the enemy attacked with such rapidity and skill, that they penetrated the trenches of our weak company by surprise and drove it out. The loss of this position deprived us of the possibility of firing at close range from that very suitable height at hostile troops moving about, or proceeding to their water-supply. Until then I had done so with success, and had even occasionally sent up a light gun to the place, withdrawing it again after it had ceased fire.

But the loss of this high ground and the casualties sustained in it faded into insignificance beside the success achieved on Gold Coast Hill. In spite of our inferiority in numbers, we completely dominated the situation. Our patrols and stronger raiding parties worked right round the enemy's rear and pushed on to his communications. Minor enterprises on his part produced no results. On the whole, the enemy suffered very considerable casualties at Kibata, and I think they should be estimated at not less than four hundred men. The operations intended by him were also completely wrecked. There can be no doubt that he waited to advance from Kilwa on Livale. Our vigorous action at Kibata forced him to move from Kilwa against us, and to leave the rest of the country and the whole of our supply and transport apparatus in peace.

Towards the end of December hostile planes appeared, cruising about over our positions and dropping bombs. Although they now used far more powerful bombs than formerly, they hardly inflicted any casualties. On Christmas Day we saw a larger mass than usual falling on the Boma of Kibata. We were disappointed in our hope that the enemy was bombing his own camp; it was only a large quantity of cigarettes as a Christmas present for the troops.

One day, during that period, I received a personal letter from the British commander-in-chief, General Smuts, in which he informed me that I had been awarded the Order Pour le Mérite, and expressed the hope that his cordial congratulations would not be unacceptable to me. I thanked him equally politely, although I at first believed that he was confusing it with the Second Class of the Order of the Crown with Swords, which I had received a short time before. I mention this letter from General Smuts as a proof of the mutual personal esteem and chivalry which existed throughout in spite of the exhausting warfare carried on by both sides. On many other occasions also the enemy intimated his great appreciation of the achievements of the German forces.

At the end of 1916 I regarded the military situation in the Colony as remarkably favourable, for I knew that the South African troops were for the most part worn out with battle-casualties and sickness, while a large proportion of the remainder were returning to South Africa at the end of their engagements. Prisoners had repeatedly assured us that they had had enough of the "picnic" in East Africa. The Indian troops also, who had been in the field in East Africa for some length of time, were reduced in numbers, while the late arrivals—we identified Indian Pathan Regiments at Kibata—consisted largely of young soldiers. Other regiments, like the 129th Baluchis, who had fought in Flanders, were no doubt very good, but they might not be expected to stand the fatigues of African warfare for a very prolonged period.

The enemy's *Askari* were, generally speaking, new troops, and only a small proportion of them had at that time been in the field. So we could continue calmly to contemplate the continuation of the war for a considerable time. I still believe that we would have succeeded not only in holding our own, but even in beating the enemy, if he had not

160

enjoyed the power of continually filling up his reduced units and of bringing up fresh ones. At the end of 1916 I did not know that this had already been effected on an extensive scale. Among other reinforcements a strong brigade of black troops had been brought from Nigeria to Dar-es-Salaam, whence it had been moved on without delay to Dutumi and Kissaki.

In the early days of January, 1917, the five companies encamped there under Captain Otto were attacked by General Smuts with at least two brigades. In planning his attack the enemy had provided for simultaneous wide turning movements, which, with his greatly superior numbers, enabled him to bar the retreat of our troops towards Kungulio. More than once our *Askari* had to clear their way with the bayonet, and in the close country some of our companies got into very awkward situations. In withdrawing to Behobeho our field howitzer, having only a weak escort, was ambushed by a hostile force of several companies, and was lost, after the whole detachment had been killed.

But in the end all portions of the detachment successfully avoided being surrounded, and in assembling at Behobeho. At this place very heavy fighting immediately took place, in which the enemy also fought with great bravery. It was in this action that the old hunter Selous was killed, who was well known even among Germans, on account of his charming manner and his exciting stories. He had joined as a subaltern. With a superior enemy before him and on both flanks, and behind him the mighty Rufiji, crossed only by the one frail bridge, Captain Otto yet succeeded in reaching the south bank of the river, with all his troops, and in destroying the bridge, in accordance with his instructions.

We had also observed a wide turning movement which the enemy was making from Kissaki further west towards Mkalinzo on the Rufiji, which now became ineffective. The hostile brigade undertaking it did not reach the south bank of the Rufiji in time to oppose Captain Otto's passage, and thus render his situation desperate; on the contrary, we gained partial successes which were quite considerable. The enemy following us from Behobeho came on very vigorously and passed a large part of his force over the Rufiji at Kungulio in boats. Captain Otto held his detachment in readiness a little to the south of the river, and now attacked the enemy, of whom part only had crossed over, and completely defeated him with heavy loss.

This partial success was favoured by the inaction of the hostile column, which, as already mentioned, was making the turning movement by Mkalinzo. It consisted principally of whites, and a part of the black Nigerian troops. Neither of them were equal to the long march involved, and had therefore reached the Rufiji exhausted and unfit for further operations. They remained out of action for quite a long time, and the unity of General Smuts' otherwise quite well-planned operation was wrecked.

In consequence of the enemy's advance in force at Kungulio, the danger arose that he might gain possession of the middle Rufiji, and of the country to the south of it. He might then easily seize the bulk of our stores, and our whole system of communications, which for the most part ran from the middle Rufiji towards Livale. It was therefore necessary for me to meet his movements with our main body, which was before Kibeta, and so I marched off with the greater part of it to Lake Utungi, where I would be in a position to help Captain Otto, or to seize any favourable opportunity that might offer.

CHAPTER 8

Anxieties and Hardships During Our Stay in the Rufiji Country

Our march from Kibata was on the first day carried out according to plan. On the following day I rode ahead with a few companions, in the expectation that the troops who had several native guides with them would not fail to find the way. In the Kissi mountains we came upon large numbers of natives who, however, were very timid and often deserted their flourishing rice plantations on our approach. Later in the day I regretted that I did not appropriate some of this abundant produce for our own use. During the midday heat we rested at Pori. Some of my companions who knew the country called my attention to the acid *Mbinji* fruit, which we found very refreshing. Unfortunately we did not know at that time that the stone of this fruit, when roasted, makes an excellent dish, tasting like our hazelnut.

The heat was overpowering, but as we were in the neighbourhood of the enemy patrols we had to keep a sharp lookout. The springs and water-courses were now dried up; after a long search we at last found a small pool of dirty water, which, however, we were told was not injurious to health. Towards evening we reached the great deserted settlement. Here we were fortunate enough to find a negro in the employ of the German Government, who informed us that we were at Ungwara, our destination for that day.

After we had walked through the place, the man showed us a pool near which we pitched our camp. My old black cook, the bearded Baba, well known to many East Africans, had very nearly kept up with our horses, and, following our trail, soon arrived. He had soon prepared his *uzeli* (boiled rice), and was sitting contentedly by the fire. We watched him enviously, for we had nothing, and were waiting for our baggage and the troops. But no one came and we lay down, hungry, to sleep. The friend in need, however, was approaching in the shape of a splendid sable-antelope, which in the brilliant moonlight was coming down to drink.

Almost simultaneously the rifles of two of my companions, van Booyen and Nieuwenhuizen, experienced Boer hunters, who had become Germans, rang out. We sprang from our blankets as though we had received an electric shock, and within a short time the first pieces of delicate flesh were roasting on the spit.

On the following day we reached Lake Utungi, where Captain Feilke was awaiting us, and we refreshed ourselves with bread, coffee and sausage made from antelope flesh. There was still no trace of the troops. They had lost us in Pori, and almost all completely lost their bearings. One detachment did not get into touch with us until several days later, when they came upon our telephone line in the neighbourhood of Utete. In view of the difficulty of communication, it had hitherto been impossible to get an accurate estimate of the state of our supplies. I had expected to find well-filled depots at Mpanganya on Lake Utungi and in the neighbourhood of Madaba. This was why I had pressed on out of the fertile country north of the lower Rufiji through Mpanganya to the line-of-communication area. The question of supplies had developed quite differently from my expectations.

In the line-of-communication area, in addition to the large numbers of bearers necessary for the transport of war material to the south, a numerous *personnel* was maintained, who were employed on road-making, building grass huts and for other purposes. Even in the small depots there were always a number of men who, whenever possible, did nothing but fetch supplies, which they ate themselves. Often the supplies were even fetched by others who, in their turn, had to be fed. In many places it was almost the case that a load of supplies collected and forwarded by the fighting troops in the north finally landed in a small depot, and were devoured by these people who had nothing else to do.

In view of the difficulties of transport, and the great distances, even the energy and thoroughness of Captain Stemmermann, who had taken charge of the depots, did not succeed in detecting and putting a stop to these abuses. Further, there were too many people in Africa whose propensity for diverting valuable energy to non-essentials to the prejudice of the really important things that it would take a very strong broom to sweep them away. The general result of all these obstacles was that thousands and thousands of useless mouths were devouring the supplies which had been collected with great effort in the region occupied by the fighting forces. The depot did nothing for the supplies, but, on the other hand, lived on them, and the most serious point was that the moment was at hand when the areas from which the supplies were drawn would have to be evacuated by the fighting forces.

It was a difficult situation. It was necessary to lose no time in putting under cultivation the territory we were then occupying—that is to say, the country round Madaba and Livale, and in the southern parts of the Protectorate, which were likely to be the scene of the subsequent operations. But months must elapse before any results could be obtained from these measures. During these months we should have to remain on the Rufigi and live there. Here, it is true, some hundreds of acres of maize were standing, but even these would require months to ripen. Until this time came the force could not move south; it would have to remain in the unproductive area which it was then occupying.

The accomplishment of this task was difficult. The order had at once to be given for the removal of every man who was not absolutely indispensable for carrying on the war during the next few months. This meant that thousands of bearers and workmen in the line-of-communication area were sent home. The most serious drawback to this step had to be reckoned with; we were sending over to the enemy thousands of men from whom he was bound to gain detailed information as to our strength, the condition of our supplies and our internal organisation. Nor was it enough to cut down the *personnel* of our lines of communication. The non-combatant *personnel* of the companies was also reduced. Among other things, it was laid down that henceforward no European should have more than five native attendants.

That sounds a generous allowance to European ears, but under African conditions native attendance is really indispensable to the European. He requires at least one man or boy to cook for him and attend to his personal needs, and, in addition, it must be remembered that all baggage, kit, rations, blankets and tent-material, has to be carried whenever he moves. When one considers that in peacetime a travelling official on a long *safari* (journey) took with him from eleven to thirteen bearers, in addition to two or three personal servants, it will be understood how drastic this new order was and what a storm of

165

indignation it aroused.

Fortunately I was in a position, when appealed to on grounds of health and decency, to point to the fact that I myself had for months managed with three, or at a pinch two, loads—that is, four negroes—and had kept in good health. I am still particularly grateful to those regimental officers who, as on so many other occasions, saw the necessity of this vexatious regulation and set the example. They upheld the tradition of our officer-corps by not claiming any special comforts for themselves, and were the first to submit to the unavoidable discomfort. I believe that among all the soldiers and non-combatants up to the highest civilian official, there is not one who still condemns this order, at first so strongly opposed.

But reduction of the number of food-consumers alone was not sufficient to solve the problem of existence; the supplies would not go round. It was already obvious that the supplies from the area of the fighting force, which were, of course, being worked at high pressure, would not suffice to feed us until the new harvest at the end of March. After close and mature consideration, we found it impossible to avoid the necessity of cutting down the rations, a measure which went very much against the grain, as even the native, if he is to be relied on, must be well fed. This gave rise to a fresh and much stronger outburst of indignation. From all sides came telegrams and messages to say that it was impossible to get the calories of nourishment necessary for a fighting man from the daily cereal ration, fixed at six hundred *grammes* of meal. But the hard fact had to be faced that only a certain quantity was available, and we must make the best of it.

The reduction of the cereal ration could not be avoided. For the rest, each man and each company would have to try to make good the shortage by hunting, which in this region, where game abounded, could be managed with the exercise of a little agility. But logic is apt to go to pieces with many people when it comes to a question of daily food, and many did not scruple to lay the whole blame for the at times barely sufficient ration at the door of the wicked commander-in-chief, and even to do all they could to have the daily ration increased to its former amount. This I had to bear calmly, and I made my own observations as to who were the men to make the best of an unavoidable necessity and who were not.

In carrying out these drastic measures new difficulties were encountered. A crowd of *Askari* women had followed the force, and had attached themselves to various camps on the Rufiji, where they were very comfortable. I was most anxious to send them south, where the question of supplies was less difficult. The necessary transport was arranged for, and the women were given rations for the march. After one short day's march, however, the women simply lay down, and declared that they could go no further. Their rations, which were intended to last a considerable time, were all eaten by the third day, and they were crying out for more. Some even went so far as to attack and beat the European who was in charge of the transport. Even under a dark skin the gentler sex did not always scruple to make full use of their prerogatives, which are usually justified.

Finally we got over this difficulty, and a tolerable solution was found to the ration problem. The *Askari,* to whom the position was explained, saw the difficulty and were very reasonable. Skilled hunters were sent to the different hunting-grounds, and the empty stomachs from time to time more generously filled. I remember that with us on Lake Utungi our two hundred blacks in one day completely devoured a big buffalo and an elephant. It was often found possible to give a piece of antelope to the passing caravans of bearers.

In the course of February the stores in our supply dumps, of which I took stock every day, ran out. I began to fear that for reasons of supply we would not be able to wait for the ripening of the corn on the Rufiji. In that case, not only would the harvest be lost, but the crops growing further south could not be used to the best advantage. There we should have to use the grain that was actually ripe and pass on, leaving the unripe portion standing. A lucky chance came to my aid in this dilemma. I went one day from Lake Utungi to Mpanganya to see Captain Tafel, who was handling the tactical and commissariat problems there with admirable efficiency. I spent the night in his camp, and he set before me an excellent dish of young maize prepared like asparagus.

This led us to speak of the maize fields of Mpanganya and the neighbourhood. These were full of women and other natives who had swarmed over them like a flock of birds, and were living on the young, unripe corn. This was as bad economy as well could be, but it gave me the idea that in case of need the maize crops could be largely used before they were ripe. This need very soon occurred, and an experiment with the ears which had ripened most showed that these could be artificially dried and a very good meal made from them. After this, the ripest ears were gathered daily, and as the whole crop ripened the food situation improved from day to day. By 1st March it was found possible to increase the ration to seven hundred *grammes*, or nearly the normal allowance.

The increasing severity of the whole campaign called for a more intensive and energetic exploitation of our food resources; the slow, deliberate supply methods of the civil authorities, which had sufficed for the first phase of the campaign, were no longer adequate. Twice, at Kissaki and on the Rufiji I had been put in a most difficult position with regard to supplies, which had almost made it impossible to carry on the operations. A more efficient supply service which would know the military needs, look ahead and work more quickly and energetically was a vital necessity for the further carrying on of the campaign. Fortunately I was able to convince the Governor on this point, and, as a result, a new supply detachment was raised from the force, and sent ahead to Massassi, *via* Livale. They established several subsidiary detachments, which were attached to the administrative stations in the Lindi area, and in this way worked side by side with the civil authorities in organizing, and, later, in carrying out, the cultivation and storing of food. In this way the desired impregnation of the supplies and transport service with the necessary military spirit was completely attained.

At this time there was no appreciable shortage of kit, and there was also an adequate supply of arms and ammunition.

With a view to the envelopment of the enemy at Mkalinzo, where he was reported to be in strong force, Captain Otto had marched his detachment south from Kungulio. North of Mawa he covered the fertile area of Madaba, and the line of transport and telephone communication running from Lake Utungi, *via* Mawa to Madaba. On 24th January, 1917, Captain Otto was attacked north of Mawa by several battalions of the Nigerian brigade. The enemy was beaten off with heavy losses and pursued several miles through the bush to an entrenched position, where he took refuge. The troops under Captain Schulz, who had been left behind after our departure from Kibeta, were gradually withdrawn to Ungwara. They had been reinforced and relieved from time to time after the fighting in the region of the Kibeta-Utete-Kissi mountains. Strong enemy forces—identified as an infantry brigade—had followed them.

In spite of his numerical superiority, the single engagements were very costly, and for the most part unfavourable for the enemy. Captains von Lieberman, Goering and Koehl, and numerous patrol leaders on many occasions completely routed more than twice their number of

Indian or negro troops, and captured rifles, machine guns and ammunition. The long war had produced a large number of capable leaders, and their example, as in the case of Lieutenant Kroeger, who was afterwards killed, roused unbounded enterprise and daring. Over and over again, and without stopping to ask the strength of the opposing force, this officer, followed by a handful of men with fixed bayonets and cheering loudly, had charged the enemy in the thick of the bush. He had even trained the *Askari*. Several of these distinguished themselves as patrol leaders, and when later the brave *effendi*, of the 4th Field Company, with his patrol, routed an entire Indian company, we owed the success to this training at Ungwara.

Our line of communication to the south, passing through Madeba and Livale, was in danger from a strong enemy force west of Kibata, and it was necessary that we should afford it adequate protection. This meant a gradual move south of our forces from the Rufiji, especially as our supplies on this part of the river were coming to an end and the rainy season was at hand.

It was particularly important that we should not evacuate this part of the Rufiji until the rains had set in. This would mean a considerable gain in time for us, as, during the actual rainy season and immediately after, the operations would, of necessity, come to a standstill, and the corn, particularly the *mtema* (millet), would have time to ripen.

When the migrations of the ants warned us that the rains were at hand, orders were given, as a precautionary measure, that the women, children and non-combatants should as far as possible be transferred to the north bank of the Rufiji, and thence transported to Dar-es-Salaam. This step, which the approaching rains and the state of the supplies made necessary, aroused much discontent, which I was obliged to treat with the same indifference as the previous outbursts of indignation. I am, however, still of the opinion that the timely removal of these people was much better for them than spending part of the rainy season on the drenched ground or in flooded dwellings with insufficient food.

The rains, which set in at the end of March, were particularly heavy in 1917. The site of our camp, which was slightly elevated, became an island, from which access to the outer world was only possible by boat through the Rufiji wood. A number of people were drowned in the wood during the rains; others had to take refuge for days in the trees. The water rose so high that in Mpanganya it reached the high-lying dwellings of the Europeans, and invaded the hospitals and disturbed every kind of filth. It was impossible for women and children, sick and wounded to remain, and after the withdrawal of the troops they had to give themselves up to the English, who took pity on their need, and provided them with food and transport.

The majority of the troops marched south out of the flooded districts on the Rufiji and Lake Utungi in good time, after using up the available crops almost to the last grain. The evacuation was carried out gradually and in *echelon*; the greater part of the troops were assembled in Mpotora, which was occupied by Captain Rothe, in a fortified camp, with his two companies which had defeated the Portuguese at Nevala. Only a few small detachments were left on the Rufiji, and these were gradually reduced to the strength of patrols. Four days' march east of Madaba the detachments of Koehl and Goering had the opportunity of some successful skirmishes against enemy detachments on the western edge of the Matumbi Mountains. Gradually, however, all these detachments were brought to Mpotora, and only Captain Otto remained in the higher regions of Madaba.

CHAPTER 9

The End of the Frontier Defence in the Subsidiary Theatres

In August, 1916, Major Kraut had gradually retired from Kilossa on Mahenge, leaving only Schoenfeld's division at Kidodi, on the Ruaha. Captain Braunschweig's force was embodied in Major Kraut's command. Of these Captain Falkenstein, with the 5th Field Company, had retired, at the end of May, 1916, from Ipyana, and Captain Aumann, with his company, from the Mbozi region in the direction of Lupembe and Maubire. During the retirement there was continual skirmishing. Our weak divisions had to make a stand against the pursuing enemy, at least a brigade strong.

At the end of June, 1916, Captain Braunschweig, who was then at Dodoma, was sent through Iringa, and his force was strengthened to five companies by the addition of the Kondoa troops and others brought from Dar-es-Salaam, including the two companies from Langenburg. One hundred of the crew of the Konigsberg from Dar-es-Salaam and a field howitzer were added to this force. At Malangali he accepted battle with the enemy, and apparently inflicted heavy losses. Then, however, he evacuated the position, and abandoned the howitzer, which was difficult to move, first making it useless. The difficulties of Braunschweig's position were increased by the action of an important Wahehe chief in his rear, who rebelled and went over to the enemy with all his people and cattle. Captain Braunschweig then retired on Mahenge, fighting a succession of minor rearguard skirmishes, and put himself under the orders of Major Kraut.

After numerous minor engagements Major Kraut's retiring divisions established themselves on the line of the Ruhudje and Ruaha Rivers. In the fertile region round Mahenge the supplies were excel-

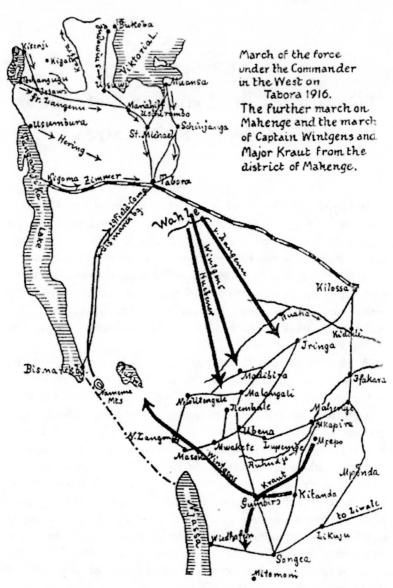

March of the force
under the Commander
in the West on
        Tabora 1916.
The further march on
Mahenge and the march
of Captain Wintgens and
Major Kraut from the
district of Mahenge.

FIG. XV. MARCH OF MAJOR-GENERAL WAHLE IN THE WEST

lent, even after the evacuation of a large part of the rice-field west of the Ruhudje. On this river the enemy had established a strongly fortified camp at Mkapira. With our insufficient resources it was impossible to take this position by force, but there was a chance that by cutting the enemy's line of communication with Lupembe, we might force him to evacuate the camp owing to shortage of food.

Major Kraut crossed the river with five companies and a light field gun, and occupied a position in a semi-circle of hills in the enemy's rear and right across his line of communication. In the enemy's front weak forces covered the river bank on the Mahenge side. Unfortunately the fortified positions of our companies were so extended that, owing to the difficulties of the country, there was no guarantee that support could be brought up in time. On the ———, before daybreak, the 10th Company on the right wing was surprised by a heavy enemy attack. The enemy also cleverly took the company's position in the rear and, after inflicting heavy losses, put the machine guns out of action. On the left wing Lieutenant von Schroetter's company was also attacked from all sides, and had to cut its way out with the bayonet, losing the light field gun and a machine gun.

In view of the heavy casualties of the enemy, Major Kraut would have been able to remain on the west bank of the Ruhudje, in spite of this partial disaster, but fighting could be heard from the direction of Lupembe, where the 25th Field Company was covering his rear. Major Kraut thought, wrongly, that there, too, a sharp attack had been made, and, therefore, retired again to the east bank of the Ruhudje. To his astonishment the enemy's strong entrenchments at Mkapira were found to be evacuated a few days later, the enemy having withdrawn in the night. Closer inspection showed that he had suffered heavy losses in the recent fighting. This, however, was not enough to explain his withdrawal; this riddle was not solved until later, on the appearance of General Wahle, with whom no communication had been established.

In expectation of the opening of the big operations of 1916 the reinforcements that had been provisionally sent to Victoria Nyanza, Ruanda, the Russissi and the Tanganyika area were brought back and embodied into our main forces along the North railway. A single command for these minor theatres of war was required, and with this object a "western command" was established under Major-General Wahle, who for the most part co-ordinated and directed these operations from Tabora.

In April and May, 1916, when the British main forces in the Kilima

Njaro area had completed their march, and, after the rainy season, were beginning a fresh advance to the south, English and Belgians from Muansa, Lake Kiwu, the Russissi and Bismarckburg began to advance concentrically on Tabora through these minor theatres of war. Our weak divisions retired on this place.

Major von Langenn retired at once from Tschangugu to Issawi, followed by Captain Wintgens from Kissenji. Heavy casualties were inflicted on the pursuing Belgian brigades in successful rearguard actions. The German detachment later continued its retirement on Mariahilf. The danger to our district from the strong Belgian forces on our heels had been correctly estimated by Captain Gudovius. When in June, 1916, strong English forces advanced across the Kagera, he retired south from Bukoba with his division. Owing to the difficulties of communication and getting information, a part of his force unfortunately ran upon strong Belgian forces in Ussuwi district. Captain Gudovius himself was wounded in the abdomen and fell into the enemy's hands. The engagement went badly for us and cost us heavy losses. Individual bodies of the detachment, however, managed to fight their way through to Muansa and Uschirombo.

In the middle of July, 1916, the English succeeded in effecting a surprise landing with about a brigade in the neighbourhood of Muansa. There, too, there was some skirmishing, favourable to us, and there the Commanding Officer, Captain von Chappuis, retired in the direction of Tabora. The troops from Muansa and those under Major von Langenn and Captain Wintgens established a new front, approximately on the line Schinjanga-St. Michael, and repulsed several Belgian attacks. Captain Zimmer had sunk the steamer *Goetzen* at Kigoma and blown up the Wami. He then retired slowly along the railway to Tabora. Captain Hering von Usumbura followed suit.

The fact that the operations were nearing Tabora gave General Wahle the opportunity to bring up quickly part of the troops from the north of Tabora, to make a dash west by rail and retire again at once. In this raid the 8th Field Company completely routed a Belgian battalion west of Tabora, and Wintgens' detachment brought off a successful surprise attack west and north of Tabora. These minor victories were often considerable, and on several different days of skirmishing the enemy losses amounted to hundreds; several light howitzers were also captured in these raids.

On 2nd June, 1916, the 20th Field Company was surrounded in its fortified position in the Namema mountains. In fighting his way through, the brave company commander, Lieutenant Franken, was severely wounded and taken prisoner. Lieutenant Hasslacher retired step by step on Tabora. In an affair of patrols south of this place he met with a hero's death.

In this way the troops of the western command were actually assembled at Tabora, and the moment had come for a systematic retirement to the south-east. These last operations and the capture of Tabora were not known at Headquarters until long afterwards. There was no means of communication with the western command. Major-General Wahle was aware that this retirement of our main forces was of first importance for the Mahenge area. Accordingly he gave orders for the march. At first the railway could be used for supplies and transport. The eastern column, under Major von Langenn, marched on Iringa, the centre column, under Captain Wintgens, on Madibira, and the western column, under Lieutenant Huebener, on Ilembule. Major Wahle accompanied the centre column.

In this way they came upon the line of communication between Neu-Langenburg and Iringa, and the enemy's dumps along this line. Huebener's detachment lost touch, and surrendered, being enveloped by a superior force of the enemy at Ilembule. Langenn's detachment was most unfortunately surprised by; a burst of fire while crossing a ford near Iringa and lost heavily. The subsequent attack on Iringa was also costly and without success.

Wintgens' detachment surprised enemy dumps and columns near Madibira, and also captured a gun and some wireless apparatus. In spite of several days of stubborn fighting, they were unable to take Lupembe and the surrounding farms. The influence of Wahle's advance immediately made itself felt in the Mahenge district. The apparently strong enemy troops, who from their fortified positions at Mkapira had carried out the successful raid against Major Kraut, now felt themselves seriously threatened in their rear. They evacuated their strong positions and retired on Lupembe. General Wahle took over the command of all the forces at Mahenge.

At the end of 1916 the troops of General Wahle's western command were grouped round Mahenge. From here he directed the operations extending approximately to the line Ssongea-Lupembe-Iringa-Kidodi.

It has been said that all touch with General Wahle had been lost since July, 1916, until in October, 1916, his patrols joined up with those of Major Kraut south of Iringa.

It was not, therefore, until after the fighting at Mkapira that Major Kraut, and through him Headquarters, learned of General Wahle's advance; the development of the situation made a very different impression on the enemy. He must have regarded the advance of General Wahle's columns against the English line of communication from Iringa to Langenburg, and Major Kraut's accidentally simultaneous threat to Mkapira, as a widely-planned joint operation, which was seriously endangering his troops at Mkapira, even after Major Kraut had withdrawn to the east bank of the Ruhudje. He avoided this danger by a hasty retirement from Mkapira in a westerly direction.

General Wahle's columns at once concentrated in the Lupembe-Mkapira area. No news was received of Huebener's western column. Its capitulation was not known until much later.

Welcome though this reinforcement of the forces in the west was, there were difficulties of supplies, and it became necessary to put under cultivation a considerable area, stretching almost to Ssongea. Major Grawert's detachment advanced to Likuju on the Ssongea-Liwale road, that of Major Kraut to the Mpepo region and Captain Wintgens' surrounded an enemy detachment in a fortified camp at Kitenda. The enemy quickly marched to the relief of this force, but the relieving troops were driven off with heavy losses. At the same time the position of Grawert's detachment took a very unfavourable turn. The enemy had succeeded in driving off this force's livestock.

As other supplies in the district were scanty, Major von Grawert, exaggerating the difficulties of supply, thought his position hopeless and surrendered in January, 1917. A transportable 8.8 air naval gun which had been brought to Lihuju with great difficulty fell into the enemy's hands, as well as a number of good machine guns. In reality the position of Grawert's force does not appear to have been so desperate as he supposed; at any rate, a strong patrol under Sergeant-Major Winzer, who refused to surrender, made its way south without being molested by the enemy, and, a few days later, found abundant supplies at small cost in the districts west of Tunduru. The conduct of this patrol gave further proof that there is almost always a way out, even of an apparently hopeless position, if the leader makes up his mind to face the risks.

Meanwhile General Wahle's supply difficulties were increasing. Whether they could have been modified by ruthlessly reducing the number of non-combatants, as had been done on the Rufiji, or whether the material welfare of the western command could have been substantially improved by greater care in procuring and rationing the available resources, could not be decided from my position on Lake Utungi. The temporary telegraph to Mahenge was very inefficient and often interrupted, and it took several days to get a despatch through from General Wahle in Mahenge to the troops. This made it difficult for me to get a view of the situation from the incomplete information at hand. Suffice it to say that the difficulties of supply in Mahenge were regarded as so acute that it was not considered possible to keep such strong forces concentrated there, and part of them would have to be withdrawn.

Kraut's and Wintgens' forces were marched west to Gumbiro, whence they were to press on across the Ssongea-Wiedhafen road. It was thought that they would find adequate supplies in the mountains south of Ssongea. The report of this move reached me too late for me to interfere. From Gumbiro Captain Wintgens turned north and, near Lake Rukwa, successfully engaged an enemy column which had been following him; on nearing Tabora he got typhus and was taken prisoner. Captain Naumann led the force on until finally he surrendered to the pursuing enemy column near Kilima-Njaro towards the end of 1917. It is to be regretted that this operation, carried out with so much initiative and determination, became separated so far from the main theatre of war as to be of little use.

Major Kraut had separated from Captain Wintgens in Gumbiro, and, carrying out General Wahle's orders, had marched south. There was no difficulty about crossing the line of communication Ssongea-Wiedhafen, but as the enemy had strongly entrenched and secured his supply dumps, no booty was captured. In the open little was to be found in March, 1917, the poorest season of the year, a few months before the new harvest. After some rearguard actions against English troops a success was scored in a surprise attack on the small Portuguese camp at Mitomoul, on the Rovuma. Major Kraut then followed the river downstream to Tunduru and himself came to Headquarters to report. Two of his companies remained at Tunduru to guard the fertile district. The other three marched further east and were temporarily taken over by Captain Loof at Lindi.

CHAPTER 10

Lindi and Kilwa

The operations of the last few months had narrowed the area from which supplies for the troops could be obtained. The productive areas of Lupembe, Iringa, Kissaki and the lower Rufiji had been lost, and the newly-occupied districts included wide stretches of barren land. The productivity of the more fertile areas was for the most part unknown; for instance, it was not known until during the subsequent operations what yield could be expected south-west of Kilwa and south-west of Livale, for example. At that time I only had a general idea that the eastern part of the Lindi area was very fertile and known as the granary of the colony. But this fertile region, owing to its nearness to the coast, was in a very precarious position, and it was already necessary to consider what should be done if it were lost.

Our eyes naturally turned to the Portuguese territory across the Rovuma, but we had even less information about this than about parts of the German colony. Fortunately, however, a number of Portuguese chiefs had immigrated into German territory out of hatred for their oppressors, and, apart from this, we Germans enjoyed a very good reputation among the intelligent natives of Portuguese East Africa, many of whom worked on German plantations. Thus we were able to get at least an approximate picture of the district east of Lake Nyassa, and to take it as probable that south of the *steppe*-like zone of the Rovuma, in the neighbourhood of Mwembe, several days' march, broad and thinly populated, lay a fertile region. An expeditionary force of a few hundred rifles under Major von Stuemer, crossed the Rovuma south of Tundura, and quickly took possession of Mwembe from where our patrols explored the banks of Lake Nyassa as far as the neighbourhood of Fort Jackson, and east half-way to Port Amelia.

In view of the difficulty of communication—messengers from the

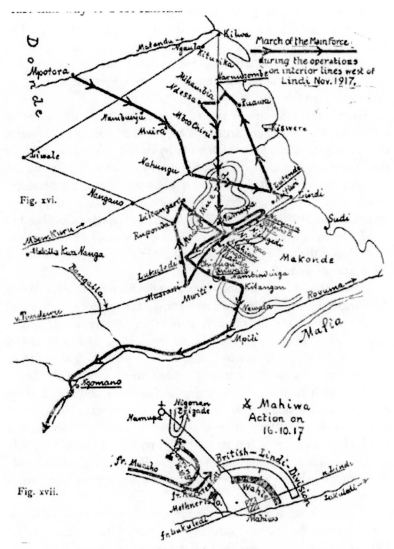

FIG. XVI. MARCH OF MAIN FORCE DURING OPERATIONS ON INTERIOR
LINES WEST OF LINDI, JUNE TO NOVEMBER, 1917.
FIG. XVII. BATTLE OF MAHIWA.

telegraph station at Livale took about three days to get to Tunduru and five from there to Mwembe—it was difficult to get a clear idea of the situation at Mwembe. We had no definite news until Lieutenant Brucher personally reported at Headquarters in January, 1917. The European potatoes he brought with him gave us good hopes that supplies could be expected there. He reported that the country was fertile, as was also the region round Tunduru, where the war had so far hardly been felt.

There were still large numbers of eggs and fowls in the richly cultivated district. When Brucher slept on the ground in Tunduru, this was regarded as a piece of bravado by the inhabitants, so little did they know about war. In view of the difficulties of transport and the constant movement of the troops, it became increasingly necessary to make the force less and less dependent on their inadequate line of communication. With this object the forces of Captains Goering and von Lieberman were also moved to the region south of Kilwa, where, according to the stories of some Europeans in the Kiturika mountains, there was plenty of food.

In order to relieve the transport of supplies from the rear the troops were marched off to Kilwa without waiting for further investigation, and it was fortunate that the reports as to the fertility of this district were realized. In order to take the enemy, who had already moved some small forces half-way to Livale, as far as possible from south of his point of debarkation, and at the same time to secure the fertile districts south of Kilwa to Mbemkuru, Goering's and von Lieberman's divisions made a *détour* from Mpotora southwards and pressed forward, Goering's force following the coast straight to Kilwa, and von Lieberman keeping further west and making for the Kilwa-Livale road. A weaker force followed this road to Kilwa and served as a reserve for the patrols, which several times surprised the enemy in his camps and threw him back.

Our patrols were soon swarming in the neighbourhood of Kilwa. Several enemy dumps were surprised and part of the garrisons killed. On one of these occasions brave Sergeant-Major Struwe, who was afterwards killed, skilfully forced his way, with a large part of the 3rd Field Company, inside a dump, and, taking cover behind the sacks of flour, inflicted heavy losses on the enemy, who appeared from outside in great force. It was difficult to get much away from the dump, so the patrol had to content itself with destroying the greater part of the stores. One patrol took a field gun with it—a strange weapon for a

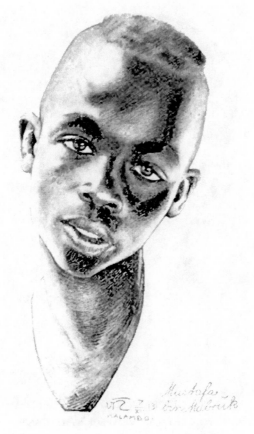

NATIVE TYPES (1). DRAWN BY GENERAL
VON LETTOW-VORBECK'S ADJUTANT.

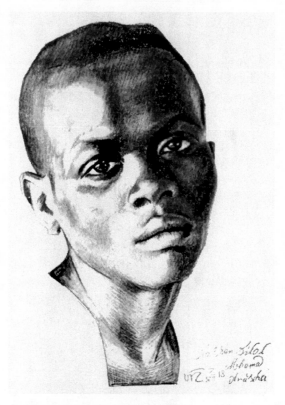

NATIVE TYPES (2). DRAWN BY GENERAL
VON LETTOW-VORBECK'S ADJUTANT.

patrol. After careful reconnaissance this reached the coast at Kilwa-Kissiwami, and bombarded some of the transports lying there.

In May, 1917, Captain von Lieberman, who, with the 11th and 17th Companies, was occupying an entrenched position at Ngaula, a day's march south of Kilwa on the Kilwa-Livale road, was attacked by eight companies with two guns. Lieutenant Buechsel, with his 17th Company, made such a heavy flank attack that he completely routed, one after the other, several of the enemy's *Askari* companies, who took to their heels, followed by the 40th Indian Pathan Regiment. The enemy left about seventy dead on the field, and, as the English related afterwards, it was only by chance that we did not find his guns, which had stuck fast in a river.

On the whole it seemed to us that the enemy's forces were once more getting exhausted. Unless he brought over very considerable reinforcements it was obvious that the forces available would before long be worn out and his operations end in failure. It was already apparent that they were involving a great strain. It had been ascertained that a battery from the Indian interior had been brought to Kilwa and that a large number of new *Askari* companies were being raised.

More dangerous than the enemy seemed to me the material position of our men. The cargo of wheat from the relief ship was coming to an end, and I thought it questionable whether bread could be baked from *Mtama* flour alone, without the addition of wheat flour. At that time I still regarded bread as an indispensable necessity for the nourishment of Europeans, and therefore I made experiments personally in baking bread without wheat flour. Unfortunately the results were unsatisfactory. Afterwards, under the stress of necessity, we all produced excellent bread without wheat. The methods differed widely. Later we made bread not only with *mtama*, but also with *muhogo*, sweet potatoes, maize, in short, with nearly every kind of meal, and with mixtures of all sorts of combinations, and later still improved the quality by the addition of boiled rice.

The necessary kit also required attention. A shortage of boots was in sight. My experiments showed me that a European can go barefoot where there are tolerable paths, but never through the bush. Sandals, which anyone can make, given an odd bit of leather, proved helpful, but did not take the place of boots. To be ready for any emergency, I had some lessons in boot-making, and succeeded, with supervision, in producing an object that at a push could be taken for a left boot, though it was intended to be a right.

It is very convenient for a European who knows the simplest rudiments of this craft to be able to kill an antelope and make a boot, or at any rate repair one, from his skin a few days later, without the help of any of the tools of civilization. A nail must serve as an awl, a tent-pole as a last, and the thread he can cut from the tough leather of a small antelope. As a matter of fact, however, we were never driven to these extremities, as we were always able to obtain the necessary kit and equipment from captured stores, and many captured saddles were cut up to make soles and heels for boots.

Every European was becoming more and more like a South-African "*Trekker*" and was his own workman. Naturally, not always in person, but within the small independent household, consisting of his black cook and his black servant, which followed him about. Many had even provided themselves with a few hens which they took about with them, and the noise of these betrayed the position of German camps even as far as the native settlements. An order issued in one force that the crowing of cocks before 9 a.m. was forbidden brought no relief.

The important question of salt was very simply solved by the troops at Kilwa, by the evaporation of sea-water. In order to secure the supply, which was beginning to run short, against the loss of the coast, salt-yielding plants were collected and the salt obtained from their ashes by lixiviation. We got this idea from the natives of the district, who supplied themselves with salt in this way. The salt thus obtained was not bad, but was never required to any extent, as we were always able to meet our requirements from the captured stores. The large numbers of elephants in this district furnished us with fat; sugar was replaced by the excellent wild honey which was found in large quantities. The troops had made an important step forward as regards supplies of grain. They found out how to ripen it artificially, and in this way provided against want.

It should be noted here particularly that the Medical Corps, in spite of the difficult and constantly changing circumstances of life in the field, had succeeded in satisfactorily solving the important questions of quinine and material for bandages. It has already been mentioned that in the north quinine tablets of better quality than the English had been added to the stock of Peruvian bark. After the evacuation of the northern area a large consignment of Peruvian bark had been sent to Kilossa. Through the efforts of the Deputy Staff Medical Officer, Staff-Surgeon Teute, a part of this was transported further south. It was of course impossible without the necessary apparatus to manufacture tablets, but liquid quinine was produced by boiling Peruvian bark. This had an infernal taste and was drunk unwillingly but with beneficial results by the patients, among whom it was known as "*Lettow-Schnaps.*"

The other difficulty was the supply of bandages. To supplement the stock of linen, which was beginning to give out, not only was clothing of all kinds disinfected and used for this purpose, and then after being boiled used again, but quite a good bandage-material was made from bark. This idea, too, we got from the methods of the natives, who for a long time had made clothing and sacks from Myombo bark. The medical service had done everything humanly possible to keep the troops alive and well. The great resource of this service and the necessary husbanding of the primitive material available deserve special recognition, as this service had always been accustomed under the special conditions of a tropical climate, and rightly so, to be very free with their stocks. The Staff Medical Officer, Staff-Surgeon Stolowsky, and later his successor, Staff-Surgeon Teute, showed exemplary devotion, energy and foresight.

The surgery was on an equally high level. The hospitals which, during the early part of the campaign, had been accommodated for the most part in solid buildings, and had worked the whole year round without moving their quarters, had now to turn themselves into movable columns, which might at any moment be called upon to pack up, with patients and baggage, and keep up with the march in various directions of the troops. All not absolutely indispensable material had to be eliminated, so that the preparations for a surgical operation had always to be more or less improvised. The operating-theatre was as a rule a newly-erected grass hut. In spite of all this, Staff-Surgeon Müller, Dr. Thierfelder, of the Imperial Medical Service, and others successfully performed even serious operations, including several for appendicitis.

As has already been mentioned, the confidence even of the enemy in the German medical service was fully justified. The successful and devoted activity of these men went far to strengthen the mutual confidence between white and black. In such ways as this the strong bond was formed which united the different elements of our force.

At Lindi the enemy had strengthened himself more and more, and it was reported that detachments were being transported by sea to Lindi, which hitherto had been posted west of Kilwa. General O'Grady, who had commanded a brigade at Kibata, also appeared at Lindi. The obvious idea that the enemy would advance from Lindi against our weak forces and our main supply area, as had been his intention earlier at Kilwa, appeared to be materializing.

Several attacks had been beaten off by Captain Looff's force west of Lindi. At the request of the Governor three of the companies which had arrived under Major Kraut were not, as had been the original intention, used to subjugate quickly and thoroughly the rebellious inhabitants of Makonde, in the south-east corner of our Protectorate, but were put under the command of Captain Looff. Two of them took part in an attack on Sudi, south of Lindi, where the enemy was strongly entrenched. The attack on the fortified position was bravely launched, but suffered heavy losses, and could not be brought to a successful conclusion.

Later, Captain Rothe was ordered to Lindi with reinforcements consisting of three companies from Mpotora. But the rains spoiled our plans. The crossing of the Matendu had already become difficult. All the ram that had fallen in Donde district collected ultimately in the valley of the Matendu, which in the dry season is simply a series of pools. It had become a strong, rushing torrent, like the Fulda in spate at Cassel. and tore up great trees in its course. By making use of some islands, tree-trunks were got into position under the direction of skilled engineers and a bridge to take transport was built; but a sudden rise in the stream repeatedly swept it away, several men being drowned. A footbridge further downstream met with the same fate; a narrow suspension-bridge of ropes made from twisted bark was only of slight service and was somewhat uncertain as, in view of the alternation of strong sunlight and wet, there was always a danger of the ropes rotting and giving way.

At Nahungu, on the Mbemkuru, similar conditions hindered Captain Rothe's march. The stream was so strong that the first attempt to cross by the few ferry-boats available failed. Driven out of Nahungu by scarcity of supplies, Captain Rothe marched into the fertile region to the north-east, in this way seriously compromising the plans of Headquarters. It was necessary that this fertile country north-east of Nahungu should be spared to serve as a reserve for the forces south of Kilwa and to provide for a strong reinforcement of these troops should tactical reasons make this necessary. The time that was lost before a message could be got through to Captain Rothe was very vexatious, but finally his division was diverted towards Lindi again in time to take part in some of the fighting.

In view of the need for reinforcement of our troops at Lindi owing to increased tension of the military situation and the projected transference of fresh troops to that area, General Wahle had been withdrawn from Mahenge and had taken over the command of the Lindi front; Captain Tafel succeeded him at Mahenge. In the middle of June, 1917, General Wahle had, after several engagements which had brought to light a considerable increase in the enemy's strength, retired so far up the Lukuledi river that the enemy seemed to be incautiously exposing his north flank.

I decided to make use of this advantage without, indeed, knowing exactly how it was to be done. So much was clear : that only a surprise attack promised success. I therefore advanced, with four companies and the mountain-battery consisting of two guns, through Nahungu, along the main road leading *via* Lutende to Lindi. At Lutende were encamped Captain von Chappuis' company and Lieutenant Wunder's company, and the rest were further back. I went on ahead to reconnoitre, with my able companion Nieuwenhuizen, who had played the chief part in the horse-drive on Erok mountain. From the height on which Chappuis' company lay, there was an extensive view : one could see the different farmhouses round Lindi and the Lukuledi River with the steamer *President*, which had taken refuge there and been rendered useless.

It was, perhaps, fortunate that no wild pigs or bush deer had come within range of our guns in this otherwise gameless district, for not far from Chappuis' camp we crossed the trail of a strong enemy patrol which must only just have passed. The talk of the natives, too, led us to suppose that they had recently seen something interesting. When we questioned them they would tell us nothing. Making a wide *détour*, we arrived in the evening, after dark, at the camp of Wunder's company. We reported our observations to the company commander and the capable guide Inkermann, who died a hero's death a few days later, warning them to keep a sharp lookout. Orders were also given that this camp, situated as it was in an open plain and exposed to fire from the surrounding bush, should be moved. After a cup of tea we returned to our main force about a quarter of an hour's march to the rear.

On the morning of 30th June we heard increasing rifle-fire from the direction of Wunder's company. Assuming that the enemy had taken advantage of the lie of the ground and was firing on the camp from the surrounding bush, I immediately advanced with the three companies to the right through the bush, so as to strike the road further south and so take the enemy in the rear. Soon, however, we met some *Askari*, who told us that a strong force of the enemy had forced its way into the camp, taking the company by surprise and driving it out.

A young *Askari* complained to an old "*betschausch*" (sergeant) of the third company that the enemy had taken everything from them. "*Niemaza we, tutawafukuza*" (shut your mouth, we'll soon have 'em out), was the defiant answer which at once shamed the excited youth into silence. The sergeant's answer indeed hit off the position. The enemy, consisting of the 5th Indian Regiment and a few natives, had thought to find only a weak German outpost. He had rashly penetrated into our badly-placed entrenchments and was now in his turn exposed on all sides to a concentrated fire from the bush.

The position was so clear that it called for the quickest possible independent action by the subordinate leaders, and Captain von Chappuis also attacked at once. Staff-Surgeon Mohn (afterwards killed), who had remained in Wunder's camp and had temporarily fallen into the enemy's hands, described the very harassing effect of our concentrated fire at short range and the panic it caused among the enemy. Nevertheless, the cover afforded by a few ravines and the undergrowth enabled some of the enemy to get away. These fled wildly.

A number so entirely lost themselves that they were picked up in the bush days afterwards by our patrols in a half-starved condition. We inflicted about 120 casualties. In addition to recovering our own ammunition, which had fallen temporarily into the enemy's hands, we captured the enemy's ammunition which he had just brought into the camp, about a hundred rifles and some machine guns. Among the severely wounded whom we took to the English camp at Naitiwi, and there handed over, was the commanding officer of the English regiment. He afterwards died of his wound.

We stayed a few weeks longer in the fertile district of Lutende and tried with our patrols to inflict losses on the enemy, whose fortified camps at, and south of, Naitiwi offered no prospect of successful attack. Far to the south we often heard the explosion of air-bombs and of the heavy guns which were bombarding Wahle's division. Von Chappuis' company was marched to reinforce Wahle's force. Apart from some skirmishing our success at Lindi was followed by a lull in the operations.

That this was only the prelude to new efforts on the enemy's part was borne out not only by the reports of the transport of strong forces to Kilwa, and also by the fact that at the end of May General Hoskins, who had taken over command from General Smuts, had been relieved by General van Deventer. Once more a Boer was in command, and the rumours that fresh European troops were being brought from South Africa seemed to be confirmed. South of Kilwa the enemy attacked our nine companies with three brigades, but Captain von Lieberman, who had taken over from Captain Goering, the latter being seriously ill, succeeded with extraordinary skill in beating off the superior forces of the enemy.

On July 6th, at least a brigade made a frontal attack on Captain Lieberman at Unindi and was repulsed with heavy losses. The bold charge of our companies cost us heavily too; among the casualties was Lieutenant Bleeck, who received a mortal wound in the stomach while leading his company. This brave and upright personality had done excellent service both as a fearless patrol-leader and on the Headquarters Staff, and I knew him intimately. Von Lieberman's right flank was covered against another enemy brigade by Captain Spangenberg with two of the nine companies. He carried out his task and attacked the enemy brigade so energetically with his two companies that, as we heard later, the English reports spoke of an attack by very strong enemy forces.

In spite of this success at Unindi, the great superiority of the enemy and the danger from enveloping movements to our supplies in the rear, induced Captain von Lieberman to withdraw gradually south, fighting all the time. I thought the moment had come to make a rapid counter-march with the available companies at Lutende, and the mountain-battery come unexpectedly to the aid of Captain von Lieberman and perhaps seize a favourable opportunity to inflict a decisive defeat upon the enemy. We moved due north from Lutende by forced marches and crossed the Mbemkuru, now once more an insignificant stream, without difficulty, two days' march below Nahungu. The only opposition we encountered was from swarms of wild bees which forced us to make a slight *détour*. North of Mbemkuru we continued our march north into the Ruawa hills.

I made use of the two days required to muster the force again to reconnoitre thoroughly the surrounding country, and on the 28th July, to my astonishment, I learned accidentally from some natives that a road through the mountains led almost in a straight line from our camp to Captain Lieberman's camp at the Narungomba water-hole, about six hours' march. A patrol of Europeans was sent at once to reconnoitre this road. In the morning of the 29th July I heard from my camp at Ruawa some explosions from the direction of Lieberman's force. I did not think this could denote serious fighting, as the sounds ceased and, further, the patrol which I had sent to Lieberman's force, and which had returned that morning, reported that everything was quiet there.

I had, however, to change my mind when at noon van Rooyen, who was very reliable, returned from a hunting expedition and reported that he had certainly heard continuous machine-gun fire. The reader will, perhaps, wonder that I had not already begun the march to Lieberman's camp, but it must be remembered that there was no water on the way, and my men were very exhausted, while some had only just reached Ruawa. By nightfall I was just three hours' march nearer the scene of action, but it was not until the night was well advanced that my companies had all come up. A continuance of the march through the bush in pitch darkness was hopeless; it was bound to lead to a good deal of misunderstanding and would have meant a useless waste of the men's strength, which had already been severely tried.

At 3 a.m. the march was continued and soon after a report came from the advance officer patrol that Captain von Lieberman had certainly defeated the enemy, but, owing to shortage of ammunition, had marched to Mihambia during the night. The rear-guard had evacuated the springs and at the time of the report was following the rest. My order to hold the springs at all costs until my arrival at 6 a.m. to join in the battle had, therefore, been disregarded owing to pressure of circumstances. I now thought that the enemy, who was stronger than we, would have strongly entrenched the springs position, as was his habit, and that I should have to carry out any attack with thirsty troops. That seemed to offer little prospect of success.

Later, when I learned the enemy's real position, I inclined to the opposite view. In spite of his superiority the enemy had suffered a severe defeat. His 7th South African and 8th European regiments were almost broken up. Again and again his infantry had hurled themselves in deep waves against the front of our *Askari* regiments, and each time they had been driven back by counter-attacks. A forest fire had broken out and spread among his ranks. Finally the main body of his troops had broken away and fled in wild disorder through the bush. Machine guns, masses of rifles and hundreds of cases of ammunition had been left on the field. In this condition, my attack, even after the withdrawal of Lieberman's force, would perhaps have sealed the doom of the enemy's main body.

It is much to be regretted that at that time large numbers of the troops did not show sufficient initiative to make good the shortage of German ammunition during the battle itself, by using the enemy rifles and cartridges which were lying about in quantities. We had been within reach of a most important success which was snatched from our grasp by accident. We must, however, be grateful for the feat of arms which the 7th *Askari* Company performed under the doubtless brilliant leadership of Captain von Lieberman, against overwhelming odds.

I did not get a clear report of this action, however, until later. For the moment I thought it right to march to Mihambia in order, by joining with Lieberman's detachment, to secure unity of command, to supply it with sufficient ammunition to carry on and, if necessary, to raise its moral after the severe battle by a visible reinforcement. This last turned out to be unnecessary; when I arrived I found Lieberman's detachment in excellent spirits, all the companies being proud to have dealt such a heavy blow to the superior enemy.

For me the operation at Narungombe was a further proof how difficult it is in the unknown African bush and in face of the uncertainty of communication, even if other circumstances are favourable, to carry through an operation in which several columns are taking part, so as to secure the necessary unity of action on the battlefield. At Narungombe, where all the conditions were as favourable as could have been hoped, the decision was finally thwarted by slight mischances, and my belief was strengthened that if I wanted to use different bodies of troops in one operation it was necessary to secure the closest connection first.

The engagement at Narungombe brought the enemy at Kilwa to a standstill for a considerable tune, and the fighting was confined to patrols, who inflicted losses on the enemy's lines of communication, firing out of the bush on his detachments and motor transport and attacked at close quarters when a favourable opportunity offered. In order, for one thing, to put this patrol work on a broader basis, but also to counter the moving of enemy troops westward, and finally for reasons of supply, I deployed the force laterally on the line Mihambia-Ndessa. A large number of aircraft appeared over the fertile Ndessa district against whose bombs we were defenceless, and some severe wounds resulted; from this air-reconnaissance we could infer the enemy's keen interest in the district and soon it was reported that he was moving still further west.

Our patrols did such good work that from time to time whole companies of the enemy were put to flight with heavy losses. But the enemy continued his efforts to obtain information. He hardly took the trouble to hide his intention when sending flags of truce. I remember one occasion when the party bearing the white flag arrived at our camp out of the bush; they had, therefore, not only avoided the roads leading to it but had deliberately crossed them. The closer proximity of the enemy made it more difficult for us to get up our supplies, which were gradually running out. It was unavoidable that the position of our requisitioning and hunting-parties should become known to the enemy and that they should be surprised. The influence of the enemy on the natives was shown by the fact that south of Mihambia several villages had been suddenly deserted. I had long regarded this phenomenon as a sign of the enemy's intention to advance in that direction.

The state of our supplies made it impossible for us to maintain so strong a force in the Mihambia-Ndessa area. As in any case the evacuation of this area could not long be delayed, and as the enemy west of Lindi was at the same time developing increased activity in strong force on General Wahle's front, I decided to join General Wahle with some of the companies from Ndessa and perhaps bring off the operation that had failed at Narungombe; a decisive success by an unexpected reinforcement. On the 3rd August General O'Grady's forces had certainly suffered a serious defeat. An Indian regiment, which had advanced through the gap between two strongly fortified German outposts, was attacked by our reserves, held ready for such a contingency, and almost annihilated. In the pursuit much valuable material fell into our hands. The enemy, however, had renewed the attack a few days later, and in face of the enveloping movement of his strong detachments, General Wahle had fallen back on Narunyu and a mountain of equal height south of the Lukuledi River.

Captain Koehl, with six companies and a battery, remained behind at Ndessa; I crossed the River Mbemkuru below Nahungu with four companies and two mountain-guns, and then marched diagonally across the Muera *plateau* to the mission-station at Namupa. The prefect in charge entertained us, among other things, with *muhogo* (a species of corn with edible roots), prepared like fried potatoes, and supplemented the scanty provisions of our Europeans with bananas and other fruit out of his extensive gardens.

In the camp at Njangao the receipt of part of a German wireless message directed to me, expressing his Majesty's acknowledgments on the occasion of the third anniversary of the outbreak of war, delighted us all.

We pitched our camp with the first company at Njengedi, on the main road between Njangao and Lindi, in the rear of Wahle's division, in unpleasant, rainy weather. I immediately set out for Narunyu to inform General Wahle of our arrival. Here, in an almost impenetrable country broken by numerous ravines, at the bottom of which lay deep swamps, friend and foe faced one another in close proximity. Our men were working at dug-outs covered by branches cut from the trees. Only five of General Wahle's seven companies were at Narunyu, the two others being on Ruho Mountain on the south bank of the Lukuledi River.

In view of the danger of a surprise attack on our weak forces at Narunyu I ordered them to be reinforced by the companies on Ruho Mountain and marched two of those that had come with me to take their place. The enemy attack on Narunyu occurred the following day. Captain Lieberman's Company from Ruho Mountain and the two companies I had brought with me all took part in the engagement. The third company had literally started their forced march to Karungu immediately after their arrival at Njengedi. I can still see the *Askari* coming up just before dawn and hear their shouts of delight at the thought of once more routing the enemy.

Our attempt to envelop the enemy's right wing, however, only served to press it back; the bush was too thick for an offensive movement which had to be developed at short range under a continuous machine-gun and rifle fire. The darkness made it still more difficult to direct the operations, and there is no doubt that in the confusion of the two fronts in this broken country our detachments often fired on one another : it was almost impossible to recognize friend or foe. For instance, hearing loud sounds of shouting in front of me, in the complete darkness of the bush, I thought this came from our enveloping attack driving back the enemy. It was not discovered till some time afterwards that this was the enemy and soon we heard him working at his trenches.

The exact location of his trenches gave us the advantage of being able to get the range for the 10.5 cm. gun of the *Königsberg*, which was with Wahle's force. This was done with good results; at any rate the enemy evacuated his trenches on the following day and retired.

The complete victory desired had not been attained and, in view of the difficulties of the ground, could not be expected, as we had discovered our strength to the enemy in the fighting of the 18th, and lost the advantage of a surprise. Once more I had to content myself with delay. In this fertile country there was no difficulty about holding our ground from the point of view of supplies. The force has rarely been so well fed as in the Lindi area. Great fields of sweet-potatoes and *muhogo* stretched as far as the eye could see, and there was an abundant supply of sugar-cane. The numerous Arab plantations indicated the fertility and the ancient civilization of the country.

We made ourselves at home, and though rifle bullets often whistled through our camp and aircraft dropped bombs on us, not much harm was done. On one occasion the dentist, who had set up his surgery in a European house and was giving us the attention we had long needed, was attending to a patient when a bomb fell into the room. It was discovered later, when the place was examined, that the planter kept his store of dynamite in this very room. Fortunately the bomb did not touch this or both patients and dentist would have been permanently freed from toothache.

It was no easy matter to decide what to do with the German women and children, some of whom had fled from Lindi and did not know what to do. A number of them had taken refuge in the planters' houses, which were within range of the enemy's guns. In view of the restriction of supplies and the difficulties of transport and accommodation, it was desirable that these women and children should be sent back to Lindi. Some were intelligent enough to see this. By means of a parley their transference behind the British lines was duly arranged, and they were able to leave for Lindi. For reasons unknown to me the English then refused to keep to the arrangement, and the women and children, as well as male non-combatants, gradually collected in the Catholic mission at Ndanda. A military convalescent home had been quartered there for some time and had developed into an important hospital. All the people who were brought here found good food and accommodation in the spacious buildings of the mission with its extensive gardens.

CHAPTER 11

In The South-East Corner of the Colony

While at Narunyu there was a lull in the fighting for several weeks, the enemy had shown considerable activity in the section of Portuguese territory occupied by Stuemer's force. Several English columns from the south-west and south had concentrated on Mwembe, and Major von Stuemer, not thinking himself strong enough to resist, had evacuated Mwembe. The different companies had then gradually retired on the Rovuma. North of this river Lieutenant-Commander Jantzen, who had been sent from Headquarters to Tunduru, and under whom the various companies of Stuemer's force had re-formed, had taken over the command. Enemy forces were also advancing on Tunduru from Ssongea.

It was difficult to obtain detailed information about the enemy. My impression was that he wanted to bring our main force to a halt, invade our supply-area in the Tunduru-Massassi-Ruponda district with strong forces, and carry off our supplies. I did not then think it out of the question that we might score a success, and I, therefore, marched on the 10th September, 1917, with five companies, from our camps at Narunyu towards Massassi. From there Captain Goering immediately marched with three companies towards Tunduru; Jantzen's division stood north-east of this place. I reconnoitred the road to Tunduru on a bicycle and feared that the difficulties of supply would be very serious. These fears were unfortunately realized. Supplies from the land could not be brought up and there was no time for a prolonged operation that would allow of additional supplies being obtained from Massassi.

The small English and Portuguese patrols which attacked our supplies and transport from across the Rovuma to the south did not cause us to hurry our movements. But the enemy from Kilwa, whom Captain Koehl's heavy attack from Mbeo-Chini and a number of lesser encounters had not been able to stop, reached the neighbourhood of Nahungu. His flying columns, for the most part mounted, outflanked Koehl's force, and pressed forward up the Mbemkuru River to Nangano. Communication with Captain Koehl by means of the telephone-line from Nahungu to Nangano was first interrupted for a few days, and then broken off completely. The supply dumps fell into the enemy's hands and were destroyed. To provide against the interruption of the exposed telephone-line a new line had been laid from Ruponda, running north-east, but connection by messenger between this line and Koehl's division took several days.

In view of the slow means of communication with Koehl's detachment, it was not possible to get an accurate view of the situation in time, and as the intended success at Tunduru could not in any case be attained, I marched the five companies from Massassi to Ruponda at the beginning of October, and then further north-east, joining forces with Koehl's force at Likangara. On receiving the report that enemy detachments were approaching Ruponda, I ordered the removal of the sick and the stores from Ruponda to Lukuledi and Mnacho. On 9th October, 1917, an enemy patrol was beaten off with some losses at Ruponda.

On 10th October a considerable force of the enemy—the 25th Indian Cavalry Regiment was identified—assaulted Ruponda from several sides. The withdrawal of our companies had, therefore, unfortunately been rather premature; otherwise the enemy might have encountered some of our passing companies at Ruponda and perhaps suffered a serious defeat. As it was, there were no troops in Ruponda except a few of our patrols; most of the sick fell into the enemy's hands, and also some 90,000 kg. of supplies. At Likangara there was no fighting worthy of notice. Some enemy patrols and weak detachments did appear, but our fighting-force, which was attacking the enemy's main line of communication along the Mbemkuru River, firing on and destroying motor-transport, and capturing mails and supplies, led me to suppose that the strongest part of the Kilwa force was recuperating further west in the direction of Ruponda.

The increased enemy activity a few days' march east of Likangara, where he established requisitioning stations, as well as the stories of the natives, made it seem probable that considerable enemy forces were marching from Nahungu towards the south, and therefore against General Wahle. Captured mails revealed the fact that in spite of his extensive intelligence and spy systems the enemy was groping in the dark. He did not know, for instance, where I was, although he seemed to place the greatest importance upon knowing. The knowledge of my Headquarters would tell him the probable position of our main force.

While one letter thought that I was in the neighbourhood of Lukuledi, another professed to know that I was at Tunduru, and according to a third I was at Mahenge. The talkativeness of these Europeans, who, in spite of all warnings, cannot refrain from communicating to one another in their private letters their knowledge and their conjectures about the war situation, had in this case done good: there was so much gossip, the rumours were so contradictory, and even the most improbable things were so indiscriminately believed, that anything at all could be read into the German correspondence. In spite of this unintentional misleading of the enemy, it is difficult to understand how intelligent people can entrust to the post important matters, the knowledge of which must be kept from the enemy, knowing how unreliable the post is, and that the letters often fall into the enemy's hands.

It was clear to me that the enemy's obvious uncertainty about the situation would give me a great opportunity if it could be used quickly and decisively. I ventured to hope that the intended decisive blow might now be struck for which I had tried twice near Lindi and once at Tunduru, and the success of which at Narungombe had hung on a hair. The development of the situation on Wahle's front seemed favourable for this attempt. His forces had gradually withdrawn from the Mtua district to Mahiwa. The enemy's whole handling of the campaign suggested that his various columns would press forward with all their weight and try to crush us by a concentration from all sides. The enemy's Lindi Division was advancing energetically with the rest. General Wahle's nine companies, fighting stubbornly, had retired before them to Mahiwa. I had a fair personal knowledge of the country at Mahiwa. It was very probable that my march in that direction would not be observed by the enemy in time.

On the 10th October, 1917, trusting in the fortune of war, I crossed the Linkangara mountains to Mnacho with five companies and two mountain guns. I arrived there at dark and left again at daybreak on the 15th. On the narrow mountain paths the force got very scattered. The guns were left far behind, and the pack-animals gave trouble.

Askari and bearers came to the rescue, and again and again Sergeant-Major Sabath rose superior to the difficulties and brought his guns forward. It surprised me that we were unable to get any information from Mahiwa, but the rifle and machine-gun fire indicated that fighting was in progress. Before dark I reached Lieutenant Methner's company, which was in reserve behind Wahle's left wing. The enemy seemed to be attacking this company with a view to enveloping it. His fire had the unfortunate effect of causing the disappearance of my bearer, with my dispatch-box, containing most important dispatches and maps: he did not return for two days.

The first two companies to come up were immediately thrown against the enemy's enveloping movement, and the enemy was thrown back. The companies then dug themselves in. On the morning of the 16th I went to reconnoitre, and found that the enemy had also entrenched himself immediately in front, at a distance of sixty to a hundred metres. When Lieutenant von Ruckteschell offered me a cup of coffee, care had to be taken, as the enemy was keeping a fairly sharp lookout, and shot with tolerable accuracy. I thought the opportunity favourable for a determined surprise attack. It was decided to launch the attack at noon, on the left (north) wing, and try to turn the enemy's flank. Goering's detachment was to lead the attack.

After we had eaten our midday meal undisturbed, I went at once to the left wing, where Captain Goering had just begun his advance with his two companies. When he had crossed a wide depression in the ground, to my surprise he changed direction still further to the left. The companies were soon in action. Only gradually I realized the significance of this surprising move. Captain Goering had come unexpectedly upon a new enemy who had come from Nahungu and was now attacking from the north. The force consisted of several battalions and two guns of the Nigerian Brigade who knew nothing of our arrival at Mahiwa and were expecting to smash General Wahle's force by an attack on his left flank and rear, while his front, facing east, was vigorously attacked by a division.

The Nigerian Brigade was as much taken by surprise as Captain Goering and was not so quick to adapt itself to the new situation. Captain Goering, closely supported by the reserves, threw himself so vigorously against the enemy in the bush that he ran through some of his detachments, threw them into confusion, and finally put them to flight. An enemy officer in command of an ammunition column took our men for his own, with the result that we captured about 150,000 rounds of ammunition. A gun with ammunition was taken by assault, and the killed did not consist wholly of Nigerian *Askari*. On Captain Goering's right, where two companies under Lieutenant von Ruckteschell and Lieutenant Brucker, wounded in this action, were fighting, the enemy was also thrown back some way into the bush.

While this fighting was going on on the flank, and on the following day also, the enemy attacked Wahle's force with all his strength. Here the enemy was in great superiority; wave after wave of fresh troops were thrown against our front. There was a danger that General Wahle's front would give way, and the fighting was very severe. There was also serious danger that our enveloping movement, in the very difficult swampy ground of the bush, would be held up so long by weak enemy forces that a defeat would be inflicted upon our front before it could make itself felt. In that case the battle was lost. I thought it expedient to increase the disadvantages that the enemy was bringing upon himself by his costly frontal attack and used all my available strength in such a way that the enemy by the increasing fierceness of his frontal attack was bleeding himself to death.

The original intention of enveloping the enemy's left wing was not developed further on the following days, but, on the contrary, every available company was withdrawn from the left wing to stiffen General Wahle's front. In this way we not only succeeded in holding our ground, but, by immediately taking advantage of the enemy's moments of weakness to make heavy counter-attacks with our reserves, we were able to inflict a real defeat.

My, perhaps surprising, tactics were prompted by the personality of the enemy commander. I had learned in the engagement at Reata (11th March, 1916) that General Beves threw his men into action regardless of loss of life and did not hesitate to try for a success, not by skilful handling and small losses, but rather by repeated frontal attacks which, if the defence held its ground and had anything like adequate forces, led to severe losses for the attack. I guessed that here at Mahiwa he was carrying out the same tactics. I think it was by taking advantage of the enemy leader's mistaken tactics in this way that we were able to win this splendid victory. Until the 18th October, for four days therefore, wave after wave of the attack broke on our front, but my own observation told me that the weight of the attack here on the right wing was diminishing and that the enemy's defeat was absolute.

On the evening of the 18th October we had, with some 1,500 men, completely defeated a whole enemy detachment at least 4,000, and probably not less than 6,000, strong. With the exception of Tanga, it was the most serious defeat he had suffered.

According to a high English officer the enemy lost 1,500 men; but I have reason to believe that this estimate is much too low. Our casualties were: 14 Europeans and 81 *Askari* killed, 55 Europeans and 367 *Askari* wounded, 1 European and 1 *Askari* missing. Considering the smallness of our forces these losses were for us very considerable, and were felt all the more seriously because they could not be replaced. We captured a gun, six heavy and three light machine guns, and 200,000 rounds of ammunition.

The situation, unfortunately, did not allow us to take full advantage of our victory; in our rear was the enemy who had occupied Ruponda on the 10th October, advanced in strong force further south and on 18th October attacked Major Kraut at Lukuledi. It must be remarked in passing that our troops which had fought under Lieutenant-Commander Jantzen near Tunduru had gradually retired northeast to the upper Mbenkuru and had reached Headquarters above Ruponda before the occupation of that place by the enemy on the 10th October. Two of these companies had reinforced the company which was guarding our supplies near Lukuledi, and it was these three companies, under the command of Major Kraut, which were attacked by a superior enemy from the north on the 18th October.

The enemy, believed to be six companies of the Gold Coast Regiment, was driven off, but in order to protect our supplies and material lying at Chigugu and Chiwata, Major Kraut retired to the first of these places. As well as Chigugu and Chiwata, Ndanda, where we had large stores of war material, was also threatened by the enemy, who had doubtless, in my opinion, been reinforced at Lukuledi. The enemy from Lukuledi might at any moment attack our lines of communication, capture our stores and supplies, and so put us out of action. We had no means of protecting our lines of communication locally, for the few thousand men we had were required for fighting. As, however, the force had to be kept alive, the danger had to be overcome in some other way.

There was only one way: to beat the enemy decisively at Lukuledi. It was necessary therefore to lose no time at Mahiwa, and, hard though it was, I had to abandon the idea of an annihilating pursuit. When, early on the 19th October, a few scattered detachments of the enemy were seen and fired on, I had already begun my march with six companies and two guns. On the next day at two o'clock we entered

Lukuledi from the east, and on 21st of October at dawn we attacked the enemy, who was apparently taken completely by surprise. North of Lukuledi, on the Ruponda road, Major Kraut's column surprised the camp of the 25th Indian Cavalry Regiment, which, with transport harnessed, stood ready for the march on Massassi; the camp was taken by storm and the regiment lost almost the whole of its transport horses, altogether 350.

Whilst I was engaged with the detachments of Koehl and Ruckteschell in a fairly serious action against the enemy entrenched at Lukuledi, I waited in vain for the intervention of Kraut's force. An attack on the camp without the advantage of surprise had little hope of success. When the force began to come under the fire of the enemy's mine-throwers on the flank, I withdrew the greater part from the zone of the effective cross-fire, after beating off a strong enemy attack, in order to avoid unnecessary losses. A fresh enemy, in the shape of a company of King's African Rifles (English East African *Askari*), who appeared unexpectedly from the bush, was quickly driven off. In this engagement Lieutenant Kroeger fell at the head of his company. The action was then broken off. No news came of Major Kraut until night; thinking he could no longer attack successfully at Lukuledi, and hearing no sounds of fighting, he had made a *détour* and then approached Lukuledi from the south.

Owing to unfavourable circumstances we had not succeeded in inflicting a decisive defeat on the enemy at Lukuledi, and the operation had only in part gained its objective, but the enemy's losses must be regarded as serious. The impression made on him was even greater than I had supposed. At any rate, it was reported that he had evacuated Lukuledi and withdrawn to the north. Among our casualties were three company-commanders killed. I can still see Lieutenant Volkwein, severely wounded in the leg, limping through the bush at the head of his company.

I had also spoken with Lieutenant Batzner and Lieutenant Kroeger shortly before they fell. Sergeant-Major Klein also fell, who had so often led his patrol on the Uganda railway. He was a capable machine gun leader. But our losses were not in vain. Our patrols pursued the enemy and fired on his camp near Ruponda and also his lines of communication. The impossibility of maintaining large bodies of troops in the neighbourhood of Ruponda—our supplies collected there had fallen into the enemy's hands—forced me to give up all idea of pursuing the enemy.

At that time I thought it possible that the enemy's withdrawal from Lukuledi might have been due to the movements of Captain Tafel's force, which was marching from Mahenge to join us. We had lost touch with him since the beginning of October. He had received orders to retire gradually before the strong enemy columns which were advancing on Mahenge from the north (Ifakara), west and south-west (Likuju, Mponda), and to try to get into touch with the main force under my command. I thought it quite possible that he had already arrived in the district of Nangano, or west of that place, and that the enemy had turned about again out of anxiety for his lines of communication.

CHAPTER 12

The Last Weeks in German Territory

On 24th October, the Governor of Chiwata, which had become the centre of the Administration, arrived at my camp east of Lukuledi for a conference. I firmly stated my opinion that, in spite of all difficulties of supply which must shortly arise in German East Africa, the war could and must be carried on. One possibility that offered was to base the operations on Portuguese territory. This could only be done by evacuating German East Africa and invading Portuguese East Africa.

The question of supplies was becoming very serious; we had in our stores only about 500,000 kg. of supplies. That would last us about six weeks. But it had been found that these figures were deceptive. The piled-up sacks had to a great extent lost weight and the grain had been eaten by insects. The new harvest could not be expected until March at the earliest. If the operations were to be continued it was necessary from this point of view alone to move south. I was still reckoning with the possibility that Captain Tafel's force might arrive in the neighbourhood of Massassi and Chiwata, in which case I should hand over to him the supplies at Chiwata, while I crossed the Makonda hills in the direction of Lindi with part of the Chiwata force and attacked the enemy's main line of communication on the Lukuledi River.

In whichever way the situation might develop, the Chiwata district was, on account of its fertility, of the greatest importance to us. Chiwata was, however, not protected and was further threatened by the fact that enemy operations were taking place in the north against Mnacho, and enemy mounted forces had been seen on the Lukuledi-Lindi road in the neighbourhood of Ndanda. Also enemy aircraft were paying our camp at Chiwata increasing attention.

These were my reasons for withdrawing from Lukuledi at the end of October with the main part of my forces. It could not be foreseen whether another opportunity would offer of making another attack from Chiwata on one of the enemy columns that would be passing before long. For the next few weeks the enemy's pressure was again directed against Wahle. Quite fresh troops were appearing there, among them the Cape Corps of South African half-castes. This corps had been stationed along the Central railway and had been brought up to reinforce General Beves' troops, apparently *via* Dar-es-Salaam and Lindi. Fortunately General Beves had not waited for this reinforcement before his defeat at Mahiwa.

General Wahle was retiring step by step up the Lukuledi River. I was, unfortunately, not able to send him any support, but even had to draw on his forces to have troops in hand ready for a favourable opportunity for an attack and to protect the supplies. In the almost daily bush-fighting of General Wahle's force heavy losses were apparently inflicted on the enemy, and he was held severely in check. There was, however, no defeat and no considerable capture of booty, and meanwhile our supplies were getting lower and lower. On 6th November, I rode from Chiwata to Nangoo, near Ndanda, where, close behind Wahle's force, I found a suitable point of attack for the Chiwata troops. On 7th November I rode back from Nangoo to Chiwata, making a detour south across the Makonde hills. On the same day enemy troops were again reported at Lukuledi, and on 9th November an affair of patrols took place at Chigugu, just west of Chiwata.

At this critical time, when the heads of the enemy columns were nearing Chiwata, it was urgently necessary for us to throw all our strength against one of these columns as soon as possible before the others could intervene. The first essential to make this blow effective was to bring the whole strength of our all too weak forces to bear simultaneously. This depended chiefly on the supply of ammunition. Our whole supply had dwindled to about 400,000 rounds, a very scanty allowance for our 25,000 rifles and 50 machine guns in a serious engagement, after which it would only be possible to continue the struggle if ammunition were captured.

For this the nature of the ground was unfavourable. In the thick bush there was a tendency for each individual to fire many rounds and make few hits, so that the supply of cartridges was quickly used up without producing the decisive results we needed. What made a satisfactory solution of the ammunition question still more impossible was that the cartridges were for the most part the smoky '71 type, whereas only about one-third of the troops were armed with '71 rifles; the other two-thirds had modern German, English or Portuguese rifles, and for these the supply of cartridges was very small. What there were were required for our most important weapon, the machine gun.

It was a difficult position. There was nothing else for it but to make the attack with only those troops who were armed with the '71 rifle and to hold in reserve the rest, who had only twenty rounds of ammunition suitable for their modern rifles, the rest being the smoky '71 type. The two forces would then be interchanged so that the first, armed with the '71 rifles, could hand them over to the relieving force, taking the modern weapons in exchange. This meant that at the best only one-third of the available strength could be in action at the same time and even then would have to be very sparing with their ammunition.

Our artillery ammunition had already been exhausted with the exception of a few rounds for the two mountain guns and some Portuguese ammunition. Our last field-howitzer, as well as the English gun captured at Mahiwa, had burst. The last two 10.5 cm. guns from the *Königsberg* had been destroyed a few days before. On the day after a German mountain gun had been destroyed and sunk at Kitangari. We were thus left with one German and one Portuguese mountain gun. During the last few months the lack of artillery ammunition had been so serious that we had rarely more than three hundred rounds all told. That was about the allowance per engagement for one of the numerous English guns.

Under such circumstances an attack could only promise success if the situation was exceptionally favourable. This was never the case. The patrols were kept active, and the enemy harassed as much as possible, but otherwise there was nothing left but for General Wahle's force and the 11th Field Company, which had been left at Mnacho to bring away the supplies, gradually to give way before the pressure of the enemy and retire to Chiwata. On 10th November the Ndanda mission, immediately in the rear of General Wahle, who was at Nangoo, was surprised by a strong enemy force and captured.

The field-hospital quartered there, and part of our stores, fell into the enemy's hands. Lieberman's force, south of Ndanda, ensured the retreat of General Wahle's force, which ascended to the Makonda *plateau*, by the road south-east of Nangoo, the road I had reconnoitred on 7th November, and, by crossing the *plateau* diagonally to Chiwata, escaped from the enemy's trap. The 11th Company also found its way to Chiwata from Mnacho, so that, with the exception of Captain Tafel's

Detachment and some small bodies of troops further south, the whole force was concentrated at Chiwata. The gradual transport of our supplies from Chiwata east to Nambindinga had begun, and with that our march to Kitangari. Meanwhile I kept an anxious lookout for a vulnerable point in one of the enemy columns. On the 14th November I thought I had discovered one.

A strong enemy column, to which belonged the 10th South African Mounted Infantry, had passed close to our position while marching from Lukuledi *via* Massassi, and had attacked Mwiti, two hours' march south of Chiwata. In this place, which until then had been only weakly held, Lieberman's force (three companies) had arrived the day before. In spite of the shortage of ammunition there was, I thought, a chance that by unexpectedly throwing into the fight Koehl's force from Chiwata, this enemy might be defeated separately. I was, however, very busy with the preparations for the withdrawal to Nambindinga and unfortunately let the opportunity at Mwiti pass without taking advantage of it.

There was nothing for it, then, but to retire gradually to Nambindinga.

Through the evacuation of Chiwata the European prisoners, as well as the Indians, who had been carried to the hospital, and the hospital itself, full for the most part of seriously wounded, fell into the enemy's hands. The march to Nambindinga was carried out under continuous fighting between the 15th and 17th November. I wanted to make the enemy complete the concentric march of his columns, advancing north-west and south, so as to effect a junction; then, when the enemy's masses were helplessly crowded on a narrow area, I could march where I liked. On November 17th I had to take a fateful decision at Nambindinga. The continual bush-fighting was threatening to consume all our ammunition. It would have been madness to go on with this fighting, which could not bring about a favourable decision. We had therefore to withdraw.

The supply question pointed the same way. Only by a drastic reduction of strength could we carry on with the stores in hand. Our supply area had been narrowed, fresh requisitioning had been interfered with by the enemy, and the produce of the land exhausted. The supply of quinine would last the Europeans a month longer. After the consumption of this the Europeans would certainly fall victims to malaria and its attendant evils; they would no longer be able to contend with the rigours of a tropical campaign. Only by reducing the number of Europeans to a minimum could enough quinine be ensured for each man to enable us to carry on the operations for months.

At the same time we had to reduce our total strength. Our large force with little ammunition was of less value in the field than a smaller number of picked men with plenty of ammunition. It amounted to the reduction of our strength to about 2,000 rifles, including not more than 2,000 Europeans. All above this number had to be left behind. It could not be helped that among the several hundred Europeans and 600 *Askari* that we were compelled to leave behind in the hospital at Nambindinga, there were men who would have liked to go on fighting and were physically fit to do so.

Unfortunately, it must be admitted that among those who were left behind at Nambindinga, even among the Europeans, there were many who were not unwilling to lay down their arms. It is, however, worthy of mention that not only the majority of the Europeans, but also many *Askari*, were bitterly disappointed at having to remain. We had repeatedly to refuse the request of a brave *Askari* that he might come and fight for us. But when, two days later, Lieutenant Grundmann, though severely wounded and scarcely able to walk, reported himself, saying that he could not, in spite of orders, bring himself to surrender, I have seldom been so pleased as at this breach of discipline. It may be mentioned here that in general the enemy, as far as I am in a position to judge, treated our prisoners with humanity, but it seems to me that he was anxious to convict us of cruelty to English prisoners, perhaps in order to justify reprisals, perhaps for other reasons.

Lieutenant Cutsch had been left sick in Nandanda, and fell into the enemy's hands. On the totally unfounded and unproved evidence of a negro that Lieutenant Cutsch had on one occasion, when commanding a patrol, burned to death a wounded Englishman, he was put in irons and sent by sea to Dar-es-Salaam, being imprisoned during the voyage just outside the ship's round-house. At Dar-es-Salaam he was locked up for several weeks in the prison without a trial.

When at last he was tried, it came out that the charge of senseless cruelty rested purely on the lying evidence of the negro. Again, General Deventer informed me that Captain Naumann, who had surrendered near Kilima Njaro, had been tried for murder. He, too, as I heard later, was kept imprisoned for a long time without a hearing, until his innocence was finally established. I find it all the more difficult to understand this mockery of justice, as the English prisoners were always humanely treated by us, and were often better cared for materially than our own people.[1]

These decisions placed the conduct of the war on an entirely different basis. Hitherto we had stored the supplies in dumps and for the most part had been able to satisfy our demands from these; the ammunition also had been maintained from stores. This system had laid us more open to attack and offered the enemy points of attack which we could not protect. But by the methods adopted hitherto it had been possible to keep the troops in the field at great strength, considering our position, and to employ a great part of them on a small area for a considerable period.

It had further been possible to give a permanent character, at any rate to some of our hospitals, where sick and wounded could recuperate in peace, and in this way we could fill the gaps in our front with refreshed and experienced men. This system had made our operations dependent to a great extent on the situation of the supplies and reinforcements, and had hindered freedom of movement. The advantage, however, in our position of being able to employ strong troops and with them successfully to engage, and often defeat decisively, superior enemy forces was so great that I held to this system as long as it was at all possible.

It was now no longer possible, and the advantages I have mentioned had to be sacrificed under the pressure of necessity. It was certainly questionable whether the reduced force could be maintained without supply dumps, and without reinforcements the prospect of remaining, after twelve days in the plains, with five thousand hungry negroes and without supplies was not attractive. Should we succeed in satisfying those requirements of the force which could not be obtained on the spot, especially ammunition and arms, by means of capture from the enemy for the only possibility of renewing our supplies lay in capturing the enemy's in sufficient quantities to make the continuation of the war possible? That was the all-important question.

If we succeeded, however, in maintaining the force on the new territory the increased independence and mobility, used with determination against the less mobile enemy, would give us a local superiority in spite of the great numerical superiority of the enemy. In the unlimited territory at our disposal it would be possible to withdraw from unfavourable positions. The enemy would be compelled to keep an enormous amount of men and material continually on the move, and to

---

1. The English Government issued to us articles of food for the English prisoners which we could not get for ourselves.

exhaust his strength to a greater extent proportionately than ourselves. There was also the prospect of tying down strong enemy forces and protracting the operations indefinitely if—my forecast proved correct. This was at that time doubtful, but the risk had to be taken.

We did not stay long at Nambindinga; this place situated on the *plateau* had no water and the springs in the valley were within range of the enemy's guns and machine guns. Under the protection of patrols, which held back the enemy at Nambindinga, Headquarters and the main part of the forces arrived at Kitangari on 18th November. The enemy did not follow, probably he could not. As had been foreseen, he had strained every nerve to strike the so long hoped-for knockout blow at Chiwata and had to re-form before undertaking further operations. At Kitangari the old experience was repeated of finding that the supplies stored there had been estimated much too highly. The supplies at all serviceable would, all told, only feed the force for about ten days; we could reckon on no appreciable addition to these stores from the region south of Kitangari. The question in which direction the march should be continued focussed itself in the main on the prospect of again finding the means of adequately feeding the force. There was no tune to be lost.

I knew that in the area along the Rovuma the English and Portuguese had systematically destroyed our supplies. Our small dumps, requisitioning stations and supply columns had been attacked and the supplies destroyed. The natives had been influenced against us. The north and south banks of the middle Rovuma were only thinly populated; at Tunduru, further up the Rovuma, strong forces of both sides had been engaged and the supplies there were probably exhausted. I could get no reliable information about the Mafia *plateau* south of the lower Rovuma.

Even if, as many reported, this had been a richly-cultivated district before the war it was very doubtful whether now, after strong Portuguese forces had been billeted there for years, there would be any food left. The most probable place for finding supplies seemed to me at that time to be the district where Major Stuemer's operations had taken place: the corner between the Rovuma and the Ludjenda Rivers and further south in the region of Nangware and Mwembe. Even this was doubtful, for here, too, war had interfered with the agriculture of the natives. Meanwhile, of the various improbabilities this last seemed to me the least improbable, and I decided to march at once up the Rovuma.

A determining factor in the choice of this direction was my wish to equip my force for a prolonged period of action by a large capture of ammunition and other war material. Previous observation and the reports of the natives led me to believe that somewhere near the Rovuma the enemy still possessed large stores. On 20th November we reached Nevale, where we were joined by the patrols which had secured our southern flank, and the reorganization of the force was finally carried through.

At Nevale the last men unfit for marching were left behind, and on 21st November we marched south to the Rovuma with 300 Europeans, 1,700 *Askari*, and 3,000 bearers and other natives. Every man was loaded to his full capacity. In general, as the supplies were consumed, the bearers no longer required were left behind, so as to keep the number of consumers as low as possible. In many cases we had to refuse the urgent requests of our good old bearers to remain with us, a large number offering to carry on without pay, some even without either pay or rations; these were ready to provide their own rations from what we threw away and Pori fruit. The quartermaster at that time, Naval Lieutenant Besch, reorganized the supplies and transport service very efficiently. He deserves the chief credit for the force's ability to carry on.

As was to be expected, only small detachments of the enemy were reported in the neighbourhood of the Rovuma. On 21st November we arrived at Mpili, on the bank of the river, and were about to pitch our camp when several shots passed close to a hunting party. On reconnoitring we found in front of us a large pond, on the opposite side of which horses were being watered. Behind rose a rocky mountain. Soon afterwards a native, apparently a spy, appeared, bringing a written message:

We are English cavalry, and we want to get into touch with Portuguese infantry regiments.

Whether this was a ruse could not be ascertained. It was clear that for the moment we had only to do with a small squadron of cavalry. By a sharp attack the enemy was soon routed and in the pursuit sustained several casualties: five European prisoners belonging to the 10th South African Mounted Infantry were, for reasons of supply, sent back to the enemy. The captured horses were welcome as chargers and as a possible addition to our rations.

The rest of the march up the Rovuma progressed very slowly. A

NATIVE TYPES (3). DRAWN BY GENERAL
VON LETTOW-YORBECK'S ADJUTANT.

NATIVE TYPES (4). DRAWN BY GENERAL
VON LETTOW-YORBECK'S ADJUTANT.

great part of the force were unaccustomed to long route-marches. The columns straggled endlessly. The *Askari* women followed singly, several hundred yards apart. It was some time before they learned to keep to a regular marching order. Incidentally it became obvious that in some companies the *Askari* who had come with us had not been selected from the most suitable point of view. In the reorganization of the companies which had had to be carried out during the fighting, many good and reliable men had been left behind, and replaced by others, stronger perhaps, but less reliable. Many went into battle with their children on their shoulders; it would have been better to choose an equally reliable man who was not burdened by having to drag about a wife and family.

But it was too late now to alter anything.

Apparently we had quite got outside the enemy's range of observation. The aircraft which usually followed our marches were absent and no bombs fell on our camps. Once an enemy supply column crossed the Rovuma right into our camp. It was a welcome capture. Of grain we found practically none in this district, but on the other hand, we shot plenty of game. Several buffaloes and quite a number of antelopes, particularly *Wasserbok*, fell to our guns. But we dared not delay; our shrinking supplies urged us continually forward. Fortunately I had with me a few Europeans who knew the country, and who, shortly before, had been working near the confluence of the Ludjenda and the Rovuma.

In peacetime a Portuguese station had been situated there, and even in war a more or less strong garrison had been reported there. It might be assumed that even now we should find some traces of the enemy. The few natives we came across even spoke of a stronger garrison, amounting to two thousand English or Portuguese. The natives' figures could not, of course, be relied on, but they strengthened my belief that in the neighbourhood of Ngomano something might be done.

CHAPTER 1

Across the Rovuma

Early in the morning of November 25th, 1917, our advance guard waded across the Rovuma, a little above the Ludjenda confluence; the main force of nine companies followed in the course of the forenoon, the rearguard about two days' march in the rear. Captain Goering with three companies had crossed much further downstream to surprise a Portuguese camp reported there. We had no news of Captain Tafel, and I thought it probable that he would strike the Rovuma much further west.

The feeling that we were cut off from all support, as well as the absolute uncertainty as to the fate before us, had produced what is popularly known as "*allgemeine Wurck*tigkeit" (absolute callousness). Undisturbed by the tactical situation, our hunting parties went on with their work, and their shots were, as afterwards transpired, distinctly heard by the enemy.

While crossing the river, many took a careful bath in full view of the enemy; in many cases it required some effort to make clear the requirements of the state of war.

On the south bank we soon came under fire. The company acting as advance guard came upon enemy scouts, several of whom were killed. I employed the next few hours, while the troops gradually came up and covered the crossing of the rest, to reconnoitre. Not far from our front, on the far bank of the Ludjenda River, signals could be heard and men could be seen. We came close to the enemy camp and saw men in white suits moving about, a few hundred yards away. Others were building earthworks and a transport column was also observed. The troops were certainly in great force.

While I was still considering whether, and in what way, a prospect

214

of attack offered, a column of *Askari* in khaki advanced from the camp towards our troops. About a company of the enemy left the camp. Guessing that the enemy was wisely about to attack our troops with all his force while they were still occupied in crossing the river, I ran back quickly and ordered those of our companies who had crossed first to put themselves in a defensive position. The favourable opportunity I had hoped for did not, however, materialize: the enemy did not come.

Thus I was again faced with the question what to do. I was doubtful whether, in view of our large numbers of bearers, it would not be more expedient to march past the enemy stationed here at Ngomano and advance further up the Ludjenda River. Either the enemy would not hinder us, or, if he did, he would have to emerge from his entrenched positions and make up his mind for a difficult attack.

On the other hand, it was not unlikely that an attack by us on the enemy camp would be successful, for its defences were not yet especially strong. Reconnaissance had established that on the far bank of the Ludjenda river a belt of thick wood led right up to the camp and offered the opportunity of surprising the enemy here in strength, and bringing off a decisive attack. I had not yet fully made up my mind when Captain Müller decided me to take that one of the two decisions which, though very risky, offered a prospect of the long awaited decisive success and the capture of ammunition and war material which had become an urgent necessity. No time was to be lost.

The attack was, therefore, made while part of the force was still crossing the river. While our light mountain-gun fired on the enemy's entrenchments from the west, and while at the same time several companies engaged the enemy on this side as also from the north, Captain Koehl's detachment crossed the Ludjenda half a mile above Ngomano, marched through the high wood on that bank and made a determined attack on the enemy's camp from the south. I took up my position on a little hill west of the camp, near our guns. Immediately behind me the last company of General Wahle's force to cross the river was advancing along a valley.

In front I had a fairly good view of the enemy's entrenched positions. The enemy's machine guns were not shooting badly, and their fire was at times directed upon our little sand hill, from which I had to send into cover a number of Europeans and *Askari*, who had collected there immediately and were visible to the enemy. The clear ring of the enemy rifles, which we had heard before, and the absence of trench-mortars, made it probable that the enemy were Portuguese. We had already learned to distinguish clearly between the dull, full detonation of our '71, the sharp crack of our S-rifle, the double report of the English rifle and the clear ring of the Portuguese rifle of a little over 6 mm. calibre. Even our *Askari* had noticed at once that in short skirmishes the speed with which the enemy trench-mortars always got the range of our positions had been very harassing.

Our '71 rifles threw up so much smoke that it was impossible to guard against this. Today, however, there were no mine-throwers, and the treacherous smoke of our good old rifles was not so bad. On the other hand, when they did hit their target they made a very considerable hole. Our *Askari* soon realized that today they were able to bring their soldierly superiority to bear without being handicapped by inferior weapons. "Today is the day of the old rifles!" they shouted to the German leaders, and from my hill I soon saw the firing line of Koehl's detachment storm the enemy's entrenchments at the double and capture them.

This was the signal for attack on the other fronts also. From all sides they charged the enemy, who was badly shaken by the concentrated fire. Scarcely more than 200 of the enemy force, about 1,000 strong, can have survived. Again and again our *Askari* troops, in search of booty, threw themselves ruthlessly upon the enemy, who was still firing; in addition, a crowd of bearers and boys, grasping the situation, had quickly run up and were taking their choice of the pots of lard and other supplies, opening cases of jam and throwing them away again when they thought they had found something more attractive in other cases. It was a fearful *mêlée*. Even the Portuguese *Askari* already taken prisoner, joined in the plunder of their own stores. There was no alternative but to intervene vigorously. I became very eloquent, and, to make an example, dashed at least seven times at one bearer I knew, but each time he got away and immediately joined in the looting somewhere else. At last I succeeded in restoring discipline.

We buried about 200 enemy dead, and about 150 European prisoners were released after taking an oath not to fight again during this war against Germany or her Allies; several hundred *Askari* were taken prisoner. Valuable medical stores, so necessary to us, and, as a result of the Portuguese experience of centuries of colonial campaigning, of excellent quality, were captured, as well as several thousand kilos of European supplies, large numbers of rifles, six machine-guns and about thirty horses. Unfortunately we captured no native supplies. Almost half of our force was re-armed this time with Portuguese rifles; and a plentiful supply of ammunition was served out.

A quarter of a million rounds of ammunition were captured, and this number was increased in the course of December to nearly a million. From captured dispatches we learned that the Portuguese-European companies had only reached Ngomano a few days before, in order to carry out the impossible English order to prevent a German crossing of the Rovuma. It was really a perfect miracle that these troops should have arrived so opportunely as to make the capture of the place so profitable to us. With one blow we had freed ourselves of a great part of our difficulties.

But yet another serious difficulty arose, which drove us remorselessly on. This was the necessity of procuring food for our large numbers of natives. Accordingly we advanced up the Ludjenda River. Day after day our patrols searched for native guides and supplies. During the next few days, however, they had little success. The natives, never numerous in this district, had fled before the advance of the Portuguese, fearing their ruthlessness and cruelty, and had hidden what stores they possessed. One after another, mules and horses found their way into our stew-pots. Fortunately this district is very rich in game, and the hunter can always shoot one of the numerous antelopes or guinea-fowl.

Though at first our marching columns were too long and straggling, here again practice made perfect. Bearers, boys, women and children, soon learned to keep pace and distance as exactly as the *Askari*. Regularly and in good order, the expedition wound along the narrow native paths, and even through the thick bush, into the unknown land. Half an hour's halt was called after every two hours' march; the rule was six hours' march a day, *i.e.*, about fifteen to twenty miles, and this was often exceeded. The force was for the most part divided into detachments of three companies, each with one supply train and one field hospital.

The advance detachment was a day's march ahead of the main body, the last a day's march behind. At the head of each detachment marched the fighting companies with their machine guns; they had with them only the necessary ammunition and medical stores, and each European was allowed one load of necessities. The *Askari* marched gaily forward, straight as lances, and with their guns reversed over their shoulders, as has always been the custom in the rifle regiments. Lively conversation was kept up, and after the plundering of an

217

enemy camp, which often yielded rich booty, cigarette smoke rose on all sides. The little signal recruits strode bravely forward, half-grown youths in *Askari* uniform for the most part, carrying all their worldly goods in a bundle on their heads.

The *Askari* would call out their friendly, "*Jambo Bwana Obao,*" or "*Jambo Bwana Generals*" ("Good-day, Colonel"), or a little signalman would express his hope of coming some day to *Uleia* (Europe) and Berlin. "Then the *Kaiser* will say to me, 'Good-day, my son,' and I shall give him an exhibition of signalling. Then he will give me roast meat and present me to the Empress. The Empress will say, 'Good-day, my child,' and will give me cakes and show me the shop-windows." During all their talk the *Askari* kept a sharp lookout, and no movement in the thick bush escaped their lynx eyes.

The head of the column investigated every trail, and from it gave the number and the distance of the enemy. Equally soldierly were the machine-gun bearers, mostly strapping Waniamwezi and Wazu-kuma. The companies and detachments were followed by bearers with the loads of supplies, baggage, camp-kit and stretcher cases. The loads, about 25 kg., were carried alternately on the head and shoulders. The endurance of these men is enormous. They became more and more attached to the troops. If ever the supplies were short and the hunting parties unsuccessful, they would say, "*Haiswu'b* (it doesn't matter), we wait, get some another time."

Many marched barefoot and often got thorns in their feet. Often one would promptly take his knife and calmly cut out a piece of flesh from the wounded foot. Then he would start off again. The bearers were followed by the women and the *bibi*. Many *Askari* had their wives and children with them in the field, and many children were born during the march. Each woman carried her own Mali (prop-erty), as well as that of her lord, on her head. Often they carried on their backs a small child, his woolly head peeping out of the cloth in which he was wound. The women were kept in order and protected by a European or a trustworthy old non-commissioned officer, assist-ed by a few *Askari*. They all liked gay colours, and after an important capture, the whole convoy stretching several miles would look like a carnival procession.

Even during the march the obtaining of supplies had to be attend-ed to. Hunting patrols marched ahead of the column or on the flanks in the bush. Often they would remain behind near the old camping sites, where game or traces of game had been observed. Other patrols followed human tracks leading to settlements to requisition supplies. On arriving at the camping-ground, four *Askari* and my boy Serubiti would cut down branches and erect a frame for the tent sections or for a grass-hut.

Sometimes a raised bivouac of branches was arranged and covered with grass. Soon afterwards the bearded Baba, my cook, would arrive and give careful directions for the arrangement of the kitchen. The bearers would come and fetch water, cut grass and firewood with their bush knives. The hunting patrols brought in what they had shot, and soon the smell of cooking rose from the camp-fires on all sides. Meanwhile, parties of bearers had been threshing in the villages, and brought back corn. In the *Kinos* (thick wooden vessels) the corn was crushed by beating it with thick clubs, the dull thuds sounding far into the bush. Messages, reconnaissance reports, and captured dispatches were brought in; a box in a shady spot served as a desk.

During the longer halts a table was built of branches. The evening meal was eaten in company with friends round the camp fire, the boys bringing cases to sit on. The more lordly had deck-chairs. Then to bed under the mosquito-nets, and in the early morning once more into the unknown. Should we find supplies, and could we make what we had last out until we did? These uncertainties cropped up every day afresh, and haunted us week after week and month after month. The eternal marching was, as will be understood, no mere pleasure. At —— I heard some remarks about myself, such as: "Still further? The fellow must come from a family of country postmen!"

When we reached the confluence of the Chiulezi, difficulties of supplies had become so serious, and the district hitherto regarded as fertile had so greatly altered, that I dropped my original intention of keeping the force together. For the moment it seemed impossible, from the tactical point of view also. From the English, who were probably following us, we need not expect any strong pressure, owing to the daily lengthening of their line of communication and the consequent difficulty of bringing up supplies.

A written message from the British commander-in-chief, General van Deventer, in which he summoned me to surrender, was brought under protection of the white flag, and strengthened me in my belief that our escape had taken him by surprise, and that our invasion of Portuguese territory had put him at a loss. Neither he nor General Smuts had ever thought of sending a summons to surrender when the situation was favourable to the English. Why should they do so in a situation like the present, or that of September, 1916, at Kissaki, which was undoubtedly favourable to us? Only because they were at their wits' end. That was indeed not difficult to see through.

The time before the setting in of the rainy season, at the end of December, was too short to prepare for a fresh operation, and after the rains had begun the enemy transport of supplies, which depended largely on motors, would be faced with new difficulties.

We had, therefore, plenty of time, and could divide ourselves into several columns without hesitation. We had nothing to fear from temporary loss of touch one with the other. Accordingly General Wahle's detachment was separated from the rest, and marched through the Mkula mountains, while I marched further up the Ludjenda.

The surrender of Captain Tafel, which I learned from General van Deventer's message, came as a severe and unexpected blow.

Captain Tafel had taken over the command at Mahenge from General Wahle, when the latter left to take over the forces on the Lindi front. He secured the fertile region of Mahenge to the north, with Commander Schoenfeldt's detachment of a few companies. The latter succeeded in holding his ground with his weak force by skilful use of his 10.5 gun from the *Königsberg*, and put his force in a very favourable position materially by the cultivation of gardens and, fields.

On the middle Ruhudje was a weak detachment under Captain Aumann, and north-east of Ssongea Captain Lincke's detachment near Likuju. The latter engaged the enemy repeatedly, and in the barren district suffered from lack of supplies. They therefore gradually retired north to Mponda. There they were reinforced by two companies and one gun from the main force. Captain Otto took over the command. In August, 1917, strong English and Belgian forces converged on Mahenge; Captain Tafel had foreseen this, and withdrawn his supplies out of the Mahenge district to Mgangira. On September nth, Mahenge was evacuated. Even though the individual engagements were often successful, the superiority of the enemy made itself seriously felt, and the shortage of ammunition handicapped more and more the *Askari* companies, mostly armed with the smoky '71 rifle.

I learned later through Captain Otto, who had fought his way through to me with one of Captain Tafel's patrols and joined me at ——, that Captain Tafel, from west of Livale, had marched south in three columns, and on the upper Mbemkuru had fought several partially successful actions, capturing large quantities of ammunition. He had then marched further south to the Bangala River, and turned east when he thought he was near Massassi. South of this place he heard from the natives that the Germans had not been fighting north of Rovuma for several days.

Captain Tafel turned towards the Rovuma and crossed near the Nangala confluence, hoping to find supplies on the south bank. His own were literally exhausted. He found nothing and had no idea that about a day's march from him Goering's detachment of my force had captured the Portuguese camp and found enough food on the prosperous farms to enable them to live well for fourteen days. Captain Tafel therefore returned to the north bank of the Rovuma and surrendered to the enemy.

The news of Captain Tafel's surrender strengthened my reluctance to detach another part of my force, though, in view of my proximity, the junction at which we were both aiming had as nearly as possible been effected. I was straightway put upon the rack by the cessation of news from Goering's detachment with which, while it was at Ngomano, we had kept touch by means of patrols. During the march up the Ludjenda, when we had to keep the different detachments and companies further apart, in order to facilitate the search for food, it was necessary to impress upon subordinate leaders the importance of keeping the whole force in touch.

It was, however, not to be expected that these officers, who later performed such excellent work as leaders of detachments, and worked so successfully in co-operation with the rest, should possess the necessary training from the beginning. The Governor had remained with the force even after leaving the Protectorate, in accordance with the regulation (certainly not intended to provide for war with a European power) that he was the military head of the Protectorate. He had interpreted this authority in such a way as to interfere most seriously with that of the commander-in-chief, and had often encroached upon my sphere of activity. I had been powerless to prevent this, and now that we were outside the Protectorate I attached the greatest importance to the fact that now, at any rate, I had a free hand. Even if I did not yield to the governor's claims, it must be understood that in the unprecedented military situation there were enough differences of opinion to overburden the commander-in-chief, who, whatever happens, is held actually, if not morally, responsible.

It was perhaps natural that at this time I was not always very gentle and considerate to those around me. So it happened that those very officers of my Staff who were working with the greatest devotion to the cause and deserved the most recognition, were the objects of much unjustified reproach. For not taking offence or allowing this to prejudice the cheerful continuation of their work, they deserve particular gratitude. It is largely to the work of these officers, often carried out under adverse circumstances, that are due the successes which the public is so generously inclined to place wholly to my credit. For me, who have always delighted in the good comradeship characteristic of our officer corps, this general atmosphere of snarling and fault-finding was naturally not ideal. Fortunately, however, it was only a passing phase.

Our position was now such that in case of an encounter with the enemy we could not investigate his strength. We had no time for prolonged reconnaissance. Perhaps this conviction, together with the determination with which we attacked the Portuguese forces whenever we met them, accounts for the fact that, during December, three more Portuguese fortified positions were taken in quick succession. Of decisive importance in these enterprises was the personality of the officer in command who first engaged the enemy. He must lose no time, and so could not wait for orders.

On the 2nd November, Lieutenant Kempner, commanding the 11th Company, which was acting as advance-guard in the march up the Ludjenda, came upon a fortified Portuguese camp at Nangwale. Like most Portuguese camps, it lay on a bare hill, with a wide range of fire. The brave 11th Company at once deployed along the edge of the bush, and advanced to the attack across three hundred metres of open ground exposed to the enemy's fire. The *Askari*, who were carrying full marching kit, could not keep up with the company commander and his *effendi* (black officer). Lieutenant Kempner and the *effendi* leapt upon the enemy's breastwork, and from there into the enemy's entrenchments, and so for a time found themselves alone among the enemy garrison, consisting of a platoon.

The latter were so dumbfounded that, hearing the cheers of the oncoming *Askari*, they at once obeyed the order to lay down their arms. In addition, a considerable ammunition dump fell into our hands, as well as enough rations to feed our whole force for several days. When the Portuguese officer invited Lieutenant Kempner to a glass of special brandy and found the bottle empty, its owner had further reason for being taken aback, but with the difference this time that his enemy was taken aback equally. An *ombascha* (black lance-corporal) had the best of the joke.

I was filled with grave anxiety about the fate of Captain Goering, of whom I had received no news. From General Wahle's force, which had marched up the Chiulezi River, we heard subsequently that they had attacked and annihilated a force of several Portuguese companies in a strongly entrenched position in the Mkula mountains. The repeated attempts to establish communication with Wahle's force by means of the heliograph did not succeed, although the Portuguese in the Mkula mountains had clearly observed our signals from Nangwale. The Portuguese Europeans captured by our detachment had refused to give their word not to fight against us again in this war. They had been sent north to the Rovuma by General Wahle owing to the difficulty of feeding them.

Captain Stemmermann succeeded, after several days' siege, in capturing another very strongly held and vigorously defended fortified position. As the storming of this offered no prospects of success, the enemy's water supply was cut off, which made his position in the trenches untenable, and forced him to surrender. Among our casualties, unfortunately, were a number of very good native non-commissioned officers. I was not present at the fighting at Nangwale, as I was occupied in dealing with delays in the rear companies and arranging that the march should be kept up to the intended standard.

By a double day's march I easily made up for the delay this had caused me, and arrived in Nangwale in time to superintend the division of the captured stores. In the most favourable circumstances we were only living from hand to mouth. At Nangwale, where six months before our troops had found such a rich neighbourhood, the position was now quite different. Apart from the captured stores there was absolutely nothing; even the game in a considerable area round Nangwale had been shot or frightened away. This was a disappointment, for I had hoped at this place to be freed from the more ordinary difficulties of supplies. The force had, therefore, to be split up. From the information of the prisoners and captured documents it appeared that the garrison in Nangwale had been fed by columns of bearers from the distant neighbourhood of Mwalis. There must, then, be something to be found there.

On 5th December Captain Koehl, with five companies, a gun and an ammunition column, left Nangwale to march to the Mwalia-Medo district. I myself continued the march up the Ludjenda. Fortunately the assurance of Lieutenant von Scherbening and other Europeans, who had already patrolled this district, that we should soon come into a region rich in supplies was confirmed. These supplies, however, were not excessive, and we were very glad that they could be largely supplemented by hunting. The enormous numbers of hippopotami which lived in the river above Nangwale, often in large herds of from fifteen to twenty, had become quite a staple dish. I myself could not resist having a shot at a huge bull; the animal sank at once, the water above it swirling as over a sinking ship. After a time it came to the surface again, feet uppermost, and made little further movement. The animal was then drawn to the bank with a rope. The numerous crocodiles made us cautious, and many a good prize had to be left from fear of these.

The flesh of the hippopotamus tastes like coarse beef; the tongue, however, is particularly delicate. The most valuable product, however, is the excellent lard which the men had very quickly learnt to prepare. Its snow-white, appetizing appearance now was quite different from the dirty yellow of the first attempts on the Rufiji. On my many reconnoitring and hunting expeditions into the bush the *Askari*, who came with me and the bearers to carry the spoils of the chase, gradually revealed some of the secrets of the bush. We had long ago learned to make excellent spinach from different foliage plants (called *Mlenda*); now they showed me many different kinds of excellent wild fruit. We also learnt that the kernel of the *Mbinji*-fruit, the pulp of which I already knew contains prussic acid, is quite free from acid, and when roasted makes an exceptionally delicate dish, tasting like our hazelnut.

On the 17th December, 1917, Headquarters arrived at Chirumba (Mtarika). Lieutenant von Ruckteschell, with his company, had gone on ahead and had soon driven off the weak Portuguese outposts. This was a station of the Portuguese Nyassa company; this merchant company also administered the northern part of the colony. Further south, too, the administration is in the hands of other private companies. The Portuguese official in Chirumba, called Fernandez, seems to have been very capable. The massive buildings of his station, situated at the top of a bare eminence, were spotlessly clean. A trench ensured it against surprise. Beautiful gardens with fruit and vegetables stretched along the bank of the adjacent Ludjenda River.

Avenues of mulberry and mango trees fringed the carefully laid-out roads. Many species of this mango fruit, known to the natives as *Emben*, were to be found in the station and the neighbouring native villages. It was already beginning to ripen and was so plentiful that it was found worthwhile to have the fruit systematically gathered. The waste to which the natives are generally prone was prevented as far as possible. The beautiful, sweet fruit was enjoyed by all the Europeans and a great part of the natives, and, in view of the shortage of sugar, for weeks provided a really valuable addition to the supplies. When, on my arrival at Chirumba, I stepped on to the veranda of the European house, Lieutenant Ruckteschell set before me some hog's lard, which I had not seen for a long time. Here, as at many other Portuguese stations, there had been European pigs.

We remained here for several weeks. One detachment moved further upstream and took possession of the small station of Luambala. At the same time General Wahle marched to the prosperous station of Mwemba, already known to us. The richly-cultivated triangle Chirumba–Luambala–Mwemba and beyond the frontier was patrolled by our requisitioning and reconnaissance patrols. The natives of this district showed themselves for the most part intelligent and friendly; they already knew that they had nothing to fear from the German troops. In spite of that they had hidden their stores of food in the bush and would let us have little or nothing.

Our men had, however, long since learned to examine closely, for example, a suspicious-looking tree stump, and often found that it had been put together by hand and was the hiding place for stocks of food. Others would drive their sticks into the hollow ground of a freshly laid-out garden and found stores of grain buried there. In short, many such hiding-places were found, and when, at Christmas, we sat down to dinner in a large grass-hut, we were relieved of the most pressing shortage of food. According to the descriptions of our men the Ludjenda River was, during several months of the year, so full of fish that they could be pulled out in basketfuls. Oddly enough, on this occasion only very few were caught. Most of them were sheat-fish, about eighteen inches long, and smaller fish which were best fried crisp. These, too, contributed their modest share towards the improvement of the rations.

Touch was kept with Koehl's detachment in the neighbourhood of Medo by means of a system of relays. I thought it probable that the enemy, following his usual tactics, was preparing a great concentric movement against us which would not be ready for at least a month. We could thus rely on there being no considerable enemy activity until after the rains, which would end at the end of February. About this time I intended to concentrate my forces in the neighbourhood of Nanungu. Until then we must husband our supplies in this area and live as far as possible on what could be obtained in the outer fringe of our present locality. At first there was not much game shot at Chirumba, but the bag increased when we found considerable herds of antelopes on the east bank of the Ludjenda, and particularly further upstream.

During the remainder of the dry season, while the river was low, caravans of bearers were continually crossing the river by several fords, carrying their loads to the dumps on the east bank. As well as the fords, canoes made from hollowed tree-trunks were used for crossing. Patrols were sent out for weeks at a time to collect supplies and reconnoitre. Lieutenant von Scherbening, with his patrol, made an expedition lasting months, marching from Chirumba *via* Mtenda, Mahua and finally south, *via* the Lurio River, then up the Malema, where they surprised the Portuguese Boma Malema. An Italian, who had been hunting elephants on the Ludjenda and had joined us in a ragged, starving condition, accompanied Lieutenant von Scherbening's patrol. The man's health was, however, so undermined by lingering malaria and his spleen so terribly swollen that he had to be carried from Mahua to a plantation near Malacotera.

At the beginning of January, 1918, the English began to move. From the south-east corner of Lake Nyassa two battalions the 1st and 2nd King's African Rifles began to advance towards Captain Goering's detachment, which had joined up with us and occupied the acute angle between the Luhambala and Ludjenda Rivers. He was covering the supply stores further up the Ludjenda. On 9th January, in the forenoon, a detachment of the enemy, attacking unsupported, was defeated.

When, in the afternoon, the enemy returned to the attack after the arrival of his reinforcements, and at the same time an enemy force pressed forward in a northerly direction toward the supply dumps on the east bank, Captain Goering crossed to the east bank with the main part of his force. Only a strong patrol was left in the old camp on the west bank, and they held the enemy in check. At the same time an enemy force—the 2nd Cape Corps of South African half-breeds was identified—was advancing on Mwembe.

Then began innumerable small skirmishes and patrol actions, which often put us in an awkward position, owing to our inability to protect the bearers bringing up supplies. The English cleverly took advantage of these difficulties to try to undermine the loyalty of our *Askari*. Many were very war-weary. Added to this, there was in many cases the feeling of uncertainty as to where the campaign was going to lead them. The great majority of black men cling to their homes and their relations. They said to themselves: "If we go further we shall come into country we don't know. We can find our way back from where we are now, but soon we shan't be able to."

The English propaganda, by word of mouth and pamphlets, fell in many cases on fruitful ground, and, as a result, a number of good *Askari* and even older non-commissioned officers deserted. Small annoyances, such as are bound to arise—the persuasion of the women and so on—all contributed to their decision to desert. One old *sol* (native sergeant-major) suddenly disappeared, who had led a brilliant independent patrol and had brought a strong detachment of bearers with their loads right through the enemy lines, and for his good service had been promoted to "*Effendi*." He, too, had deserted the impulsiveness of the black makes him very sensitive to insinuation.

But even if the English colonel can boast of having lowered the *moral* of certain elements, this was only a passing phase. The old lust of battle and the old loyalty returned, even among those who had begun to hang their heads. The example of the faithful *Askari*, who simply laughed at the mountains of gold the English promised them if they would desert, won the day. In so long and trying a campaign the *moral* was bound to be low from time to time. It was no use to be astonished and discouraged, the important thing was to fight against it firmly, and for this the loyal elements, of which there were many, both among Europeans, *Askari* and bearers, had firmly made up their minds.

CHAPTER 2

East of the Ludjenda

The patrol of Captain Otto, who had been sent from Captain Tafel to me after the latter's surrender, and gave me details about the events leading up to it, had arrived at Chirumba. Captain Otto, with two additional companies, now marched to Luambala and took over the command also of Goering's detachment (three companies). As was expected, the main pressure of the enemy was felt at Luambala, as also on the east bank of the Ludjenda. It was clear that if the enemy advanced downstream my position at Chirumba on the west bank of the river, in a district where the supplies were being gradually exhausted, and with the river swollen by the rains in my rear, was extremely unfavourable.

It was necessary to evacuate this position and to move my force, while there was tune, to the east bank of the Ludjenda. Unfortunately the fords were impassable, owing to the height of the river, so that the whole crossing had to be effected by means of the three canoes available.

Gradually, and without interference, the companies were transferred to the east bank. The supply question was beginning to become very serious. Fortunately Captain Koehl, who, in the neighbourhood of Medo and Namunu, had kept the very intelligent natives to the cultivation of the quickly ripening grain, reported that a good harvest could be relied on as early as the middle of February. But that was not for another month, so we should have to try by every possible means to hold out a bit longer at Chirumba. Welcome as the *manna* to the children of Israel, the fungi which shoot up at this season helped to keep us from starvation. I had already in Germany interested myself in mycology, and soon found fungi closely related to our German species of mushrooms and yellow *boleta* and others, in the African bush.

228

I had often gathered basketfuls in a very short time, and even though an excessive diet of mushrooms is indigestible and not very sustaining, they were a considerable help.

In torrential rain we marched east. The usually dry ravines had become raging torrents. Trees, felled in such a way as to fall over the stream, formed bridges, a hand-rail being improvised from poles or bark lashed together. The mule I was riding on account of fever—I am apparently very sensitive to malaria, from which I suffered a great deal—as well as the few other riding animals that had not found their way into the cooking-pot swam across. When we arrived at the camping ground my men soon built me, on account of the damp, a raised shelter of branches over which both my tent-cloths were laid as a roof. Veterinary Surgeon Huber, who was responsible for the material welfare of the staff, and under him our capable black cook, old bearded Baba, at once got to work and, no matter how wet the wood, we were always able in a short time to sit down to our meal beside the camp-fire. Dr. Huber often managed even to have a grass roof erected for our protection.

On sunny days tobacco was eagerly dried and cut. The efficient Quartermaster-Lieutenant Besch, who was full of resource where the comfort of the men was concerned, had thought of this and had collected very good tobacco from the natives. But in spite of everything the deprivations were very great and the insidious whisperings of the enemy, that every native who deserted should be free to go home and there live in comfort on his own land, did not always fall on deaf ears. Even the faithful boy of one of our officers, whom he had served for years, had one morning disappeared; probably his *Bibi* (wife) had had enough of campaigning.

Captain Otto's detachment marched from Uambala due east to Mahua, and there, on the Lurio River, found a district rich in supplies. Goering's detachment, marching from Luambala across country to Mtende, found considerable supplies on the way. In this district the harvest was very much earlier than in German East Africa; the maize was beginning to ripen and could to a large extent already be eaten. Headquarters next moved from Chirumba to Mtende and, some days later, on to Nanungu. Wahle's detachment, which had followed us from Chirumba to Mtende, was here cut off by several enemy companies which appeared unexpectedly on a height on their rear and interrupted the messenger service and the transport. General Wahle extricated himself by a *détour* from this uncomfortable position and advanced nearer to Headquarters at Nanungu.

At Nanungu we found abundant supplies and we thought it expedient, as before, to establish requisitioning stations and supply dumps in the district between Nanungu and Namunu and further south. There was good shooting, and the natives readily brought garden produce and honey to exchange for meat or, preferably, clothing. Very welcome was a delicate sweet, cherry-like *Pori* fruit, which ripened in millions in the neighbourhood of Nanungu. I preferred to have it made into jam. We also occasionally obtained other dainties, particularly pig-nuts, and the crowing of cocks proclaimed far and wide that there were fowls and eggs in the camps and among the natives.

The setting in of the rainy season did not quite coincide with the forecasts of the natives. There were some sharp downpours, but in the undulating country the water quickly ran off and collected in the main artery of that region, the Msalu River, which was soon swollen so as to form a strong obstacle. Over the Msalu River the post-service official, Hartmann, who had joined the force as a sergeant-major, had built a pontoon bridge which connected us with General Wahle's force, which was still on the west bank. The floating supports of the bridge were boats made from bark. The necessity in this well-watered country of being able to cross the swollen rivers without difficulty had drawn my attention to this question.

Hitherto our sole provision for such contingencies consisted of a few hollowed canoes. Their continued transport, however, was too difficult and their capacity too limited. A planter named Gerth, who had joined us as a volunteer, interested himself particularly in this matter and had himself instructed by the natives of the district in the building of boats from bark. The ensuing experiments soon produced good results, after which the building of these boats, which took barely two hours to put together, for crossing rivers was enthusiastically taken up by every company. Most of these boats were not used, but they gave us a feeling of security that, if necessary, even a full stream would not be impassable for our unwieldy caravans and baggage.

When we became better acquainted with the neighbourhood, we found fords over the Msalu which could be used even when the river was in flood. Our patrols, in charge of Sergeant Valett and others, left our fortified camp at Nanungu, crossed the river which formed the boundary of our camp on the west, and went to look for the enemy in his camps at Mtenda. One of these patrols, which was particularly strong and armed with two machine guns, succeeded in surprising an enemy column west of Mtenda. Our men, however, did not get away quickly enough to escape the enemy's covering force and, attacked from all sides, found themselves in a difficult position. Both machine guns were lost and the Europeans working them fell. Gradually the *Askari* all returned to Nanungu, but the patrol leader, Sergeant-Major Musslin, who had got away from the rest during the march, had fallen into the enemy's hands.

Another patrol, with which Captain Müller crossed the Msalu to the north, quickly drove off an English outpost at Lusinje. In the neighbourhood of Lusinje, also the camp of the English, Lieutenant Wienholt, who, as has already been mentioned, escaped from arrest and became one of the best English patrol leaders, was captured. The natives were thoroughly exploited by the English patrols and acted as spies for the enemy in return for articles of clothing. The volunteer, Gerth, who has been mentioned in connection with boat-building, was attacked and killed by an English patrol while in the house of a native chief.

In the second half of March, 1918, our spirits were greatly raised by the news, received by our wireless, of the powerful German March offensive on the Western front. I laid a wager with the Staff Medical Officer, Staff-Surgeon Taute, that Amiens would soon fall. I used the period of rest that now set in for several weeks during the lull in our operations to have my foot attended to. It had been bitten by a sand-fly, and for the last six months had caused me inconvenience. These sand-flies, which infested many of the camps, bore their way into the flesh, round the edge of the toe-nails, causing painful inflammation. If care is not taken they attack the flesh round them and, according to medical opinion, the maiming of the feet frequent among the natives is very often to be traced to the sand-fly. I, too, was suffering from this inconvenience, and on the march the inflammation constantly recurred. Fortunately Staff-Surgeon Taute, using a local anaesthetic, was able to extract the nail.

I was also inconvenienced in another way. On a reconnoitring expedition a blade of the tall grass, which grows above a man's height, had pierced my right eye. During the subsequent treatment it was feared that the use of the lens might be affected by *atropia*; the result was that I could not see properly with my right eye and was unable to read hand-writing or sketch-maps. This was very awkward, as my left eye had been so seriously injured by a shot wound received during the Hottentot rebellion in South-West Africa, that I could only see through it with the help of spectacles. Suitable spectacles could not, however, be obtained, and so I was compelled to carry out various enterprises without being able to see properly.

The patrols of Koehl's detachment in the Medo-Nanungu district had meanwhile reached the coast, after taking Portuguese fortresses on, and far south of, the lower Lurio River, and carrying off a few guns and, what was more important, rules, ammunition and considerable supplies. The natives showed themselves very friendly towards our men, whom they regarded as their deliverers from Portuguese oppression. Patrols from Otto's detachment from Mahua had also reconnoitred as far as the region south of the Lurio. Lieutenant Methner, so experienced in the ways of the natives, and first *referant* of our government, praised the capacity and cleverness of the Portuguese natives and the intelligence and far-sightedness of their local chiefs.

Lieutenant von Scherbening, who with his patrol had taken the Boma Malema, reported that this neighbourhood was very productive. As a specimen he sent us a captured pig to Nanungu. As it refused to walk it was carried the 500 km. Unfortunately it turned out eventually not to be a European pig at all, but a *Pori* pig, like those we frequently shot in the bush.

Once more a time had come when it was difficult to obtain news of the enemy, but a good deal could be conjectured from the incomplete maps at our disposal. I could have no doubt that the imminent enemy operations would be launched from the neighbourhood of Port Amelia with their main force from the coast. The appearance of strong enemy forces at Mtende, as well as the report, unconfirmed it is true, that troops were on the march from the south-west towards Mahua, showed me that other troops from the west were going to co-operate with the approaching attack of the enemy main force. A situation seemed to be developing in which I could make use of my inner line to attack one part of the enemy singly.

The enemy's position with regard to reserves and supplies made it obvious that the columns marching from the west could not be over strong. This seemed to be the chance I had so long been awaiting. I, therefore, remained with my main force at Nanungu and also recalled Captain Otto's detachment from Lurio. With these forces I intended to assume the offensive in a westerly direction. Captain Koehl, whose detachment was assembled at Medo, was charged with the duty of holding up the enemy's main force advancing from Port Amelia and retiring gradually on my force.

Captain Müller, who, after years of work at Headquarters, had taken over an independent detachment of two companies, was sent on from the neighbourhood of Nanungu to Mahua to harass the enemy as far as possible. He passed round Mahua and surprised, south-west of this place, the fortified supply depot of Kanene. The defending English European troops saw that all the stores were lost. To prevent this, at least to some extent, they fell upon the stores of liquor in the camp and were captured in a thoroughly intoxicated condition.

For myself, I, likewise, advanced in the middle of April in the direction of Mahua, and during the march could hear from afar heavy sounds of firing. At Koriwa, north-east of Mahua, Captain Müller had attacked an enemy battalion under Colonel Barton, which had been making a reconnoitring expedition and was at once attacked by our troops on the march. In spite of the fact that on our side scarcely 70 rifles took part in the action, our troops succeeded in enveloping the enemy's right wing, and from a large ant-hill poured upon him such a vigorous and effective machine-gun fire that he fled wildly. He lost over 40 men in this action. Lieutenant-Commander Wunderlich, who had received a severe wound through the abdomen, had to be taken to the hospital at Nanungu, two days' march distant, and died shortly afterwards.

The blow which I had intended to strike with the main force had already been successfully carried through by Müller's weak detachment. I, therefore, turned with my main force to the district west of Nanungu. A large force of the enemy had arrived meanwhile on the Msalu River and had crossed it with several patrols. My calculation that I should be able to surprise a strong body of the enemy immediately after crossing the river was not fulfilled: the reports received had been incorrect.

However, in a whole series of minor engagements on the Msalu River and further west our fighting patrols inflicted, gradually, severe losses on the enemy and his patrols soon evacuated the east bank of the Msalu. On 3rd May our supply patrols, whose duty it was to obtain further supplies from the direction of Mahua, surprised, in the neighbourhood of Saidi, strong enemy detachments which were seriously threatening our field hospital and supply depots at Makoti.

Part of our stores had been brought to Makoti in readiness for the operations planned to be carried out further west. Our fighting patrols, which were sent out immediately, had several encounters with the enemy near the Kireka mountain at Makoti. I thought at first that these were only enemy patrols, so sent Captain Schulz there with a strong patrol as a reinforcement, and myself marched on the 4th of May, with the main body, to the Nanungu-Mahua road. From here I expected to be able to carry out a swift attack on the enemy forces, which were trying to surprise us somewhere in this neighbourhood. The general situation was made clear when it was known that patrols had, in the course of the day, encountered a new enemy near the Kireka mountain.

An enemy detachment had been thrown back and it was probable that strong forces were in entrenched positions in the rear. In the morning of the 5th May I marched from my camp to Makoti. During the march I hoped sincerely that the enemy would spare us the necessity of making the attack on his fortified positions and that, as in view of the general situation was not improbable, he would emerge from his entrenchments and offer battle in the open. If this happened, and we succeeded in attacking with our main force before the enemy was aware of our arrival, a considerable success was probable.

At eleven o'clock in the forenoon I arrived at the Kireka mountain and went on ahead to see Captain Schulz who, with his patrol, had occupied some rocky grottos in the copse. As soon as I had arrived a *sol* (native sergeant-major), who had just returned from a patrol expedition, reported that the enemy was advancing in great force and must soon appear at close quarters. I passed on this report to Lieutenant Boell, who had just brought up his company in the rear of Schulz's detachment, and instructed him to go up at once in case of an enemy attack. I then went back and ordered the advance of our companies which were gradually arriving.

Meanwhile the fighting in front began. The enemy, advancing in close order, had quickly thrown back our patrols out of the grottos, but had then been completely taken by surprise by the effective machine-gun fire of Boell's company and partially driven back. Goering's detachment, coming up at that moment, began an enveloping movement on the right, completely surprising the enemy, who was rapidly driven back with very heavy losses.

After several miles of hot pursuit we reached the enemy's entrenchments. On our left wing, where two more companies had been sent into action, the fight wavered, and it was difficult for me in the thick bush to distinguish friend and foe. It was, therefore, some time before I could get a clear idea of the situation on the left wing, and it was not until I received a report from Major Kraut, whom I had sent to investigate, that I realized that, in advancing, our left wing had come under a withering enemy fire in a clearing which had brought it to a standstill. A counter-attack by the enemy, which had brought him very near to the position of our Headquarters, looked very dangerous. Fortunately for us, however, just at this moment Lieutenant Buechsel, whose company had been detached from the main force and so arrived late, came upon the scene of action and was able to avert the danger.

Meanwhile, on the right wing, Captain Goering had realized that a frontal attack on the enemy entrenchment offered no prospect of success. He had, therefore, sent Lieutenant Meier with a strong patrol round the enemy's position to fire on the enemy mine-thrower from the rear and if possible to capture it. This capture was not brought off, for the enemy had at his disposal unexpected reserves which were able to keep Meier's patrol at a distance.

The action thus came to a standstill. When it had grown quite dark we were close in front of the enemy. Shots were still being exchanged from both sides, but only occasionally. The clerical work—even in Africa there was writing to be done, though not as much as is usually the case—was postponed during the fighting. A number of charges and other tiresome details had to be written up. I was able from time to time to talk personally with the company leaders, and called them together for this purpose. I changed my own position as little as possible to avoid difficulties and annoying delays in the dispatch and receipt of messages. A meal was cooked further in the rear, where the dressing station had also been established. We at Headquarters had our meal prepared as usual by our black servants, who brought it up to the firing-line.

In order to get the force in hand ready for further action, some parts of it were withdrawn from the front line and mustered. I came to the conclusion that it would be expedient to remain where we were for the night, to be in readiness to renew the action on the following day, and especially to cut the enemy off from his water-supply, which must be somewhere outside the camp.

About midnight it was reported that one of our patrols had encountered a strong enemy force on the Nanungu-Mahua road. I was afraid that this force, which I took to be strong in view of its independent movement, would advance further on Nanungu and capture our company's stores (ammunition, medical stores, supplies, etc.), which were on this road as well as the depot at Nanungu. I therefore withdrew during the night with the greater part of my force, *via* Makoti, to the Nanungu-Mahua road. Only strong patrols remained in front of the enemy, but these did not notice that the enemy, too, evacuated his position during the night and withdrew towards Mahua.

On 6th May it became apparent that the report of strong enemy forces on the Nanungu-Mahua road, which had caused my retirement, was incorrect. There was no enemy there. Captain Müller, hearing the firing of the English trench-mortars, had, with admirable initiative, immediately begun a forced march from his camp north-east of Mahua, towards the sound and had apparently been taken for the enemy.

When he arrived on the battlefield he found that the enemy had retired. The enemy, consisting of four companies and a machine-gun company, and to judge from his fortifications a thousand strong, had been completely defeated by our force of little more than 200 rifles—we were 62 Europeans and 342 *Askari*. He had lost 14 Europeans and 91 *Askari* killed, 3 Europeans and 3 *Askari* taken prisoner. In addition, his hospital with about 100 wounded had fallen into our hands, and according to the natives he had taken other wounded with him. Our casualties were : 6 Europeans, 24 *Askari*, 5 other natives killed; 10 Europeans, 67 *Askari* and 28 other natives wounded.

While this gratifying success against the enemy's western columns was being attained, Koehl's detachment had been engaged in continuous fighting, often on a considerable scale, against the enemy divisions which were advancing on Nanungu from Port Amelia. At Medo the enemy, according to his own statement, suffered heavy losses in one engagement west of Medo. Captain Spangenberg, with his two companies, had succeeded in getting round the enemy, falling on and capturing from the rear his light field howitzer battery. Nearly all the men and horses of this battery were killed.

Unfortunately it was not possible to remove the guns and ammunition. They were rendered useless. But in spite of this individual success, Koehl's detachment had to retire. The moment was approaching when the timely intervention of my main force with Koehl's detachment might bring about a decisive success against General Edwards. Once more, however, the question of supplies dragged our movements. The crops of the district had all been consumed, except the Mtama, which ripens much earlier in this country than in German East Africa. But it was not yet ripe. In order to avoid having to withdraw simply for reasons of supply, we ripened the Mtama artificially by drying it. This made the grain quite edible, and as there was plenty of it in the district everyone got as much as he wanted, and there was no want.

The condition of the crops prompted me to march with the main body of the force further south-west, in the direction of Mahua, and pitch my camp beside the Koroma Mountain, not far from the Timbani Mountain. I intended, if necessary, to march further south, to avail myself of the abundant crops in the fertile districts near the confluence of the Malma and Lurio Rivers. West of the Timbani Mountain the country was favourable for a decisive action against General Edwards, who was following Captain Koehl's detachment south-west from Nanungu. The extraordinarily rocky and broken country near the mountain, and four miles north-east of it, as far as the place to which Koehl's detachment had retired, was not favourable for the decisive attack I had in view.

On 21st May smoke indicated fresh enemy camps west of the positions of Koehl's detachment. I guessed that this new enemy would march on 22nd May to take Koehl's detachment in the rear from the west. Unfortunately I omitted to give Koehl's detachment definite orders to withdraw their main force immediately from the unfavourable country to the south-west of the Timbani Mountain. Instead of a positive order I gave him instructions which left him too much freedom of action.

Thus it came about that Koehl's detachment did not get their bearers with the ammunition and baggage on the march until the forenoon of the 22nd of May. Even then all would have been well if the Governor, who had attached himself to Koehl's division, had not marched at their head. Not understanding the seriousness of the situation, he made a considerable halt in the middle of this unfavourable country, where he was exposed to a surprise attack from the enemy at any moment, without being able to put up an effective defence. The bearers of Koehl's detachment, in spite of Captain Koehl's orders, allowed themselves to halt likewise.

During the morning of this day, I once more personally reconnoitred the very favourable country south-west of the Timbani Mountain, and met, among others, Lieutenant Kempner, who had been wounded the day before with Koehl's detachment and carried to the rear. From Koehl's detachment itself, where, since the morning, several enemy attacks had been beaten off, sounds of distant fighting were to be heard. There was telephonic communication with Captain Koehl, and I returned about 11 a.m. to the Koroma camp without having any idea of the situation of his transport.

NATIVE TYPES (5). DRAWN BY GENERAL
VON LETTOW-YORBECK'S ADJUTANT.

NATIVE TYPES (6). DRAWN BY GENERAL
VON LETTOW-YORBECK'S ADJUTANT.

At noon I had just entered the camp when suddenly there was a loud sound of firing, from a very short distance, of trench-mortars, beyond doubt between us and Koehl's detachment. Immediately afterwards telephonic communication in that direction was broken off. There was no alternative but to march my whole force immediately from the Koroma camp against this new enemy. I secretly hoped that, in spite of the unfavourable country, we might perhaps succeed in taking him by surprise, and in inflicting a decisive defeat. Barely an hour later we reached the Timbani Mountain and quickly threw back the advanced detachment of the enemy.

A few scattered men reported that the governor and Captain Koehl's transport had been surprised by the enemy and all the baggage lost. The governor himself had only just managed to get away; others said he had been taken prisoner. The enemy had opened a fairly lively fire with several mine-throwers, and was attacked by our companies from several sides. He had, however, taken up a good position, in which he entrenched himself and had hidden part of the captured baggage. Unfortunately we only recaptured a small quantity. But the enemy position was surrounded and subjected to a concentrated and gruelling fire. According to a dispatch captured later, the 1st King's African Rifles alone lost about two hundred men.

Several companies and patrols of Captain Koehl's detachment took part in this envelopment of the enemy. Captain Koehl himself had turned his main force against the new enemy, attacking his rear, and hoped to be able to defeat him while a strong patrol facing northeast held his former enemy in check. This patrol, however, was much too weak. It was pressed back, and had again to be reinforced with troops from Captain Koehl's detachment. Even though the enemy had without doubt suffered on the whole considerable losses, a decisive success was unattainable. The fighting was broken off at dark, and we withdrew to the favourable country I had reconnoitred between the Timbani and Koroma Mountains.

Meanwhile the governor had found his way to the camp by the Koroma mountain. He had lost all his belongings in the adventure, and was looked after by Heder, a non-commissioned officer, and the trustworthy and cautious leader of the supply column. I, too, came up to help the Governor in his adversity, and honoured him with a pair of blue socks, which his wife had made me at the beginning of the war, but which unfortunately had faded.

Apart from the serious loss of about 70,000 rounds of ammunition, we had also lost a considerable amount of notes—I believe it was 30,000 *rupees*. My desire to give requisition notes in preference to bank notes, and so save a lot of transport of securities and avoid unnecessary losses, had not been acceded. Millions of *rupee* notes had been printed, the dragging about of which, in the present war situation, was particularly burdensome. In order, at least, to avoid similar losses in the future, the quartermaster, on my instructions, destroyed a great part of the notes which had been obtained with so much trouble.

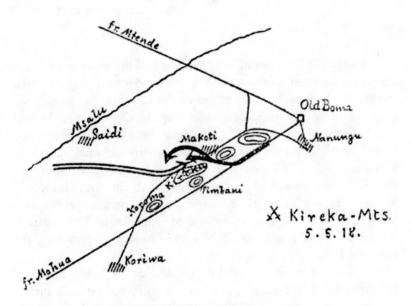

FIG. XVIII. THE ACTION AT KIREKA MTS.

CHAPTER 3

In the Region of the Lurio and Likungo Rivers

On May 23rd the rest of our transport and the main body of the troops were started off from Coroma camp on a track right through the bush to Koriwa. The bulk of our carrier columns and the sick had gone on ahead. The rearguard under Captain Otto remained a few days longer on the Koroma Mountain and there successfully repulsed several hostile attacks. It looked as if our enemy had once again collected the bulk of his troops at Timbani, after the conclusion of a concentric operation, and needed some time to reorganize his supply before resuming his march. Returning patrols reported heavy motor traffic on the Nanungu-Timbani Mountain road. Other patrols informed us that hostile forces from the east were approaching the northern bank of the Lurio River.

Unmolested by the enemy, I now made for the fertile district of Kwiri, south of Mahua, and from thence on to the Lurio. It turned out, however, that some of our seriously wounded and sick would not be able to endure several days of such marches in their *"maschille"* (litters). Nor was it easy to ensure medical attention. We had too few attendants to be able to leave the sick behind individually. So there was nothing for it but to collect our invalids from time to time, turn them into a complete Field Hospital, under a single medical officer, and take our leave of them finally. Even the senior medical officer of the Protective Force, Dr. Meixner, was left behind at Kwiri with one such hospital.

On that occasion I said farewell to Lieutenant Schaefer who had rendered us such exemplary service in the preparations for the action at Jassini, and was now stricken with black-water fever. This experienced "African" was fully aware of his situation, but was as cheerful as ever and faced his inevitable end, which was approaching fast, with composure.

I did not wish to linger long north of the Lurio, for I thought that this river, which had been very high only a short time before, would be a serious obstacle. For that reason I proposed to cross it with our large quantity of transport quickly and without let or hindrance. When we actually reached the Lurio it appeared that at this time of the year there were plenty of fords which offered a comfortable crossing. We left some of our troops on the northern bank without anxiety as to the drawbacks involved, and established a camp for the main body on the southern bank. The country was very fertile and the inhabitants trusted in us; good relations had been established by the earlier visits of the patrols and raiding parties. One of my orderlies had a hearty reception from some old acquaintances.

I was pretty sure that the English would attack us here and be compelled to bring up ever more troops. If I only withdrew slowly enough, the strong enemy forces would, I believed, probably follow, but in view of their immense supply difficulties, it would be in vain. In this way I might achieve my main purpose of gaining enough time to raid the weaker hostile camps and posts further south. Captain Müller's detachment, which had been sent south, discovered one such camp at Malema, the same place where our troops had won heartening successes before.

After fighting for several days Captain Müller captured the Boma Malema. It had been occupied by an English half-battalion which retired south at night. Simultaneously a Portuguese patrol had gone north from the Boma Malema and returned. Captain Müller took the latter for the retreating English, attacked them on the march and was very astonished to find that the killed were Portuguese.

After the action Captain Müller shifted his camp. In the move, Lieutenant von Schroetter, who was ill with malaria, was left behind for a short time and taken prisoner by an English patrol which suddenly appeared upon the scene. When this patrol marched off to the Boma Inagu he managed to escape, and rejoined us at length, quite exhausted. But he lost all his belongings, and had nothing on his head—a very serious matter under a tropical sun.

From the reports of the natives and our own patrols there was no longer room for doubt that strong enemy forces, which had disembarked at Mozambique, were marching west on the Boma Malema, and were already only a few days' march from that place. Simultane-ous reports were received that troops were also marching towards the Boma Malema from the west, the direction of Malacotera. A few days later the enemy following us from the north reached the Lurio, so we evacuated its northern bank. From captured documents and the fight-ing that took place on the northern bank, we judged that this hostile force was stronger than I had suspected. Thanks to its light motor transport columns it had been able to follow us up quickly with all its supply as well as a body which I estimated at about three or four battalions with auxiliary arms.

The country along the River Malema in which we had our camp was quite extraordinarily fertile. The *mtama* was perfectly ripe, and there was an abundance of tomatoes, bananas, sweet potatoes (*bata-tas*) and other fruits. The food was also very varied. Game and fish were plentiful. The natives knew the German troops from previous acquaintance, and were very friendly. When I rode from one detach-ment to another the women came running out of their houses to see the "*njama*" (animal, game, flesh), a creature quite unknown to them. I was riding a horse, of course!

The fertile country was so extensive that we could not even ap-proximately exploit or protect it. We could not prevent it supplying the necessities of life to the large number of *Askari* and non-combat-ants with our enemies, as well as ourselves. We could not deprive the enemy of the possibility of also making this prolific region in a large measure into a new base and shortening his line of supply. From our point of view the country was, if anything, too fertile and we were not in a position, as on earlier occasions, to exploit it to such an extent before we left that it was insufficient to support the enemy masses. But at any rate it had the result that for the moment we were very mobile as, thanks to our sojourn of several weeks, our wounded and sick were so far recovered that all, even the inmates of the field hospitals, were quite fit for marching.

This advantage would have been lost once more by any consider-able actions. I decided gradually to evacuate the region, in spite of its extraordinary fertility, and slip through the ring in which the enemy columns were enclosing me in the fertile district of the Malema River. My idea was that a small part of my troops should hold off these enemy columns and keep them so busy that they would think they were in-volved in a serious affair, and attack my rearguard properly. In coming to this decision, good service was done me by the orders of the English commander which had fallen into our hands. He had no intention of being "foxed" by us a second time, as he had been at Koriwa, and had therefore arranged that whenever contact was established with us at any point, several detachments should immediately execute a flank march round us at a distance of five or six English miles.

I told General Edwards about this later on, and he was extraordinarily amused that this had given me an intimation of his intentions, and enabled me to take my counter-measures against them. It was obvious that if I only *echeloned* my troops deeply enough the enemy's enveloping detachments would be placed in the greatest peril. They would find themselves sandwiched between my detachments and in this way could be taken by surprise in the flank or rear by my troops *echeloned* further back. Unfortunately the execution of this plan was only imperfect. In the very thick bush, however carefully one watched camp fires and the dust, there were too few indications to follow a column properly and it was very difficult for a column to keep its direction. In addition there were a number of factors that threw out one's calculations, factors such as dense bush, marshes and watercourses. In spite of all these obstacles, we succeeded every now and then in taking one of the hostile enveloping columns by surprise and bringing it under fire.

The inevitable difficulties of moving separate columns in the thick bush were even greater on the English side than on the German. When a collision occurred there was often a complete mix-up in which neither friend nor foe knew whom he had before him. On one occasion Lieutenant von Ruckteschell's detachment, which had been nearest to the enemy, fell back on some of our troops which had been *echeloned* further back. In so doing it came across a reconnoitring party in the bush, at a distance of about thirty paces. This patrol was recognized as an enemy. The machine guns were brought into position under the nose of the enemy and without any interference on his part, and the patrol, which had taken our men for English, was fired on lustily at point-blank range and put to flight in a second.

In the same way our own patrols continually found themselves in the middle of enemy troops. On one such occasion *Vizefeldwebel* Schaffrath made his patrol lie down in the high grass and then opened an effective fire on the head of approaching enemy columns. Then he took cover again. In this way he succeeded in the course of a few hours in inflicting sensible losses on the enemy several times and capturing some material.

I wanted to gain time by these holding actions, so that I could get my main body into the country further south, which was supposed to be fertile, according to report, and fall upon and drive away the small-ish hostile garrisons we expected to find there. The first objective of this nature was the Portuguese *Boma* Alto-Moloque. A captured map showed that this had been the seat of a higher administrative authority in peacetime and the military station of a force exceeding a company. Both natives and food must certainly be there. Between us and Alto-Moloque lay the high range of Inagu.

An English battalion in its entrenched camp at Inagu barred the road which led from the Boma Malema round the west side of the Inagu Mountains to Alto-Moloque. It was therefore probable that our advance by that road would be contested, and that would have been unpleasant in view of the length of our carrier columns. In any case we should have been delayed and our intended surprise attack on Alto-Moloque would have been spoilt. But surprise I regarded as ab-solutely essential, as we suspected the presence of ammunition and arms at Alto-Moloque.

Accordingly we left the enemy in peace in his entrenchments at Inagu and marched round the east side of the Inagu Mountains on Alto-Moloque. The strategic situation was somewhat remarkable, and well described in the words of an old Boer, words that were not quite pure High German: "*Is das eine Komische Orlog; ons lopt achter de Por-tugies an, und de Englanders lopt achter ons an*" (This is a funny war. We chase the Portuguese, and the English chase us).

We marched by native tracks or straight through the bush. Several considerable streams had to be negotiated on the way. This district, too, was fertile, and we soon came across unmistakable human tracks leading towards Alto-Moloque, not to mention *kraals*, the first I had ever seen. They were grass huts, very thick and carefully built. Ashes were smouldering in places and the heads of hens which were lying about were still fresh. We exchanged shots with some Portuguese pa-trols and a few rifles with ammunition were captured.

No time must be lost, so Müller's detachment, made specially mo-bile by being relieved of all its transport, went on ahead and found in Alto-Moloque only a few Portuguese officers and non-commissioned officers who were just drinking coffee on the verandah of the very fine European house. These were taken prisoner.

I now followed slowly with the main body. Our rearguard, under Captain Koehl, had quite a series of little collisions, which in bulk caused the enemy not inconsiderable losses. One of our *Askari* patrols had been surprised and captured by a stronger enemy patrol when engaged in foraging for food. These *Askari* subsequently looked on while this English patrol fought quite a bloody action with another English detachment in the thick bush and the occurrence gave them their opportunity of escaping. The lack of caution which many of our Europeans continually showed, in spite of all warnings, caused us many unnecessary losses.

There was one *Askari*, a particularly reliable and intelligent man, whose father, the old Effendi Plantan, had already been with Von Wissmann's Zulu *Askari*, whom I had been only too glad to take with me on patrol. He never came back from some quite unnecessary mission on which he was sent, and was probably taken prisoner. It was a phenomenon common to both sides that a large part of the losses in the war in East Africa were unnecessary and due solely to thoughtlessness.

Koehl's detachment gradually came up with the main body, which had reached the Alto-Moloque-Inagu road at a European plantation which was well stocked with provisions. From this place it had rung up Alto-Moloque on the enemy's telephone and received a reply, first from a Portuguese, then from Captain Müller. Müller reported that only a small amount of ammunition had been captured, and that the bulk must have been got away to the south-east just in tune by several carrier parties. Strong patrols were immediately sent out after them.

When the main body entered Alto-Moloque on June 16th we found some very fine and massive European houses. They were charmingly situated on a little hill, and had a view for miles over the neighbouring forests to the mighty rugged mountains in the distance. There were thousands of orange trees in full bloom and our coloured men immediately christened it the "*Boma ja machungwa*" (Orange *boma*).

The numerous maps and documents of all kinds which were found at the station gave us a tolerably clear idea of the country towards Quelimane. We could see that there was a telegraph wire from Alto-Moloque to Quelimane *via* Ili. A large company, the Lugella Company, had its headquarters at the confluence of the Lugella with the Likungo. There were great plantations and factories and large supplies of food. Above all, it looked as if preparations were in progress to make this station a main supply depot for food and ammunition for considerable bodies of troops.

If we wished to exploit the opportunity that this situation presented, our subordinate commanders would have to act very promptly and must not be hampered by too rigid instructions. The impression that I formed in my mind rested in many respects on unproved assumptions. Our pursuing patrols must be able to act according to circumstances independently and rapidly if that original impression was not confirmed subsequently. Time must not be lost, or the enemy would be able to get his supplies away in time. He would have the advantage of a railway which began not far south of the Lugella Company's station and led south to the River Namacurra, as well as the steamer which plied on that stream.

As so often happens, our pursuing patrols and companies were occasionally found wanting in some respects. Yet it must not be forgotten that besides many other qualities a very mature tactical judgment is required to give an independent decision on the question when the very exhausting pursuit of a fleeing foe is to be continued at top pressure or should be broken off. To exploit the promising situation to the greatest possible extent, on the very day of my arrival at Alto-Moloque I had sent in pursuit the whole of Müller's detachment, which I had hitherto kept by me. In the course of various patrols and raids in the neighbourhood we caught individual Portuguese *Askari* who in many cases had set up off their own bats as little tyrants in the villages of the district. The natives reported their presence to us.

The region of Alto-Moloque turned out to be very fertile, as we anticipated. We were therefore in a position to give Müller's detachment a greater start in following up the enemy. One of the patrols of this detachment had captured a hostile supply depot near Ili. An enemy carrier column, turned off by an Anglo-Portuguese detachment which was now several days' march east of Alto-Moloque, and trying to pass through Alto-Moloque in ignorance of our presence, was a welcome acquisition to our *Intendant*, who needed it to carry the supplies captured at Ili. Unfortunately this intended removal succeeded only partially, for a fresh English detachment appeared at Ili, apparently from the direction of Inagu, and drove off our patrols.

The advance of our main body on Ili was contested by considerable hostile patrols which were approaching the Alto-Moloque-Ili road from the north. One of these patrols was immediately pursued energetically and attacked in its camp, but I gained the impression that larger enemy forces were advancing on us from the north of Ili and Alto-Moloque. I had no intention of delaying, but wished rather to join up as soon as possible with Müller's detachment, which was on its way to Lugella. Accordingly I marched south, skirting Ili and occupied the Portuguese post of Nampepo. In this district, at about a day's march from each other, the Portuguese companies had established a number of clean, well-arranged stations around which lay the fields, which they cultivated.

A whole series of these posts and their field-depots fell into our hands during the march. Nampepo was one of them, only larger than usual, and the centre of an extraordinarily fertile district. A special feature of the Nampepo camp was our chase after domestic pigs. Large numbers of these were running loose in the bush, so that we had excellent sausages to eat, as well as roast pork and brawn. A German planter named Hauter, from the district of Morogoro, who had delivered large supplies of sausages to Morogoro during the war, had acquired expert skill in preparing them, and this now came in very useful. He now had the insides of pigs to practise on instead of the insides of cows, and our enjoyment of this unwonted luxury was so great that we did not allow ourselves to be disturbed even by the shots that fell into our camp.

For as a matter of fact a considerable enemy column from the north was approaching the station of Nampepo, which was held by Captain Spangenberg with our outposts. From the commanding ground the approach of a large enemy column could be noted quite easily. As a particularly favourable opportunity for attacking it presented itself we did not disturb the enemy in his approach. However, contrary to expectation, he did not attack us. Pillars of smoke arising from the bush about 1,500 yards away showed us that he had encamped there. Our patrols which went round the enemy crawled up to his camp at night and fired into it. Koehl's detachment had come up meanwhile and I marched off with the main body to follow Müller's detachment in the direction of Lugella. Captain Spangenberg remained with our rearguard in touch with the enemy, and then followed us at a distance of a day's march.

Meanwhile Captain Müller's detachment had succeeded in crossing the Likungo River, near the confluence of the Lugella, at a ford. It had been able to give an apparently severe drubbing to a Portuguese battalion which had rushed up from the south to protect it. Several machine guns were captured. The great depot of the Lugella Company fell into our hands. It was possible to distribute a large amount of food and clothing. The buildings themselves, which had been adapted for defence, and about 300,000 kilograms of food were burnt.

As no other remunerative objective presented itself Captain Müller considered he had fulfilled his mission for the time being, retired to the southern bank of the Likungo and there awaited my arrival.

I was afraid that our wonderful captures of the last few weeks would tempt some of our Europeans to help themselves to things improperly, and I took advantage of the occasion to point out the evils of such behaviour. It must not be forgotten that war booty belongs to the State, and that the individual soldier has to notify to his superiors if he happens to want any particular object he has captured. An estimate is then made of the value of the object and he has to pay the amount. It was important for me to maintain the *moral* of our troops unconditionally if I was to be able to appeal to their sense of honour and make calls on their endurance.

A certain amount of ammunition was captured here and there, and, further, a small Portuguese gun had fallen into our hands, but the great haul of cartridges for which we had hoped and striven had not materialized. I thought it extremely doubtful whether there ever had been such large stocks at Alto-Moloque and Ili, and suspected that the whole thing was a case of exaggeration of the approved native type. That did not imply evil intentions on the part of those concerned. On the contrary, the natives were well-disposed towards us. For example, they brought back of their own accord one of our captured Portuguese officers who had escaped. They also brought us some German black boys who had been enjoying themselves looting, and had been caught and well beaten by the natives, excusing themselves on the ground that they had taken them for Portuguese!

It is an extremely difficult matter even for a European to estimate, for example, the numerical strength of a detachment on the march. The native finds it much more difficult, especially when it comes to larger numbers. The words he so frequently uses, *mingi* (much) or *kama majani* (as thick as grass) can mean 50 just as well as 5,000.

CHAPTER 4

On to the South

However, wherever these large ammunition depots might be, they had certainly not fallen into our hands. We had to start out on the search again. The whole strategic situation, as well as the documents we captured, showed that they *must* be somewhere in this region. There was a high degree of probability that the more considerable stocks, whose existence we suspected, were further south, either because they had been there from the start or because they had been moved there as a result of our approach. It seemed likely that before long they would be transported to the coast and transferred to ships, in case of emergency.

During our march considerable patrols had reconnoitred the region within a radius of a day's march, and captured a few small enemy food depots, but no arms or ammunition. Müller's detachment, with which we had joined up at Mujeba on June 27th, marched further south again the same day. The natives told us of a large *boma* at Origa, which was said to be somewhere further south, near the coast, and to have large ammunition supplies. Müller's party was to find this *boma*. Our directions were thoroughly inaccurate, as usual. I was quite certain that on the march other and conflicting reports would infallibly arrive. Unfortunately we had not a long time in which to test the intelligence that came in. All we could do was to trust that it contained at least an element of truth.

As the situation demanded, Captain Müller was given the greatest freedom of action. If any promising objective presented itself during his march, he was to decide without hesitation what his best course was. I would bring up our main body and intervene unconditionally in his support, and, in any case, I would accept the situation he had created. The main thing was that he should not wait for special orders and instructions. I realized that in acting thus I was in a large measure placing the conduct of our operations in the hands of a subordinate commander. It was only possible because that subordinate commander possessed a very sound, tactical judgement and great initiative.

Our leading troops, with their three weak companies, had to perform the double function of cavalry sent out far and wide to reconnoitre, and that of an advance guard led with the greatest energy. In any other circumstances I should have been with the advance guard myself, in view of its important task, so that I could have a surer hold on the course of operations. Experience had taught me, however, that in view of the distance between our columns, my presence with the main body was indispensable, both to overcome obstacles quickly and to be able to act in face of some unforeseen change in the situation. It must not be forgotten that our whole advance was based on combination, and that, as actually happened often enough, the unsuspected appearance of hostile detachments from some other direction transformed the situation at a blow and made fresh dispositions necessary.

Accordingly we marched by small native tracks or right through the bush in single file. Owing to the great length of our columns, on a day's march of nineteen miles or so the head had to start off in the dark—about 5 a.m.—if the tail was to reach the camp appointed the same day, that is, late in the evening and just before darkness fell. It was inevitable, because camping material had to be procured, wood to be chopped, grass to be cut and shelters to be built, in case of need, for the sick. For that reason our whole force could not march concentrated. It was much too extended. Müller's detachment, forming the advance guard, marched one or two days' march ahead. The rearguard, Spangenberg's detachment, followed the main body at a distance of about a day's march. Communication was maintained by means of runners.

In the reports which reached us by the runners of Müller's detachment, the name "*Kokosani*" was now perpetually recurring. Considerable enemy depots, strongly protected by hostile troops, were to be found there, so it was said. But where was this Kokosani? The word could not be found on our maps. It gradually came to light that Kokosani was the same place that figured on Portuguese maps as Namacurra. In any case, all our previous intelligence, as well as a glance at the situation on the map, showed that Kokosani must be our most promising objective. We had no means of knowing whether it would be possible to capture this place, probably very strongly fortified, with our relatively limited resources. Only the attempt itself could enlighten us on that point. Captain Müller had turned west towards the place independently. On the way it became clear that, as the natives had told us, there actually was a ford over the River Likungo.

I now marched on quickly with our main body, in order to join up, and gave orders to the same effect to our rearguard under Captain Spangenberg. In the afternoon of July 1st, the main force reached the Likungo and immediately crossed it. The water of this great river, more than four hundred yards wide, came up to our necks at the deepest parts of the ford. It took each man about an hour to cross. When the troops had successfully reached the western bank, we bivouacked, and next morning continued our march in the tracks of Müller's detachment ahead.

On the way some thirty natives met us. They had worked in Kokosani, and told us that a large number of Portuguese and *Askari* were encamped there, and that a number of chests had arrived. We had to employ interpreters in our talk with these men, as they did not know Kisuaheli. Several of our *Askari* were masters of the local tongue or related dialects.

Before long we received an important report from the advance guard. On the previous day Captain Müller had completely surprised the enemy at Kokosani by an encircling move. Marching on the factory buildings from the north in broad daylight, through a field of knee-high *agaves* and without any cover, he had succeeded in getting into the Portuguese entrenchments and, in several hours of very severe hand-to-hand fighting, defeating the three Portuguese companies holding them, with very heavy losses to the enemy. In the course of the action a number of rules, as well as two field guns with their ammunition, were captured.

I myself went on a little ahead of our main body, and in the morning came across several extensive and well-arranged plantations. Next I followed the track of a field railway, which ran along the main road right through the fields, and after a short time joined up with a standard-gauge line. As was to appear later, the latter led from the River Namacurra northwards to the neighbourhood of Lugella. When Captain Müller struck this standard-gauge line the day before, he held up a train which had just come from Lugella. It is easy to realize the mutual amazement when there descended from the train several Portuguese non-commissioned officers whom Müller had captured at Lugella and released again.

When I reached the factory buildings, Captain Müller came limping up to me, pretty lame. He expressed his astonishment that I had brought my detachment direct to Kokosani by the main road and without opposition, for he thought that there must be quite two English companies somewhere in the neighbourhood. He had not yet been able to ascertain their whereabouts, but documents which Captain Müller had captured pointed conclusively to their presence in the district. Müller also told me that he had not yet found the considerable quantity of infantry cartridges. All his people were still busy trying to find them and anything similar.

When I considered the matter more closely, it seemed to me more probable that the ammunition stores we were hunting for would not be near the factory, but must be somewhere directly on the railway, and, indeed, at its southern terminus. That was the place for a large ammunition depot, for it must be the unloading point where the stuff was transferred to rail from ships on the Namacurra. We had to find out whether these deductions were sound. I went back immediately and met the leading files of our main body among the plantations. The leading companies were anything but pleased to have to retrace their steps in order to follow the standard-gauge railway southwards. After the long, tiring march a few complimentary remarks about my arrangements were comprehensible enough. Fortunately for me, I did not hear them.

It was in a rather bad humour that the men at the head of the column arrived in the neighbourhood of the railway-station. They did not seriously believe in the possibility of a fight. It was upon them suddenly, however, and several *Askari* were struck by hostile bullets at quite short range and fell. The rest of our main force, which was near at hand and ready for action, was brought up. When I arrived, the situation was not at all clear; the enemy was obviously entrenched and closer reconnaissance was in progress. An indecisive exchange of shots now developed. It began to rain and was unpleasantly cold, so that everyone felt thoroughly uncomfortable. I myself went to Lieutenant von Ruckteschell's company, which was lying opposite to and about ninety yards from the corrugated-iron buildings of the station and directing a well-aimed rifle and machine-gun fire from some high ant-hills every time anything showed.

I considered that the situation at the moment was unfavourable to storming the station. We would have been compelled to rush at the enemy's position through the thick bush, which was commanded by a most effective hostile fire. That offered but little prospect of success. A number of our men would probably not have joined in the rush at all, and those who did and got close to the enemy's fortress would probably have been held up and found themselves unable to get on. We should, therefore, achieve nothing.

On the other hand, my reconnaissance had brought the idea to my mind that on targets, some of which were very visible, artillery fire would be effective, especially from two sides. It would frighten the enemy's *Askari* and make them run away. That would be a favourable moment for good machine-gun fire. But the day was already too far advanced, and our gun was smashed, so that nothing definite could be ventured on for that day. The larger portion of the troops retired to our camp, and only three companies of Captain Poppe's detachment remained in close contact with the enemy.

The next day, July 3rd, we got our gun into working order again, after strenuous efforts. As luck would have it, it was of the same model as the guns Captain Müller had captured, and so, by interchanging the individual serviceable parts of these three guns, we produced a field-piece fit for use. There was thus a prospect of putting to good use the two hundred rounds we had captured two days before. In the after-noon the gun was to be brought up to within a few hundred yards of the station, and open fire upon it. Another smaller, 4-cm., gun was ready in the foremost infantry line—and therefore about a hundred and twenty-five yards off—to start a cross fire. All our machine guns were held ready. In the morning I had been to the factory buildings again for a conference, and had told the civilian personnel there they need not get frightened if they heard the sound of firing in the after-noon. The white women and children had been very frightened by the fighting, and some of them had fled into the bush.

I had gone back to our camp, extremely tired, when the sound of fighting at the station suddenly made itself heard. We received a telephone report that loud yells and cries of "hurrah" could be heard coming from the station. By degrees the following facts were estab-lished: the enemy was apparently tired of the well-aimed, concentric fire which had been directed at them since the afternoon. They were now being subjected to artillery fire from two sides at once, and the moment there was the slightest movement machine guns opened on them.

Their young troops could not stand it, and were very restless. Our companies recognized that this was their weak moment and used it immediately, showing splendid initiative. They leaped up with loud hurrahs, and the next minute were in the enemy's position. The enemy began to run away. The English maintained that they had been infected by the example of the Portuguese. However that may be, they ran away and our companies immediately went after them as hard as they could. Our flying foes reached the river Namacurra, which ran immediately behind their position, quickly pulled off their boots and dashed into the water. Here most of the hostile troops were drowned, including their commander, Major Gore-Brown.

Between July 1st and 3rd the enemy had 5 Europeans and 100 *Askari* killed, 4 Europeans and about 100 *Askari* drowned, while 421 *Askari* were taken prisoner. Of the Europeans (5 English and 117 Portuguese) who also fell into our hands, 55 Portuguese escaped and 46 sick and wounded Portuguese were left behind in the hospital at Kokosani. We had 8 *Askari* and 1 machine-gun carrier killed, 3 Europeans, 11 *Askari* and 2 machine-gun carriers wounded. At first it was quite impossible to estimate, even approximately, what amount of ammunition and food we had captured at the station. Seven heavy, 3 light machine guns and 2 guns had fallen into our hands, but these 2 guns had been rendered useless.

More and more cases of captured ammunition were brought into our camp. The *Intendant*, Lieutenant Besch (retired naval officer), was in despair because he did not know where he was going to get enough carriers to remove such vast stores. They included more than 300,000 kilograms of food and the stocks from the Kokosani sugar factory. The amount of booty enabled all our coloured men to receive as much clothing material as they wanted, and my boy, Serubili, said to me: "This is a very different matter to Tanga; we're all getting as much sugar as we want now."

It is a fact that the whole camp was littered with sugar. Each of the blacks was so well-off for food and clothing of all kinds that they stopped stealing, as if by word of command. Everyone knows what that means where blacks are concerned.

The booty included large quantities of European food and preserves. Every European found himself well provided for for months ahead. Unfortunately it was not possible for us to get away the whole stock of excellent wine we had captured. After a sufficient quantity had been set aside as a restorative for the sick, the rest had mainly to be drunk on the spot. The risk of a wholesale "jollification" *that* involved was gladly taken, and everyone was allowed to let himself go for once, after his long abstinence.

In addition there was some fine *schnapps* in a large number of casks in the Kokosani factory. These were being stored ready for the English troops. With the best will in the world it was impossible to drink it all, so we had to empty a large number of the casks into the Namacurra.

Column after column of carriers arrived in the camp with booty, and the *Intendant* became more and more desperate. Affairs reached a climax when a telephone message came from the station that a river-steamer had arrived. An English medical officer, all unsuspecting of what had happened at Namacurra, disembarked from it and closer examination of the boat revealed the presence of a considerable consignment of cartridges, exceeding three hundred cases.

In all we had captured about three hundred and fifty modern English and Portuguese rifles, a welcome addition to our resources, which brought our armament once more up to requirements. We were able to discard our '71 pattern rifle almost entirely.

CHAPTER 5

Back North to the Namacurra River

In face of the enemy's orders we had captured I had to anticipate that within a short time comparatively strong hostile forces would be coming from Quelimane to attack us. The country between the Namacurra and the Zambesi, however, offered a large number of river barriers, so that a march to the Zambesi would be full of difficulties for us and hinder our freedom of movement to an extraordinary degree. Equally unfavourable for campaigning, from our point of view, was the country south and south-west of our present halting-place. In the last resort we should find ourselves cooped up on the Zambesi without being in a position to effect a crossing of that mighty river which was commanded by the enemy's gunboats.

I thought it better to abandon our previous march direction. Yet in view of the total absence of news it was very difficult to say where I ought to make for. Only one thing appeared to be clear that the enemy was not directly on our heels. At any rate our rearguard and the patrols they had sent out behind them were not being pressed at all by the enemy. It seemed probable that if hostile bodies were following us at all they were engaged in trying to overhaul us on some route parallel to that we had taken. If I were right in that view—and it seemed to be confirmed by such reports as the natives brought in—we could assume that the enemy was insufficiently informed of our presence at Namacurra and further that the Portuguese soldiers among our prisoners whom we had turned off could give him no clear or trustworthy information.

We had, therefore, to devote all our efforts to making those fellows believe we intended to fortify and put up a stiff defence of Namacurra and, further, that we had our eye on Quelimane.

The unexpected disaster at Namacurra was bound to speed the

steps of the pursuing enemy. It was probable that his columns, advancing on a parallel line to us, would overshoot the mark, especially as they must be anxious about the important port of Quelimane. I therefore decided to wait at Namacurra until the pursuing enemy columns had actually shot ahead of me and then turn about to the north-east. What chiefly influenced me in this decision was that a march in this direction, leading towards Mozambique, on the main line of communication, would cause the enemy anxiety, and as soon as he became aware of it he would at once turn about to protect the neighbourhood of Mozambique with its wealth of stores. If he did not do so we should have a free hand at Mozambique. As the position would then develop the enemy would be forced to undertake marches that would exhaust his troops, while we gained time to recuperate our strength and allow our sick and wounded to recover.

It was difficult to decide on the most favourable moment for our change of direction north-east; we should have to rely to some extent on the fortune of war. Even if I made the movement too soon and encountered one of the enemy columns there was always a chance of defeating it when cut off from the rest. The first thing, however, was to get safely across the Likungo River again. The available information as to the fords was very unreliable. In order not to use the same fords as before I marched with my main body on the evening of 4th July to a crossing further to the south. Lieutenant Ott, however, ascertained by personal reconnaissance that no ford existed at the place of which we had been informed.

On the other hand, it was apparent from native information as well as from tracks discovered that on the same day an English patrol had halted in this neighbourhood. The position might become awkward. In order to lose no time in investigation I marched along the west bank of the Likungo to our previous ford. Unfortunately I had withdrawn the covering force that had hitherto been left there and I did not know whether it was free. I was therefore very relieved when on 5th July the crossing was effected without further interference. Koehl's detachment was still at Namacurra and followed as rearguard.

When we were again marching as a single column through the bush, the great length of the column was unwieldy and, in the event of an encounter with the enemy, would be a source of danger. We therefore tried to shorten the column and to march in two, and later in several parallel columns through the bush. The disadvantage of this arrangement was that instead of one head of a column having to cut a way through the bush this had now to be done by several. But the advantages of the shorter length outweighed this disadvantage.

Information from our patrols and from the natives indicated that the march of the enemy columns to the south-west had not been pressed so far as I had anticipated. Enemy troops were reported both between the Moniga and the lower Likungo and also at Mujebain; in some cases they were ascertained to be marching south-west. This brought about the extraordinary situation that the enemy troops were marching in several columns south-west while we were passing between these columns in the contrary direction, north-east. This fact could not long remain hidden from the enemy, especially as the patrols soon began to come in contact, and the enemy troops, marching along the line of telephone communication from Mulevalla to Murubella, crossed our track.

We continued our march to Oriva, threw back a weak Portuguese detachment west of this place, and occupied Oriva itself on 14th July. Unfortunately the abundant stores of supplies and ammunition that we had expected to find at this station were not forthcoming; apparently either the numerous enemy troops had drawn heavily on the resources of the neighbourhood or the stores that had been originally left here had already been removed. A small patrol, sent out to Muatama under Sergeant-Major Hüttich, succeeded in surprising a small mixed detachment of English and Portuguese; as it was unfortunately impossible to get away the supplies found in this station the stores had to be burned.

Meanwhile our attempts to get information from the natives as to the whereabouts of supplies met with no success; it was impossible to wait for the reports of other patrols dispatched to Murua in search of supplies. Various patrol actions showed us that the enemy had meanwhile become aware of the change in the situation and had accordingly turned his columns about. Want of supplies forced us to continue our march, and the attack of a mixed Portuguese-English column on our rearguard under Captain Koehl could not be developed into a complete success as our main force was already on the march. We halted for a few days in the tolerably fertile territory between Oriva and Murua. Captured papers showed us that an English patrol had closely observed our movements.

It was interesting to notice that the English prisoners whom we took with us, for the most part, accepted as a matter of course the hardships of the long marches, the constant crossing of rivers and the countless difficulties connected with supplies and transport; they realized that we Germans had exactly the same hardships to endure as themselves and were in addition burdened with a number of further duties such as patrol expeditions, fighting, carrying of supplies and watch-keeping. They bore everything with a certain humour and it was obviously interesting to them to see the war from the German point of view. It was quite otherwise with the Portuguese officers.

It is true they were in an unenviable position: for the most part they were infected with syphilis and were carefully avoided by the English prisoners. In addition they were not real campaigners. They had received a generous share of the booty captured at Namacurra, but had not learned how to make the best of it. They had at once consumed the precious oil with rice and it was too much to expect that the Germans should now share with them their own meagre ration. Marching was a burden to them, their boots were torn to pieces—in short, their spokesman, the general staff officer captured at Namacurra, was continually complaining to me of the inconveniences which with the best will in the world I could not help. He was continually asking to be released. I should have been only too glad to consent if he would have given his parole not to fight against us, but this he would not do. I could not be expected to release people without any obligation and so put them in a position to attack us again immediately.

Considerations of supply drove us on. After the failure of the Oriva neighbourhood to come up to our expectations in this respect, I planned to reach the territory east of the Ligonja, which was marked on the map as thickly populated and well cultivated. On the way the advance guard, under Captain Müller, quickly took Boma Tipa, where several days' supplies, particularly pig-nuts, fell into our hands. The weak Portuguese garrison offered only slight resistance and then fled at once; the leader, a Portuguese sergeant, was the only prisoner captured.

We had reached a high degree of efficiency in the rapid and systematic distribution of booty; the main force hardly lost a day's march and I can still see the approving smile of one of the English prisoners who seemed to have entirely forgotten that the Portuguese were his allies. Apparently it amused them to see with what little ceremony we took from them their depots one after the other, together with their supplies. The captured enemy papers repeatedly gave us valuable information. Two days' march from Tipa lay another *boma* called Namirrue, where the Portuguese garrison had been strengthened by an English company. Apparently considerable stores lay here. At any rate, according to information, supply columns had been sent to replenish at Namirrue.

The English troops there probably belonged to an enemy force newly appeared from the direction of Mozambique. It was impossible for the enemy force to which we had hitherto been opposed, and which had taken part in the general march south-west north-east, to have established such a lead on us. Accordingly the advance guard with our gun at once marched on Namirrue (the smaller gun had been put out of action at Namacurra and left behind after firing its few cartridges). Captain Müller was instructed to reconnoitre the position at Namirrue and act independently as might be required. For the time being the main force remained at Tipa, on the east bank of the Moloque. It was to obtain supplies and hold up the enemy advancing from the south-west long enough to allow Captain Müller the necessary time at Namirrue.

It was not long before small enemy reconnoitring forces appeared at Tipa, on the west bank of the Ligonja, which at this point offers no obstacle worth mentioning. There was a series of unimportant patrol engagements on the east bank also. The rearguard, under Captain Koehl, carried out a number of delaying actions at places along the Tipa-Namirrue road which for the most part have already been mentioned. As I was not clear whether the main force would find the best opportunity to attack in Koehl's position or at Namirrue I began by following cautiously with him Müller's detachment. The report then came in from Captain Müller that an enemy force of some two companies was entrenched on the heights at Namirrue and that he could not get at them even with his gun.

On the other hand, he reported that in all probability English troops would come to the support of the enemy from the north or north-west. There was a favourable opportunity for us to defeat these troops in the open. I therefore marched the main force to Namirrue and on the 22nd July crossed the Namirrue River, about three miles above the rocky hill occupied by the enemy. Camp was pitched on the east bank and immediately there were patrol engagements. I myself, with Lieutenant Besch, made a detour of the hill to join Captain Müller, who was encamped immediately south-east of it. The enemy position had been encircled with patrols and machine guns. On the heights above several horses could be seen and, here and there, men too. Wherever a target offered the enemy was fired on to prevent him from sending down men to fetch water. It appeared, however, that the enemy must have been able to keep himself supplied with water from a source unknown to us.

After drinking a cup of coffee with Captain Müller we went further round the hill and came upon Lieutenant Kempner and other patrols, keenly engaged on reconnoitring work. In order to keep under cover we had to work our way partly through the thick bush and came on large quantities of cow-itch: contact with this plant produces an intolerable irritation of the skin. We were just in the middle of a thicket of this plant when we heard lively firing from the camp of our main force. At the same time the enemy in the hill fired several salvoes, apparently as a signal to their friends. I was immediately convinced that a not very strong enemy detachment was approaching which was unaware of the arrival of our main force.

I was seized with the desire to use this rare opportunity at once with my full strength. I tried with all haste to get to the main force, but the cow-itch hampered my progress and the irritation was maddening. Eventually we reached the camp before dark. My second in command, Major Kraut, had begun the attack with small forces. In the bright moonlight I could still hope to use the approaching night for a successful battle. All available forces, with the exception of a company left to protect the camp, were at once prepared for action.

On the left wing, Captain Goering, who was to undertake an enveloping movement, took his force round to a position in the rear of the enemy. There he heard the barking of a dog, ran forward at once and found the English commanding officer, Colonel Dickinson, with his adjutant and a medical officer, telephoning in a ravine and took them prisoner. Captain Goering at once attacked and the detachments of Captains Spangenberg and Poppe, in front and on the left wing, did the same. In a very short time the enemy, consisting of one battalion, was completely overwhelmed and routed. All the detachments engaged in a hot pursuit, but in the darkness and the thick bush touch was lost with the enemy.

It turned out later that the enemy's troops marching parallel with us had crossed the Namirrue at the same time a little further upstream. In view of the constantly changing situation, due to the continuous movement of the forces and the impenetrable screen of the bush which made it impossible to see far in any direction, and also owing to the large number of his marching columns, it was quite impossible for the enemy, in spite of the unremitting labours of his wireless service, to obtain a clear picture of the situation as a whole and to keep his subordinate leaders informed in time of all the changes of the situation. In this case a column had become detached and had run upon us with only a part of its strength: only one battalion had crossed the river. In an exposed and very dangerous position this battalion had been badly handled by our main force.

A company detailed for the further pursuit of the retreating enemy returned the following day without having achieved anything more; here, again, after such a favourable action the subordinate leaders and the troops themselves could only with difficulty be persuaded to throw themselves in to the last ounce to wring every possible advantage from their success. Lieutenant Schroetter, who then for several days carried on the pursuit in a manner in keeping with the situation, was unable to effect more than a few patrol skirmishes. The enemy had, in the meantime, gained too great a start. No information was obtained except as to the very hurried flight of the enemy.

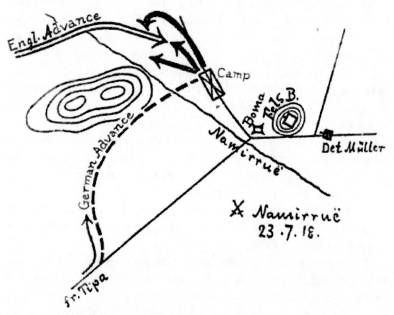

FIG. XIX. THE ACTION AT NAMIRRUE, JULY 23, 1918.

I, with the main part of my forces, stood my ground. The full exploitation of the success lay less in the pursuit of the beaten enemy than in the chances offered by the situation of the enemy we were surrounding on the hill, now that the help intended was for the moment unavailable.

For the first time in this campaign we had captured a trench-mortar with ammunition. The various parts were collected on the field of action and the seventeen rounds of ammunition made ready for firing. Experiments made with practice ammunition gave satisfactory results, and we were able to arrange for the bombardment of the enemy among the rocks at four o'clock in the afternoon. The command of this attack was entrusted to Captain Müller, whose detachment had not taken part in the fighting on the previous day and had known nothing about it. To this detachment was added Lieutenant von Ruckteschell's, which had remained in the camp. The trench-mortar was placed in position on one side of the hill, the gun on the other; our machine-guns were disposed round the hill in readiness for the attack.

At 3.45 Lieutenant von Ruckteschell took leave of the English Colonel Dickinson, who had been placed in his charge, saying that he expected to be back in an hour. At 4 o'clock the first round from our trench-mortar burst in the centre of the enemy's position. The enemy commander was just considering whether he should make a sortie during the night. In a moment the hill burst into life : everywhere men could be seen running up and down the rocks. They were brought under the fire of our gun and machine guns. Very soon the enemy showed the white flag, but continued to fire.

Lieutenant von Ruckteschell returned to his guest as he had promised, an hour later, but unfortunately with a shattered leg. His orderly who, when he was wounded, had tried to carry him out of the fight, was shot down under him. Meanwhile Captain Müller had climbed the hill from the other side and stormed the camp. It was occupied by a squadron of mounted infantry of the Gold Coast Regiment of whom hardly one came out alive. Even the horses were killed almost without exception.

On our side brave Lieutenant Selke was killed by an enemy bullet shortly before the storming of the camp. He was buried on the battlefield. The *matériel* captured was small, but the two days of fighting had cost the enemy heavy losses in men. His detachments, which were numerically hardly less strong than our own, were literally annihilated.

Here, as at Namacurra, it turned out that the English had conscripted black troops from German East Africa into their fighting force, including a considerable number of old German *Askari*.

Our thorough work at Namirrue had been made possible by Koehl's detachment, consisting only of three companies, which had kept us free from interference. This detachment had fallen back gradually from Tipa on Namirrue, daily fighting rear-guard actions with the enemy who was pressing on with all his strength. They were now within half a day's march of Namirrue and I ordered them across to the east bank of the Namirrue river. Patrols sent out to reconnoitre had meanwhile learned from the natives that there was an enemy depot with a garrison at Pekera. This seemed to me very probable, as Pekera lies in the thickly populated area east of the Ligonja River, said to be a fertile district. Our expectations were realized when after two days' march we arrived at Pekera.

The mounted squadron of the Gold Coast Regiment stationed there was at once destroyed and several motors were captured. In the same way we quickly took possession of the Boma of Chalau and a number of other stations where the Portuguese had stored large quantities of supplies, particularly pig-nuts. Our patrols advanced as far as Angoche and in a very short time we were masters of the wide and exceptionally fertile district. One night some of the Portuguese officer prisoners escaped and succeeded in joining the enemy troops at Angoche. Apparently there were among these gentlemen some who knew the country well by reason of their occupations in peace.

The period of rest during our stay in the Chalau district made it possible for our sick and wounded, who had been brought with us on the long marches, to recover; the fit, too, benefited by the respite. All had suffered more or less from the uninterrupted marching and exertions they had just gone through. It was noteworthy how the recent successes brought out the warlike spirit of the bearers, who were for the most part a very sound and reliable lot of men. A large number offered their services as *Askari*. Even my old cook was not disinclined to take up arms.

On 5th of August supplies began to run short and there remained as our chief article of diet only the still bitter *muhogo*. Several enemy patrols approaching us from the north-east showed me that the enemy columns following us from the south-west had actually overtaken us during our halt and were concentrating or an attack at Wamaka, north-east of our camp.

CHAPTER 6

Back to the Lurio River

In order to confirm the enemy in his mistake as to our objective I marched on 7th August along the road to Wamaka and pitched my camp three hours' march north-east of Chalau, in a good supply area. Several enemy patrols were driven off. From Wamaka an enemy officer appeared with a flag of truce to announce that the English commander-in-chief would like to arrange for an exchange of medical prisoners. He was also instructed to inform me as to when and where equipment for the English prisoners could be handed over to us. These very transparent proposals showed me that the enemy had something serious in hand from the north and was trying to make his task easier by enticing me into a trap. Various enemy spies were captured and confirmed my belief. Their report that the enemy intended to attack in three columns was in accordance with the usual plan of such undertakings.

When several patrol and outpost actions on 10th and 11th August indicated that a strong enemy column was advancing along the Wamaka-Chalau road, I assumed that at least one other column would be marching parallel with this further south; their objective was obviously Chalau. I decided to engage this southern enemy column by itself. The prospect of the success of my plan was certainly not great, as the enemy was marching for the most part through the bush, avoiding the paths. To meet such a development of the situation I had had a path reconnoitred and marked. In spite of this our march, begun in the evening of nth August, lasted through the whole night. Not until daybreak did we arrive east of Chalau at the place I had selected. Strong patrols, among them a whole company under Captain Koehl, were still on the march.

My general idea was a march west to enable me to turn either to the Blantyre district or east of Lake Nyassa. Without any hindrance from the enemy we crossed the Ligonja at Metil and the Tipa-Namirrue road. There the grave of an officer of the 1st battalion 2nd King's African Rifles proved that the enemy column, which had first followed us from Tipa to Namirrue, had gone round us to the north to Wamaka: for this 1st battalion 2nd King's African Rifles belonged to the force which was now approaching from Wamaka.

On the further march to Ili we passed through the camps of the enemy forces which had come from the south-west and had continued their march in the direction of Alto-Moloque. They too had made a wide detour and had accomplished correspondingly long marches. It was strange that all these enemy columns should suddenly display such a high degree of mobility; they had changed their supply system and, partially at any rate, left their lines of communication. According to the reports of prisoners they sent requisitioning parties on ahead to commandeer supplies from the natives, which were then distributed among the troops. This requisitioning of supplies seems to have been carried out with great ruthlessness. The confidence which the natives had shown during our recent stay in the Ili district had vanished. They now saw an enemy in every *Askari* and individual men who were left behind were on several occasions attacked by the natives.

When we came to Ili, the English telegraphic station situated there was quickly captured. The papers found there gave useful information as to the movements of the enemy troops. According to this there were considerable stores at Numarroe and Regone; strong forces were to try to overtake us from Alto-Moloque and Mukubi, while one column followed immediately on our track. The enemy, who up to a short time back had been groping in the dark, had apparently received, a few days before, reliable information as to our movements. It was very difficult to find the road to Regone, as no guides could be raised.

From Ili, however, a newly erected telephone line of copper wire led to Numarroe. If we followed this line we were sure to come upon something useful. As a matter of fact parts of the enemy columns were near us when we left Ili. The patrols we had left behind even met some *Askari* whom they took to be friends: they exchanged cigarettes and lights with these and did not realize until afterwards that they were enemies.

During these days I was much occupied with a domestic question. The supply of bread for the European prisoners became difficult in view of the prolonged marches. The men were unskilled and not in a position to help themselves. At last I succeeded in getting over the difficulty, and had considerable quantities of flour prepared by other methods. Captain Krüger, who had charge of the prisoners of war and died soon afterwards, was already very ill and exhausted by hardships; with the best intentions he had not always managed to find the ways and means of meeting the wishes of the prisoners, which were often very exacting.

In the morning of 24th August we crossed the Likungo River, and continued our march towards Numarroe. We could already see, several miles in breadth, the hill and the buildings of Boma Numarroe. During a halt we lunched in the congenial company of Lieutenant Ott, Sergeant-Major Nordenholz and the other officers of the advance guard. We had long grown accustomed during the halts to bring out, without ceremony, a piece of bread and a box of lard or hippopotamus fat. Naval Lieutenant Freund even still possessed some butter from Namacurra. Even the *Askari* and bearers, who formerly used to wait for their meal until camp was pitched, adopted more and more the "*desturi*" (manners, customs) of the Europeans. As soon as a halt was called every black would bring out his lunch. It was very jolly when the whole force bivouacked in this way in the forest, in the best of spirits, and refreshed themselves for fresh exertions, fresh marches and fresh fighting.

We were still two hours east of Numarroe when the advance guard was fired on. An enemy company had camped on our line of march and was slowly and cleverly retreating before us from *kopje* to *kopje* in the direction of Numarroe. Lieutenant Ott, who was shot through the chest, was in a very serious condition. With the main body led by Goering's detachment, I made a detour, and, passing the enemy to the south, made straight for the Boma of Numarroe. Before dark our gun was brought into position and fire opened on the *boma* and its entrenchments. Goering's detachment, without loss of time, made a still wider detour to the south in order, by using a ravine, to come close up to the *boma* in the rear. The advance guard (Müller's detachment), which was out of sound of the fighting, was also quickly brought up. The enemy shooting was not bad, and in spite of the distance the rifle bullets of the infantry came very close whenever one of us exposed himself.

It soon grew dark; the firing increased and died down again, until suddenly heavy firing was heard from the direction of Goering's detachment. Then there was silence. Goering's detachment had surprised the enemy in the rear and stormed some stubbornly defended trenches. The retreating enemy was, however, not recognized as the enemy by another German detachment and got away. The night was unpleasantly cold; it was pouring with rain and our baggage had not yet come up.

On the following day 3 enemy Europeans and 41 *Askari* were buried by us; 1 European and 6 *Askari* wounded, 1 European, 7 *Askari* and 28 other blacks unwounded were taken prisoner. Among the prisoners was the enemy commander, Major Garrod, who commanded the half of the 2nd battalion 4th King's African Rifles here. On our side, Sergeant-Major Nordenholz was shot through the head; 6 *Askari* and 1 machine-gun bearer were killed; 3 Europeans, 18 *Askari* and 4 machine-gun bearers were wounded; 40,000 rounds of ammunition and two light machine guns, in addition to hand-grenades, medical stores and large quantities of supplies, were captured. Among our wounded left behind in the clean, massively built houses was Lieutenant Ott, cheerful as ever. Fortunately, his wound was not so serious as was feared at first, but it was not possible to take him with us.

On August 25th I wanted at all costs to reach the camp of Regone. From captured papers I knew that valuable stores had been taken to Regone to be safe from us, including trench-mortar ammunition. Regone was probably, for the moment, still weakly garrisoned. In view of the proximity of the enemy columns it might, however, be assumed that August 26th would already be too late for a *coup de main*. The path led through a pass in the steep rocky hills.

During the march our advance guard soon came upon the enemy and engaged him, while I, with the main force, passed round this enemy and marched direct on Regone. During the climb over the hilly country, where it was only possible to see a short distance ahead, two German detachments, mistaking each other for the enemy, nearly became engaged. The machine guns were already in position when the mistake was fortunately discovered.

We then advanced further over the hills, while below us, already considerably in the rear, could be heard the machine-gun fire of our advance guard. The march was so difficult, and as we could only cross the hills in single file, our column was so long that Regone, my objective for that day, was not nearly reached. As a matter of fact we had no exact idea where Regone was. Only the fact that we could see in the distance the converging of several paths led us to conclude that Regone must lie there. Half way to Regone we saw a large encampment of tents which I took to be the other half of the battalion which had marched from Regone to the support of Numarroe.

In pouring rain we had to pitch our camp in the bush. On the next day the camp we had observed had been struck. The Boma of Regone was held in considerable strength. An attack on this place over the bare hills offered no prospect of success, and we confined ourselves to skirmishes with patrols and single detachments. As I had seen from his papers, the enemy had given orders that we should be allowed to strike at Regone unhindered and then attacked in the flank or rear by the strong reserves which lay outside.

It was therefore necessary to exercise particular caution, and the impetuosity with which Lieutenant Boell's company, in spite of all these considerations, advanced on the *boma* might have had serious consequences. Several enemy camps and columns outside the entrenchments were surprised by our fire and some supplies captured. The captured papers informed us of the approach of strong enemy columns from the south and south-east towards Regone. But there were also troops to the north; whether these were in the neighbourhood of Lioma-Malacotera or at Malema could not be ascertained. It was, however, certain that they were at hand and it was probable that they were approaching Regone, and that from the north.

As a *coup de main* against Regone offered no prospect of success, and a prolonged enterprise, in view of the intervention to be expected from outside, could not be relied on, I determined to resume the march. On account of the obstacles formed by the rivers and swamps south of Lake Nyassa, the line of march I had formerly decided on to the west appeared ill-advised, especially as the enemy could, with the help of steamers and railways, easily concentrate and maintain a force there. A further march north seemed to me more practicable, passing the lake on the east; it seemed probable that our return to German East Africa would be a complete surprise to the enemy, who would take our objective to be the natural capital of this district, Tabora.

Under this impression he might be expected, in order to save his main force the difficult overland march to Tabora, to withdraw to the Portuguese coast, take ship from there to Dar-es-Salaam, and proceed by rail to Tabora. These calculations were to a large extent realized. It was natural that, having reached the north end of Lake Nyassa, I should continue my march, not to Tabora but in another direction, probably west. In any case, the first thing was to reach the north end of the lake. This could not be done in less than a month and meanwhile the situation might alter considerably.

At Regone we observed the concentration of strong enemy forces, who examined our camps immediately after our departure but followed us only slowly. The country, with its numerous ravines and water-courses, was particularly favourable to us. On the way to Lioma a considerable enemy supply dump was captured, including a large quantity of tobacco. Müller's detachment, which had gone on ahead to Lioma, soon reported the enemy occupation of this place, but could not obtain any exact information as to his strength. I reached this advance detachment on 30th August with the main force. The position of the enemy entrenchments in the thick bush had not yet been located with any exactness. Apparently he had only just arrived and had not yet completed his works. I therefore attacked immediately. The detachments of Müller and Goering marched round the enemy to take him from the north. Meanwhile the main force gradually closed in along several ravines in the forest.

In view of the lack of information I could get no clear picture of the situation. Suddenly lively firing was heard from the rear, where our carrier columns were still on the march. A strong enemy patrol had unexpectedly opened fire on our bearers. A great part of our baggage was lost. Captain Poppe, who with two companies was standing by in case I required him, was sent to attack. He could no longer find the patrol, but followed their line of retreat and came upon an entrenched camp which he immediately stormed. Sergeant-Major Schaffrath was severely wounded.

These events were personally reported to me by Captain Poppe, who was brought back severely wounded in the chest. He reported that the enemy had been completely defeated, and that large captures of arms and ammunition had been made. The companies of Poppe's detachment had pursued the fleeing enemy and come upon a fresh and larger camp. This same camp was also attacked from the north by Goering's detachment, so that the enemy was taken under an effective cross fire. Meanwhile, a new enemy, advancing from the north-east, was held up by Müller's detachment.

I did not get anything like a clear view of these different events until I personally reconnoitred the position long after dark. On one of these reconnaissances an enemy rifle-bullet, of which many were being fired, passed through the trousers of one of my companions (Hauter, of the *Landsturm*), struck my other companion, Lieutenant

Besch, in the thigh and severed the artery. Fortunately we were near the dressing station. I was thus able to take leave of this officer, who had hitherto acted as quartermaster and at the same time had undertaken the duties of orderly officer, with the knowledge that he would recover. His few possessions he gave to his companions together with his wishes for good luck for the future. I, too, was honoured with a handful of cigarettes. It was my habit to smoke continuously during serious fighting.

In the middle of the bush I met Lieutenant Von Ruckteschell with some bearers, on his stretcher which he was forced to use temporarily because of his wounded leg, which had not yet healed; he had kept the column together as far as possible during the long march and now, rifle in hand, was beaming with joy at the possibility of taking part in the engagement with the enemy patrol which appeared on the flank and in our rear. Part of our columns had lost their way in the thick bush and only found us some hours later. After nightfall the dressing station in a ravine had been filled with wounded. It was reported that Lieutenant Schroetter and Naval Lieutenant Freund had fallen. In a further patrol-attack, Sergeant-Majors Bolles and Hüttig accidentally came close to the enemy positions and were fired on suddenly; Bolles fell, Hüttig was captured, severely wounded. Sergeant-Major Thurmann had come within five yards of the enemy trenches, and being an excellent shot he repeatedly picked off from an ant-hill any of the enemy inside the camp who exposed himself, until he, too, received a mortal wound.

Captain Goering, regarding it as hopeless to storm the camp, did not attempt this and, after dark, withdrew the force, leaving only patrols in front of the enemy. The main force was thus collected in several groups north of the enemy camp, and I decided to evacuate the scene of action on the following day and march on.

By force of necessity we had to leave behind part of our sick and wounded, as well as the sick prisoners, in charge of an English medical officer, and at nine o'clock in the morning we began our march north in several columns. We had no guides; the country was quite unknown to us and I could only give the Commander of the advance guard general instructions that I intended to pass round one of the hills that lay before us to the north. Soon firing could he heard from the advance guard.

It gradually became clear in the bush that our advance guard had turned against an enemy who had attacked in the rear from the left.

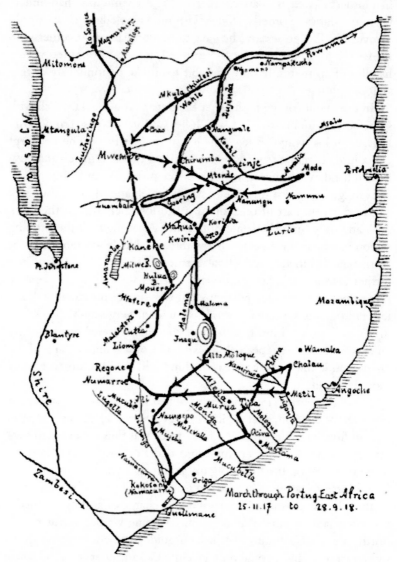

FIG. XX. THROUGH PORTUGUESE EAST AFRICA.

The shooting was at close range, and from Headquarters, which was with the main body, seemed to come from a considerable force.

I sent back an *Askari* to lead the head of the main force to the place where I was. The position certainly invited us to catch the enemy between our advance guard and our main force, and overwhelm him. I waited, but our main force did not arrive. At last I ran back and saw from the tracks that the main force had been wrongly guided and had marched past us a long way to the side. On the other hand, I saw the head of Stemmermann's detachment, to which the greater part of our columns and our sick belonged, in the very act of marching unwittingly straight into the enemy. There was just time to head off this detachment.

I myself now joined the advance detachments of Müller and Goering, who had meanwhile continued their march further north. They were following a road which led up the hill and was then completely lost. I paid no further attention to the firing which I heard from time to time further to the rear. In the late afternoon I was astonished to notice that the rest of the troops had not followed the detachments of Müller and Goering, but were marching along the valley to our right. I had no idea that our column had meanwhile been fired on again by a new enemy from the east and that a great part of a field hospital had fallen into the enemy's hands.

In order to bring the force together, I tried to descend from my hill. The descent, however, proved impossible; the rocks were steep, almost perpendicular. We continued along a native path, and evening was falling when Captain Müller reported that this path, too, ended abruptly in a precipice. Fortunately there was another small bypath. This we followed and succeeded in climbing down. Even here it was very steep in places, but the bare feet of the carriers gave them a good foothold and I, too, after taking off my boots, managed the descent. It was pitch dark and we had no water. At last, however, we found some, and a load fell from my heart when we came upon the rest of the force which, under General Wahle, had, on their side, been trying to join us.

On the 30th and 31st of August, we had lost 6 Europeans, 23 *Askari* killed; 11 Europeans, 16 *Askari* wounded; 5 Europeans, 29 *Askari* missing; 5 *Askari* taken prisoner; 48,000 rounds of ammunition, important medical and surgical stores, a considerable number of rifle parts and the whole transport of Müller's detachment had been lost. The enemy losses were also severe, as appeared from a casualty list of the 1st battalion 1st King's African Rifles which was captured later. In addition to this battalion part of the 3rd battalion of this regiment and the 2nd King's African Rifles had taken part in the fighting against us.

Our men fought brilliantly; some of the carriers, it is true, had been somewhat unnerved by the unexpected fire and more than 200 were missing. There was no news of Koehl's detachment, but our leaders had become so experienced and skilled in bush warfare that there was no need for me to be anxious. On the next day, on arrival at our camp, we surprised an English supply column.

We then crossed the Cutea-Malema road on which enemy troops also appeared, and then crossed the Lurio River at Mtetere. An English requisitioning force fled and some supplies were captured. Here Koehl's detachment rejoined the main force. They had followed the enemy who was following us and had ascertained that he was several battalions strong. We then marched down the Lurio to the fertile district of Mpuera. Here Sol (Sergeant-Major) Salim, who, during an earlier patrol expedition, had married a wife who had followed him faithfully, left her behind with her father, the local *Jumbo*, in view of her approaching confinement.

As there was plenty of food in this district, I gave our troops, who had been very exhausted by recent events, a day's rest. It was necessary, anyhow, in the interests of our numerous invalids. Captain Koehl had been left behind with his company without transport so that he could do the enemy as much damage as possible. He reported that strong bodies of enemy troops had arrived in the neighbourhood and east of Mtetere. It was clear that for the time being the enemy was devoting his whole energies to pursuing us, and for that purpose had concentrated all his forces. On that account I did not think the moment favourable for some partial success, because it could not be exploited, and an action would have cost us wounded whom we could not take away with us. As my idea was to forage the district north of Luambala for food, I was unwilling to postpone the march thither any longer.

The day of rest, September 5th, was employed in completing our food supplies from the fertile region of Mpuera, and early on the 6th we continued our march in a northerly direction. It was to be assumed that the enemy would march downstream, and therefore in a north-easterly direction, in several columns. Our troops advanced in order of echelon through the bush, and I expected any moment to come across the most northerly of the enemy columns, but we crossed its probable course without discovering its tracks.

About midday we were approaching our objective, a water-hole on Mount Hulua. Here our advance guard was shot at and before long a lively action was in progress. Captain Müller, in command of the advance guard, had stumbled on the rear of a hostile column which was marching north-east on a course making an acute angle with ours. He had immediately attacked the 2nd battalion 2nd King's African Rifles, which was at the end of the column, and put it to flight, capturing the enemy's field-hospital and his mule train.

I deployed Goering's detachment on the right of Müller's detachment, and it quickly threw back part of the opposing forces, but did not press on as the enemy deployed larger bodies—the 1st battalion of the 2nd King's African Rifles and apparently parts of the 3rd battalion as well.

Our left wing, which had arrived in rolling, open country in its advance, and also collided with fresh hostile troops, had retired a few hundred yards and occupied a slight eminence, giving a field of fire of several hundred yards. I was not able to get a clear picture of the situation until I went from the right wing, where I had joined Goering's detachment, back to the left.

The action was pretty violent and at length came to a standstill. We now heard the sound of trench-mortar fire coming from the rearguard, under Captain Spangenberg, whose arrival I was awaiting. The rearguard had beaten off the attack of another enemy column at Mpuera and driven part of it away in disorderly flight. In accordance with its instructions it had followed the main body at seven o'clock in the morning. It arrived on the battlefield about five in the afternoon, and I considered whether I ought not to throw in all my reserves to inflict a decisive defeat on the 2nd King's African Rifles there and then on Mount Hulua. I gave up the idea, however. Time was very short, for there was only an hour to darkness, and I felt perfectly certain that very early next morning fresh hostile forces would appear on the scene.

If we were to achieve a decisive victory it would certainly cost us appreciable losses, and I was anxious to avoid such losses in view of the small numbers—176 Europeans and 1,487 *Askari*—which our strength return of September 1, 1918, revealed. Lieutenant Wenig (Navy), who had been employed with his gun in Goering's detachment, told me that he had taken over the command of that detachment, because all the other officers were incapacitated. Before long, Captain Goering, with a severe wound in the breast, and Lieutenant

Boell, with one in the head, were brought to the dressing station. Accordingly I would not commit our reserves to the confusion and uncertainty of a night battle in the bush, and determined to slip away from the battlefield in a north-westerly direction. It was soon quite dark and our progress was very slow in the thick, high grass. After going three miles we bivouacked.

Our losses in the action of September 6th had been 5 *Askari*, 4 machine-gunners killed; 13 Europeans, 49 *Askari*, and 15 other natives wounded; 3 Europeans, 13 *Askari*, and 12 carriers missing; 3 *Askari* and 3 bearers captured. The enemy were seen to have some 10 Europeans and 30 *Askari* hit, while 8 Europeans and 45 *Askari* were captured; those of the prisoners who were sick or wounded, and our own more severely wounded, were left on the battlefield under the charge of English R.A.M.C. Documents captured later on at Mwembe showed that "*Karturol*" (abbreviation for "Column of the 2nd King's African Rifles") had heavy losses on the 6th September and was put out of action for a time.

The enemy did not molest our further progress. Captain Koehl had remained behind with his company to the west of Mpuera, in order to operate from the rear against the enemy and his communications. He followed our trail, having slight encounters at Milweberg with the 1st battalion of the 4th King's African Rifles, which arrived at that point from the south on the 8th September. We moved in several columns right through the bush, a region rich in game. We even killed several buffaloes on the march. At Kanene we crossed the road that ran from Lake Amaramba to Mahua.

The enemy had burnt down the store at Kanene, but we found ample supplies in the country itself, and the material condition of the troops would have been good, if only the influenza epidemic had not made such strides. About half had bronchial catarrh, and from three to six men in each company had inflammation of the lungs; as it was only possible for some eighty sick to be carried in the whole force, about twenty men suffering with slight inflammation of the lungs had to march at times. No satisfactory solution of the problem of transport of sick was to be found, short of abandoning the campaign; we could not simply leave the sick to die in the bush.

This difficult position inevitably placed the greatest possible strain on the nerves of Surgeon-Major Taute, our splendid senior medical officer. It was the greatest good fortune that this officer, singularly gifted both in medicine and in organization, proved equal to his grave responsibility. We owe it to the measures adopted by him, as well as to the change of district and climate forced upon us by circumstances, that the epidemic soon abated. A number of *Askari* and other natives not in a fit state for heavy work followed the force slowly; many of them lost courage when they continually found our camping-places empty. A large number, however, caught up with us, especially when the force did one of its short marches, or was able (a rare occurrence enough) to take a day's rest.

CHAPTER 7

On German Soil Once More

But we could not afford many halts. The military position impera-
tively demanded that we should pass quickly through the districts to
the east of the centre of Lake Nyassa, which were not fertile and had
been largely stripped in the latest period of the war. Rapidity was all
the more essential as it was possible for the enemy to move troops by
sea to the north end of the lake and thus anticipate us by strongly occupying the district there. As we approached the River Ludjenda, the
ground became more mountainous and was scored with many water-
courses and ravines. We could not simply march by the compass, but
had to have regard to the watershed and keep along the mountain
ridge. Fortunately, the leader of the advance guard, Captain Spangenberg, found some natives who acted as pathfinders and made it much
easier to discover a good route. But a certain amount of doubling was
unavoidable, and that retarded our progress, while the enemy were in
a position to move troops and supplies swiftly from Malacotera along
a good road to Luambala.

I was somewhat anxious to know whether the water of the River
Ludjenda would have fallen sufficiently to enable us to use the fords. It
would no doubt have been easy to construct bark boats, but the transport of the whole force could hardly have gone smoothly forward,
having regard to the violence of the current. In any case, I thought
it most important that there should be no enemy opposition, and
that again made haste essential. Fortunately patrols which we sent
ahead found a ford below Luambala, where the wading of the river
presented no difficulty. Several slaughtered hippopotami enabled us
to prepare some fat again, and in the neighbourhood of Mwembe,
which we reached on the 17th September, we were able to replenish
our supplies once more. At this point we took our first day's rest for

a long time.

It was here at Mwembe that the lung epidemic reached its crisis. Since the middle of August, 7 Europeans and about 200 natives had been attacked, of whom 2 Europeans and 17 natives had died. The stores at Mwembe had been destroyed by the weak enemy posts, but there were still ample supplies to be had in the district. The question of carriers began to cause anxieties. The men had been severely tested by the continual marching, by the epidemic, and by the carriage of the sick; and we were approaching their home districts. It was probable that the Wangoni carriers would desert the moment they reached their home, which lay to the north of the Rovuma. In the district of Mwembe and the well-cultivated valleys of the River Luscheringo, several patrols of the enemy "Intelligence Department" were encountered; true, they were easily driven off, but their presence showed that the enemy was in the main aware of our movements.

We sent long-distance patrols towards Mitomoni and Makalogi. To the south of the Rovuma, after leaving the Luscheringo valley, the steppe through which our march led us was amazingly rich in game, as was the Rovuma itself, which we reached on the 28th September. But the big game had its drawbacks, for once again a sentry was killed by lions. We came on to German soil again, and stayed two days at Nagwamira; we surprised several enemy depots and columns, which had had no news of our appearance. The country was amazingly fertile, and the troops were able to get thoroughly fit again.

Our patrols sent out towards Mitomoni reported a camp somewhat strongly held and the arrival of reinforcements coming from the west. Ssongea, too, was occupied by the enemy, but in what strength could not be ascertained. Various reports, as well as the geographical position, made it likely that reinforcements were also on their way to Ssongea from Lake Nyassa.

We continued our march, moving in the direction of Ssongea, and southwards of this place came into thickly settled country. The enemy wireless disclosed that enemy troops were present in Ssongea, and that another column had arrived in the neighbourhood, in all probability from Mitomoni. On the 4th October I passed Ssongea on the west and continued to the north. When the advance guard under Captain Spangenberg reached the high road from Ssongea to Wiedhafen, it was attacked with trench-mortars by three enemy companies, which had come from the west. The enemy was forced back a little. On account of the hilly and ravine-scored nature of the ground and the advanced hour, it was improbable that we could achieve a really effective success on this day. By the morrow, however, there would be further enemy troops on the spot. I accordingly carried the attack no further, and marched by to the west of the enemy into a camp at the Peramiho mission station.

As we passed through the Wangoni territory, a large number of our carriers deserted, as we had feared would happen. It would after all have been asking too much of human nature, to expect that these men, who had not seen their people for years, should now march straight through their native district. The nigger's love of home is too strong. Even Samarunga, one of my own carriers and a very devoted and trustworthy fellow, asked for leave to visit his village, which lay nearby. He came back faithfully enough and brought his brother with him. The two then marched on with us, and Samarunga stayed on even when his brother left. To revive his depression, I gave him some of my meat ration, but on the next morning he proved to have disappeared after all, having first put all my things in order.

To the north of Ssongea a few enemy reconnoitring patrols were again met with. Day after day we moved through territory formerly fertile and well settled. Thousands of farmers could settle there in a healthy and beautiful climate. On the 14th October, we reached Pangire (Jacobi), a pleasantly situated mission station, in which, before the war, the missionary Gröschel had entertained me on my last tour. The missionary's family had been removed, but the natives, who were of the Wabena tribe, had remained, and received us as in peace time, in a most friendly manner. Several old *Askari*, also, who had left the force for one reason or another, now reported again. Here, too, some patrols were met with and driven off.

In the Wabena country, which is well stocked with cattle, our very scanty stocks were replenished, and a mobile food-reserve thus constituted, which helped greatly to lighten our transport. After we had quitted Pangire, a patrol that we had left there was fired on by an enemy detachment. Near Ubena our rearguard, under Captain Müller, was attacked by several enemy companies arriving from the south. A fairly strong enemy column was thus following our track. The free open *steppes* of Ubena were not favourable ground for us to fight on, as they were commanded from long range by rifle and gun fire. Several reports were also received of the advance on Ubena of strong enemy forces from Mwakete; these reports proved to be in part incorrect, and led to a short fight between two German patrols.

It was highly probable, and later it proved to be the case, that enemy troops would be moved by water to the northern end of Lake Nyassa and march from there on Ubena or further to the north. If I desired to give up the march towards Tabora, and to move instead between Lakes Nyassa and Rukwa, and later between Lakes Nyassa and Tanganyika, to Rhodesia, the time for the change of direction was now approaching and there was not a day to lose; this was all the more so as our freedom of movement was severely restricted by the steep slopes of Mount Livingstone and the hills round Mbeja. In settling our line of march we had to bear in mind that our stocks of provisions had dwindled considerably and required replenishing. Native information pointed to this being possible in the region of Kidugala and Sombowano, while famine was said to be raging in Ussangu, and especially round New Utengule.

On the 17th October, I quitted Ubena with the main body, leaving behind there, sick or wounded, General Wahle, two other Europeans, and some *Askari*. I reached Kidugala on this day. Koehl's detachment followed on the 18th October. On the same day, the Boma Ubena was occupied by some 100 enemy *Askari*, while 200 to 300 advanced northwards to the Iringa road. We learnt from captured newspapers that Cambrai had fallen on the 29th September and that the Belgians had advanced three kilometres west of Roubaix. We read, too, of the cessation of hostilities in Bulgaria, of the retirement of Count Hertling, and of the capture of St. Quentin and Armentieres. But positions could be given up for so many different reasons that I did not attribute any decisive importance to this news.

Our further march past Ngombowano and Brandt led us through a district well stocked with cattle. Missions and schools had been deserted, but we were very glad to find garden fruits, especially mulberries and peaches. In the bush we also found great quantities of wild figs and other sweet and tasty fruits. Small patrol encounters indicated that enemy troops were moving direct from Lake Nyassa northwards into the Brandt district. In Ruiwa we found large English depots, and we had to destroy a whole warehouse full of leather. We went on to the mission of Old Utengule, also well known to me from peace time, and now lying deserted. We then reached Mbozi mission, where the English had assembled the men from the district, examined them, and sent them to New Langenburg, probably in order to turn them into *Askari* there. At Mbozi there was a large English depot, containing, among other things, 75 loads of salt and 47 loads of coffee.

It was difficult to feel our way through the district. In the main it was but little known to us, and for years the enemy had been altering it by building storehouses and transport roads. To have reconnoitred in advance would have made too great a demand on our time and strength, besides depriving us of the advantage of surprise. The inhabitants were very hostile to the English and rendered us valuable service, but their information was too often very vague. While we rested a day in Mbozi and replenished our stores, our patrols were far afield, one towards Galula (St. Moritz' mission), another towards Itaka, one in the direction of New Langenburg, and one in that of Fife. Some of them would be away for weeks, and we could not wait for their reports.

This much, however, became clear, that a main communication road of the enemy ran past Mbozi from Fife *via* Rwiba to New Langenburg. On this road we captured a lot of stores and several supply columns on the march. The existence of this road showed that a large English depot must lie in the neighbourhood of Fife. It would probably be possible to capture this by swift action, before stronger enemy forces arrived there. On the morning of 31st October a fighting patrol was dispatched against Fife. On the evening of the same day natives and patrols reported the advance of strong enemy forces on the New Langenburg-Rwiba road. In the early morning of the 1st November I moved off with the whole force, advancing in the first instance towards Mount Rwiba. There the track showed that a strong enemy column had passed the Rwiba hill shortly before us, in the direction of Fife. This enemy force had not been observed by a German fighting patrol that had been sent out to Mount Rwiba.

CHAPTER 8

The Advance Into British Rhodesia

The second patrol dispatched by us on the 31st October towards Fife had halted at Mount Rwiba. I had now to advance with the whole force towards Fife, in order to reach it before the enemy, or to attack if our first patrol should prove to be engaged there. The ten-hour march (actual marching time) from Mbozi to Fife was a tremendous strain on the force, but the reports of our patrols, the track of the enemy, and his notes found on the trees, proved beyond a doubt that the enemy was doing everything possible to reach Fife on the same day, the 1st November. The great distance which they, too, had to march justified us in assuming that our patrol, which I expected would reach Fife on the 31st October, or at the latest on the 1st November, would be equal to preventing the enemy occupying the depot at Fife on the 1st.

In the course of the afternoon we fired on several patrols, without halting in our advance. Late in the afternoon weak enemy detachments in the hills near Fife were quickly thrown back. I myself, with Spangenberg's detachment, which had moved off the road to the right, advanced along a mountain ridge on to a point where we judged that Fife would lie.

The ground was becoming more open, being mainly covered with knee-high bush and grass, when a few hundred yards before us we observed men moving about and tents pitched close together. The men were moving about in such unconcerned fashion that I almost took them for our own patrol, but at 200 yards we were received with violent and at first very well directed rifle and machine-gun fire. It was fortunate that our men did not answer it, for I had happened to get in advance and was between the two parties. After a time the enemy, who had apparently become very excited, began to fire high. It started to grow darker, so that my patrol was able to get back to our line. We

285

had, at any rate, reached certainty. We knew that the enemy with a strength of several companies was lying before us in an entrenched position with a good field of fire. His advanced detachments had been thrown back. His depots lay in part outside the trenches, and later fell into our hands.

I did not want to undertake the storming of the position, which would have been costly, but the opportunity seemed favourable to bombard the enemy, massed as he was in the position, with our trench-mortar, and also from a height with our gun, as well as with rifle and machine-gun fire if he should show himself. Our machine guns were accordingly moved forward in the night close to his position and en-trenched. Reconnaissance for a good gun position was postponed to the next day.

It was probable that the opening of our trench-mortar and gunfire would lead the enemy advancing from New Langenburg to attack us. Such an attack against our heights would have been very difficult. But in spite of the bombardment on the 2nd November, which was observed to cause some losses, no new enemy appeared. The defi-nite success for which we hoped against the camp was not achieved, since our trench-mortar was destroyed at one of the first shots by a prematurely bursting shell. Flat trajectory fire alone could do noth-ing against the well-protected enemy. In the afternoon, therefore, our main body, with its herds of cattle more than 400 strong, marched off, between Fife and the Mwenzo mission towards Rhodesia. When we had reached camp, we saw heavy columns of smoke rising from the depots at Fife, to which Müller's detachment had set fire after our departure. From the direction of the Mwenzo mission we heard short bursts of fire on several occasions.

Reports came in gradually from that direction. In addition to our fighting patrols dispatched from Mbozi, other patrols of ours had ar-rived, and had fought with English patrols, and also with each other. One report stated that one enemy patrol had been observed with quite dark uniforms, hitherto unknown, and that it must be some re-cently arrived body. After many inquiries I finally ascertained that one of our own patrols, whose equipment was certainly no longer quite in accord with regulations, had been continually mistaken for the enemy. In the Mwenzo mission itself there was a stationary enemy hospital, from which we were able to replenish our medical stores. Our quinine stocks were brought up to over fourteen kilos., supplies thus being insured until June, 1919.

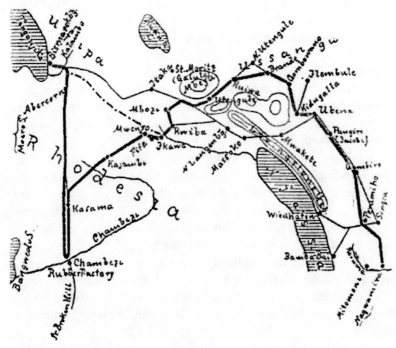

FIG. XXI. THE MARCH INTO RHODESIA.

Various reports and statements of prisoners showed that enemy transport was moving from the Broken Hill district to Kasama, and from there onwards to Fife, with motor-cars and ox-wagons. Kasama itself seemed to be a large place and an important road centre. In any case, we could expect enemy depots on the way from Fife to Kasama, and Kasama itself would be a valuable objective. So far as one could tell from the map, the position also seemed to be such that we should be able there to decide to go further southwards round Lake Bangweolo and reach the Zambesi-Congo watershed, or to march further westwards between Lakes Bangweolo and Moero. The information was certainly very uncertain, resting almost exclusively on several *Askari*, who as children had been employed in trade caravans in the neighbourhood of Lake Moero.

The important question of the nature of the rivers, and in particular of the Luapala, which flowed from Lake Bangweolo into Lake Moero, was for the time quite unsolved. We did not clear up these points until we captured some maps and notes. About this time, according to these, the Luapala was a mighty barrier; deep and in many places very broad; it is enclosed by extended marshes. In the rainy season that was just approaching, any attempt to cross the river in canoes would meet with difficulties, since on our approach the canoes would certainly be removed to the opposite bank or concealed. I devoted every minute to the study of maps and travel-descriptions, burying myself in them at every halt in the march. There was great danger that in ignorance of our position we might run into an impasse in this region of great rivers and lakes.

The first thing was to sweep rapidly along the communication road Fife-Kajambi mission-Kasama. Mobile detachments were sent on by forced marches, capturing several small depots, taking their guards prisoner, and also securing a few ox-wagon teams. Captain Spangenberg followed immediately with three companies, and then the main body, at a distance of about one day's march.

The heavy marches and the deviation to the south-west, into quite new and unknown territory, was too much for a number of carriers. On one single day there deserted from the staff 20 Wafiri, who had their homes in the region of Bismarckburg, and 13 carriers from other districts.

The main body arrived at Kajambi on the 6th November. The Catholic mission station there consists of wonderful, spacious and massive buildings. The missionaries had fled, quite unnecessarily. In the nuns' house there was a letter for me from a Catholic nun. She was a native of Westphalia, and as a fellow-countrywoman appealed to my humanity. She would certainly have spared herself many discomforts if both she herself and the other people attached to the mission had remained quietly at their posts. We should have done as little to them as we had done earlier to the old English missionary at Peramiho, near Ssongea. The soil was extraordinarily fertile; in the mission garden magnificent strawberries were growing.

At midday we heard rifle fire from the rearguard, which was encamped two hours' march north-east of Kajambi; Captain Koehl had remained there to gather supplies, and his Europeans and *Askari* had largely been distributed into separate supply patrols. In this situation he was attacked by an enemy patrol. Captain Koehl extricated himself from this unpleasant position and on the next day established his front by Kajambi mission, and we had the opportunity, which we used with great success, to take the enemy under our fire by surprise.

On the 7th November our main body resumed its march on Kasama. The enemy were not observed to be following up. If, however, they were to press on behind us, it was to be assumed that questions of supply would prevent their doing so in really great strength. We had the prospect of swiftly seizing Kasama, and then of making this place our base and giving battle under favourable conditions.

But these were hopes of the future; the first thing was to take Kasama itself quickly; according to our information it was not strongly held, but was well fortified. Captain Spangenberg with the advance guard kept increasing his distance from the main body by longer and longer marches. I followed with the main body; ample supplies were found, and we also met with confirmation of the descriptions given in various books to the effect that the forest is well stocked with tasty bush fruits.

On the 8th November Spangenberg's detachment had several patrol fights to the north of Kasama, and on the 9th it took Kasama, whose garrison, in the strength of half a company, retired to the southward. Only a little ammunition was captured and there was little else of value in the armoury. There was a large repair shop for motor and other vehicles, and more than a score of Boer wagons were taken. There was considerable booty in food supplies for Europeans. It was noteworthy that an English company in Kasama—I think it was the African Lakes Corporation—had given written instructions for the destruction of its depots by the natives. These came in large numbers to loot, and Spangenberg's detachment found buildings and their contents largely destroyed by looting natives. It is due to his action that among other things the house of the British Commissioner, which was built and furnished with great taste, was preserved.

During our advance from Fife it had appeared that the further we went the fuller were the enemy depots. We gained the impression that we were working up a line of communications which started around Broken Hill or somewhat to the north of it, and was only just being established. We had grounds for hoping that if we moved rapidly forward, we should find depots even more plentifully stocked; and the documents taken, besides information from natives, seemed to confirm this. Three days' march further along the telephone line, large stores were said to be lying at the Chambezi Ferry, which had in part been brought thither by boat. I myself on the 11th November cycled to Kasama and met Captain Spangenberg there, and he immediately resumed his march, with two companies, southwards, in the direction of the Chambezi Ferry.

On the 12th November the main body reached Kasama. Towards evening rifle and machine-gun fire was heard from the direction of our march. Our rearguard had been attacked in its camp, two hours to the north of Kasama. The enemy who had fought at Kajambi had not followed us directly, but had taken a parallel course. In the evening Koehl's detachment arrived in Kasama. I had now formed the opinion that the attempt on the Chambezi depot was the more promising and important undertaking, especially as the whole position made it probable that the pursuing enemy would continue to follow and thus again afford us an opportunity to give battle.

CHAPTER 9

The Armistice and Our Return
Home

Accordingly only Koehl's detachment remained at Kasama, with instructions to follow us a day's march behind. Early on November 13th I followed Spangenberg's detachment with our main body. I had gone on ahead on a bicycle, selected the site for our camp and was waiting for the troops to come up when Captain Müller appeared before me, also on his bicycle, and reported that an armistice had been concluded. An English motorcyclist who was to have brought the news to the British troops had apparently passed through Kasama and been captured there by Koehl's detachment. Thanks to the English telephone line, along which we were marching, we were soon able to understand each other, and thus did we get the news of the armistice. The telegram of the motorcyclist ran as follows:

12. 11. 18. To be fwded. *via* M.B. cable and despatch rider.
Send following to Colonel von Lettow Vorbeck under white flag. The Prime Minister of England has announced that an armistice was signed at 5 hours on Nov. nth, and that hostilities on all fronts cease at n hours on Nov. 11th. I am ordering my troops to cease hostilities forthwith unless attacked, and of course I conclude that you will do the same. Conditions of armistice will be forwarded you immediately I receive them. Meanwhile I suggest that you should remain in your present vicinity in order to facilitate communication.—General van Deventer. As message is also being sent to Livingstone, it is important Karwunfor receives this same time as enemy; every effort must be made to get message to him today.

Our feelings were very mixed. Personally, as I had no knowledge of the real state of affairs in Germany, I felt convinced that the conclusion of hostilities must have been favourable, or at least not unfavourable to Germany.

Spangenberg's detachment, which was on ahead, had to be told as soon as possible, and I immediately set out on my bicycle after it, taking with me Hauter, a *Landsturm* soldier, as my sole companion. About half-way, Reissmann's cyclist patrol of Spangenberg's detachment met me and reported that Captain Spangenberg had arrived at the Chambezi. Although I had no doubts about the correctness of the English news, our position was very uncomfortable. We were in a district where there was little food, and were therefore compelled to move on from place to place. This circumstance had already compelled us to reconnoitre and secure for ourselves the crossings of the Chambezi. If hostilities were resumed we must be certain of a safe crossing.

This was a burning question, as the rainy season, meaning a great rise of this river, was near at hand. We had already encountered heavy storms. I had, therefore, much to discuss with Captain Spangenberg and the English officer who would presumably be on the far bank of the river. In any case we must continue to devote our energies to buying or getting food. Full of that idea, I sent my companion back and cycled myself with Reissmann's patrol to Spangenberg's detachment.

We arrived about eight o'clock, when it was quite dark. Captain Spangenberg was away on a reconnaissance, but Assistant-Paymaster Dohmen and other Europeans looked after me well as soon as they learnt of my arrival. I was able to convince myself that the supply depot of Kasama really existed. I tasted jam and other good things which had been unknown to me hitherto.

When Captain Spangenberg came back he told me that he had already heard of the armistice through the English. After I had gone to bed in his tent, he brought me about midnight a telegram from General Deventer which had been brought in by the English. It had come from Salisbury. It stated that Germany had accepted the unconditional handing-over of all troops operating in East Africa. Deventer added that he demanded the immediate surrender of all our English prisoners of war, and that we should march to Abercorn. All our arms and ammunition were to be given up at Abercorn, but our Europeans were to be allowed to keep their weapons.

The full text of the telegram ran as follows:

13. 11. 18. To Norforce. Karwunfor *via* Fife.

Send following to Colonel von Lettow Vorbeck under white flag : War Office London telegraphs that clause seventeen of the armistice signed by the German Govt. provides for unconditional surrender of all German forces operating in East Africa within one month from Nov. 11th.

My conditions are. *First*: hand over all allied prisoners in your hands, Europeans and natives to the nearest body of British troops forthwith. *Second*: that you bring your forces to Abercorn without delay, as Abercorn is the nearest place at which I can supply you with food. *Third*: that you hand over all arms and ammunition to my representative at Abercorn. I will, however, allow you and your officers and European ranks to retain their personal weapons for the present in consideration of the gallant fight you have made, provided that you bring your force to Abercorn without delay. Arrangements will be made at Abercorn to send all Germans to Morogoro and to repatriate German *Askari*. Kindly send an early answer, giving probable date of arrival at Abercorn and numbers of German officers and men, *Askari* and followers.

This was news enough if it were confirmed, and showed the desperate situation of the Fatherland. Nothing else could account for the surrender of a force still maintaining itself proudly and victoriously in the field.

Without being in a position to examine the ground in detail, I had to tell myself that the conditions imposed upon us were inevitable, and must be loyally carried out. I met the British Commissioner, who had come from Kasama to the Chambezi rubber factory, at the river at eight o'clock on the morning of the 14th. There I handed to him a telegram to His Majesty, in which I reported what had happened and added that I would act accordingly. The commissioner told me that the German fleet had revolted, and that a revolution had also broken out in Germany; further, if he was to accept a report which was official but had not yet been confirmed, the *Kaiser* had abdicated on November 10th. All this news seemed to me very improbable, and I did not believe it until it was confirmed on my way home months later.

All our troops, native as well as Europeans, had always held the conviction that Germany could not be beaten in this war, and were resolved to fight on to the last. Of course it was doubtful whether our resources would last out if the war lasted several years more, but we faced all possibilities tranquilly for at least another year. The men were well armed, equipped and fed, and the strategic situation at the moment was more favourable than it had been for a long time. The *Askari*, it is true, saw that our numbers were dwindling—we were still 155 Europeans., comprising 30 officers, medical officers and higher officials, 1,168 *Askari*, and about 3,000 other natives—but whenever I discussed this topic with one of my orderlies he always assured me: "I will always stick by you and fight on till I fall." Many others spoke to the same effect, and I am convinced that it was not merely a case of empty words.

In the afternoon of the 14th November, I cycled back to our main body and told the Europeans what I had learned at the Chambezi, and that it was my intention to carry out the conditions which had been officially communicated to me, conditions the accuracy of which I did not doubt.

Before the prisoners were released Colonel Dickinson, the most senior of them, came to look for me to say goodbye. He said that his period of captivity (it had been more than three months) had given him an interesting insight into our camp life, our marching methods, and the way in which we conducted our actions. He was full of praise for the simplicity of our arrangements and the absence of friction which distinguished our operations. There is no doubt he had been using his eyes.

Our *Askari* were now informed of the turn of affairs. It was to be anticipated that there would be difficulties when it came to settling up with them for their pay, which was years overdue, and the same applied to the carriers. Yet it was a matter of honour for us to see that these people, who had fought and worked for us with such devotion, should receive their rights. The sum involved—about one and a half million *rupees*—was relatively small, and so Lieutenant Kempner was sent out on a bicycle to get this sum from the English, or induce them to procure it as quickly as possible. Our repeated efforts were without result. We were told at different times and places that the matter was "under consideration" by the War Office, and there it remained. I never even received a reply to my telegram to the German Government in Berlin. There was nothing for it but to draw up lists of all the back pay that was due, and give the individual carriers and *Askari* certificates against it.

We then marched by short stages through Kasama to Abercorn. The British gave us further details about the armistice conditions. It appeared that not "unconditional surrender" (as General van Deventer had said originally) but "unconditional evacuation" was what was required. I made several protests against the interpretation of the British War Office, which made the word "evacuation" include surrender and disarming, but I received no answer either from the governments of the allied countries and the United States, or from the German Government.

In view of the doubtful interpretation of the word "evacuation," I considered whether I should not cut short negotiations and march to join the Belgians or somewhere else. But in comparison to the whole series of peace conditions which affected the Protective Force, this seemed a small point, and in the end I decided to go to Dar-es-Salaam, as General van Deventer required, though certainly in the expectation that in accordance with the terms the English would immediately send us back from there to Germany. As will appear later that expectation was not fulfilled.

Not far north of Kasama we came up with the enemy with whom we had fought our last engagement. They were the 1st battalion of the 4th King's African Rifles. I had to refuse the invitation of Colonel Hawkins (their estimable commander, who was barely thirty years old), communicated to me on the march by Colonel Dickinson, to bring all the German officers to lunch, much though I appreciated such an expression of chivalry. Yet Colonel Dickinson did not neglect to pay me his promised visit on one of the following days, and we had a very pleasant hour over a cup of coffee. I must record that the officers of this battalion, even in the somewhat difficult circumstances in which they were placed, behaved with great tact and with that regard which is due to an honourable foe. Hawkins told me that for reasons of supply he would not have been able to follow us any further, and in fact we had to help him out with cattle, of which we had an ample stock.

Lieutenant Kempner had gone on to Abercorn on his bicycle. When he came back I went there myself in a car which General Edwards had sent for me. My reception by General Edwards, as well as his Staff, was very kind. I put forward my point of view to General Edwards that I did not recognize any duty to surrender of our arms, but was ready to do so if I was thereby conferring some advantage, not on ourselves individually, but on the German Government. I was then informed that the arms we surrendered would form part of the quantity which Germany had to hand over to the Allied Governments in accordance with the terms of the armistice. Further, the surrender of our arms should not have the character of a laying-down of arms.

As regards the *Askari* and carriers, I was informed that the English would take them to an internment camp at Tabora, until the question of their pay had been settled and their repatriation arranged. The Europeans were to be interned at Dar-es-Salaam until their ship left, presumably, therefore, for a few days. Not only the *Askari* but the Europeans at Dar-es-Salaam were kept behind barbed wire for a month and a half and more.

The troops arrived at Abercorn on the 25th November. The English flag was waving on the parade-ground where the handing-over of arms took place, and this shows that the character of a surrender of our arms was not altogether avoided. What we handed over was as follows:

1 Portuguese gun, 37 machine guns (7 German, 16 heavy and 14 light English), 1,071 English and Portuguese rifles, 208,000 rounds, 40 rounds of artillery ammunition. The English were mighty quick at getting away the surrendered material. There was not a single modern German rifle among it! The strength of our troops was: the Governor, 20 officers, 5 medical officers, a doctor of the Voluntary Medical Detachment, a senior veterinary officer, a senior chemist, a field-telegraph officer, 125 European other ranks, 1,156 *Askari* and 1,598 carriers. The arrival of individual detachments was delayed for hours by heavy rain.

The camp for the *Askari* was surrounded by a thick thorn hedge, and was much too small. This led to a good deal of bad feeling among our *Askari*, which vented itself in frequent demonstrations against the English *Askari*. But at length our people resigned themselves to the uncomfortable conditions, and even General Edwards realized that the treatment provided an opportunity for unnecessary friction. We were not ordinary prisoners of war, whose escape he had to fear, but had given ourselves into his hands voluntarily in the performance of an unpleasant duty. He took precautions against similar occurrences during our march to Bismarckburg, and we went there with Hawkins' battalion and without the slightest friction.

On November 28th we bivouacked by the mighty waterfall of the River Kalambo, three hours' march from Bismarckburg. Here we remained several days, as the departure of the steamer from that place was being continually delayed. Many of my officers continually badgered me to know whether we could not fight on. These suggestions were far from comfortable, as I had already quite enough to do to consider how we should get out of so unpleasant a situation. But putting aside the difficulties involved, I could only feel glad and proud of such a revelation of true soldierly spirit, a spirit which did not shrink, even after we had handed over all our arms, from storming an enemy camp and once more procuring for ourselves the means to continue the war.

On December 3rd I received a telegram, dated the 2nd December, from General van Deventer. It ran as follows:

> I beg to acknowledge receipt of your telegram setting forth your formal protest against your troops being treated as prisoners of war. This will duly be forwarded to the War Office. Meanwhile I am sure you will recognise that pending the receipt through the War Office of a communication on the subject of the German Govt. I have had no choice but to act in accordance with the orders of the War Office, and treat your force as prisoners of war.

The same day the first lot of troops for transport went on board four ships. One of them, the *St. George*, had, in addition to its crew of English bluejackets and an escort officer, only the Governor and the officers of our force with their black servants. For food the English gave us corned beef, dates and biscuits, and Dr. Huber, the veterinary officer, looked after our bodily welfare here on board as carefully as he had done for so many years in the bush. The British commander, the escort officer and the whole crew were extraordinarily kind. After a short stop on the evening of the 3rd, at the Belgian station of Vua, a violent storm arose in the night. It tore away the awning and, among other things, carried off Dr. Huber's coat. The English sailors did all they possibly could for the Germans, who were quite wet through.

On December 5th we arrived at Kigoma. The place was under Belgian control, and the Belgians received us with a hospitality which could not have been anticipated. They displayed a tactful reserve to us which had never been shown before. Tables covered with cloths had been set out for all the Europeans, a sight we had not seen for years. Some red wine was produced. The Belgian Governor had sent his orderly officer, who spoke German fluently, to receive us officially, and I was glad to take the opportunity, before we started on our railway journey, to thank the Belgian commandant for the *camaraderie* shown us, *camaraderie* which always exists among soldiers, even between enemies, when they have a mutual regard for each other.

Among the English, too, examples of discourtesy on the part of individual officers, who apparently had not been brought up in the South, were absolutely exceptional. The senior men immediately adopted a tactful attitude, whereas one or two juniors did otherwise—for example, they were inconsiderate enough to want to keep a German invalid out of the compartment. We Europeans were very well looked after on the train, and it was like peacetime to get a good night's rest by letting down the bunks and using a leather pillow.

There was quite a crowd of Germans on the station at Tabora. They complained of many cases of theft on the part of the Belgians and English. It is undoubtedly true that such outrages had taken place. We stopped for the night at Dodoma and next morning had an opportunity of fetching water and having a bath.

The news of the approach of our train had reached Morogoro, and when we arrived there in the afternoon we once more found the German women whom we had left behind us in and about Morogoro two years before. They had tea and coffee waiting for us. They had arranged tables and baked plenty of rolls and cakes. In addition they had got the finest fruit for us. The English were almost as much interested as the Germans. Besides a very amiable elderly medical officer I have a particularly lively recollection of a tall, lanky corporal who had apparently drunk a whole series of glasses to our health before our train arrived. I managed to slip away from him at last.

We reached Dar-es-Salaam at seven o'clock on the morning of December 8th. The Europeans were well housed in tents in a camp within a barbed-wire fence. Food was good and plentiful, and we were able to buy necessaries of all kinds cheaply from the English canteen. Governor Schnee and I were received by the Chief of Staff of the British commander, General Sheppard, and conducted to our very pretty house outside the camp. General van Deventer had very kindly sent a luncheon there as a welcome to us. Major Kraut, Captain Spangenberg, and Dr. Huber were all quartered here.

We found General Wahle, who had been left behind sick at Ubene and fallen into the enemy's hands a few months back. He had quite recovered. We had a common mess and our freedom of movement out of the house was only limited to the extent that we had always to be accompanied by a British officer as escort. At the start these gentlemen were very unpunctual, but gradually quite tolerable relations were established between us, and I had an opportunity of visiting acquaintances in Dar-es-Salaam and arranging my personal affairs. A car was also usually placed at my disposal. Major Hosken, the commandant of the prison camp, who had previously shown himself extremely considerate to the captured German women and children in Tanga, now again devoted himself to preserve us from unnecessary annoyance.

On our railway journey we had already been surprised to find almost more English Europeans at every station than we had in the whole of the Protective Force. Dar-es-Salaam itself literally swarmed with white troops. I estimated their number at not less than five thousand, and hundreds and hundreds of motor lorries and cars were awaiting repairs in the motor transport park.

This close concentration of human beings revealed its dangers when Spanish influenza made its appearance. Escort officers told me that frequently five or seven English officers had died of this disease at Dar-es-Salaam. We soon came across its traces among ourselves. Infection had probably taken place while we were on the ship on Lake Tanganyika, and subsequently on the train. It spread from man to man in the concentration camps in Dar-es-Salaam. Captain Spangenberg was going about with me in the town shortly after his arrival at Dar-es-Salaam. Then he felt ill, and though his iron constitution had successfully overcome all the hardships of the campaign, he died in hospital on December 18th of influenza and inflammation of the lungs.

Almost all the Europeans in our camp were attacked by it, and it was very sad that in addition to Captain Spangenberg, nine other Europeans, in all, therefore, ten *per cent*, of our strength, succumbed. Numbers of our *Askari* interned at Tabora also died.

My comings and goings often took me to the Administration Staff (corresponding more or less to our Commandant on the Lines of Communication). After much questioning I had found it in my old house which I had occupied before the war. Among intelligent Englishmen I found the view prevailing that Germany must have colonies on economic grounds, as well as on account of her over-populousness. England was considered to have too many colonies. For the time being, at any rate, she had not sufficient suitable personnel to manage them.

If the English, when telling us of the armistice, insisted on our coming to Dar-es-Salaam at once, in order that we should be transported punctually—that is, by the 12th December—they showed no haste on their own part to carry out the terms of that armistice. Our embarkation was continually postponed, and, finally, it did not take place until the 17th January, 1919, five years to the day after I had landed at Dar-es-Salaam.

To describe my return home in detail would furnish material for a whole book and could hardly be excelled for tragi-comic events. In addition to 114 German soldiers, we had 107 women and 87 children on board, and an escort of 200 British soldiers.

Voyaging by Cape Town, we reached Rotterdam at the end of February. The large crowd of Germans who turned up to meet us at the quay showed me, to my surprise, that our East African war had been watched very closely in the homeland. Many Dutch also gave us proofs of goodwill.

In cold truth our small band, which at the most comprised some 300 Europeans and about 11,000 *Askari*, had occupied a very superior enemy force for the whole war. According to what English officers told me, 137 Generals had been in the field, and in all about 300,000 men had been employed against us. The enemy's losses in dead would not be put too high at 60,000, for an English Press notice stated that about 20,000 Europeans and Indians alone had died or been killed, and to that must be added the large number of black soldiers who fell. The enemy had left 140,000 horses and mules behind in the battle area. Yet in spite of the enormously superior numbers at the disposal of the enemy, our small force, the rifle strength of which was only about 1,400 at the time of the armistice, had remained in the field always ready for action and possessed of the highest determination.

I believe it was the transparency of our aims, the love of our Fatherland, the strong sense of duty and the spirit of self-sacrifice which animated each of our few Europeans and communicated themselves, consciously or unconsciously, to our brave black soldiers that gave our operations that impetus which they possessed to the end. In addition there was a soldierly pride, a feeling of firm mutual co-operation and a spirit of enterprise without which military success is impossible in the long run. We East Africans know only too well that our achievements cannot be compared with the military deeds and devotion of those in the homeland. No people in history has ever done more.

If we East Africans received so kindly a reception in the homeland it was because everyone seemed to think that we had preserved some part of Germany's soldierly traditions, had come back home unsullied, and that the Teutonic sense of loyalty peculiar to us Germans had kept its head high even under the conditions of war in the tropics.

It is true that that feeling has suffered eclipse in many of our people under the impression of the present, (at time of first publication), tribulations of our Fatherland. But it is part of the flesh and blood of us all, and it is just that enthusiastic welcome which hundreds of thousands of our countrymen gave us that strengthens our conviction that, in spite of the momentary distractions and perplexities, the healthy spirit of our German people will prevail again and once more tread the upward path.

LEONAUR

ALSO FROM LEONAUR
AVAILABLE IN SOFTCOVER OR HARDCOVER WITH DUST JACKET

THE RELUCTANT REBEL *by William G. Stevenson*—A young Kentuckian's experiences in the Confederate Infantry & Cavalry during the American Civil War..

BOOTS AND SADDLES *by Elizabeth B. Custer*—The experiences of General Custer's Wife on the Western Plains.

FANNIE BEERS' CIVIL WAR *by Fannie A. Beers*—A Confederate Lady's Experiences of Nursing During the Campaigns & Battles of the American Civil War.

LADY SALE'S AFGHANISTAN *by Florentia Sale*—An Indomitable Victorian Lady's Account of the Retreat from Kabul During the First Afghan War.

THE TWO WARS OF MRS DUBERLY *by Frances Isabella Duberly*—An Intrepid Victorian Lady's Experience of the Crimea and Indian Mutiny.

THE REBELLIOUS DUCHESS *by Paul F. S. Dermoncourt*—The Adventures of the Duchess of Berri and Her Attempt to Overthrow French Monarchy.

LADIES OF WATERLOO *by Charlotte A. Eaton, Magdalene de Lancey & Juana Smith*—The Experiences of Three Women During the Campaign of 1815: Waterloo Days by Charlotte A. Eaton, A Week at Waterloo by Magdalene de Lancey & Juana's Story by Juana Smith.

TWO YEARS BEFORE THE MAST *by Richard Henry Dana. Jr.*—The account of one young man's experiences serving on board a sailing brig—the Penelope—bound for California, between the years 1834-36.

A SAILOR OF KING GEORGE *by Frederick Hoffman*—From Midshipman to Captain—Recollections of War at Sea in the Napoleonic Age 1793-1815.

LORDS OF THE SEA *by A. T. Mahan*—Great Captains of the Royal Navy During the Age of Sail.

COGGESHALL'S VOYAGES: VOLUME 1 *by George Coggeshall*—The Recollections of an American Schooner Captain.

COGGESHALL'S VOYAGES: VOLUME 2 *by George Coggeshall*—The Recollections of an American Schooner Captain.

TWILIGHT OF EMPIRE *by Sir Thomas Ussher & Sir George Cockburn*—Two accounts of Napoleon's Journeys in Exile to Elba and St. Helena: Narrative of Events by Sir Thomas Ussher & Napoleon's Last Voyage: Extract of a diary by Sir George Cockburn.

AVAILABLE ONLINE AT **www.leonaur.com**
AND FROM ALL GOOD BOOK STORES
07/09

LEONAUR

ALSO FROM LEONAUR
AVAILABLE IN SOFTCOVER OR HARDCOVER WITH DUST JACKET

IRON TIMES WITH THE GUARDS *by An O. E. (G. P. A. Fildes)*—The Experiences of an Officer of the Coldstream Guards on the Western Front During the First World War.

THE GREAT WAR IN THE MIDDLE EAST: 1 *by W. T. Massey*—The Desert Campaigns & How Jerusalem Was Won---two classic accounts in one volume.

THE GREAT WAR IN THE MIDDLE EAST: 2 *by W. T. Massey*—Allenby's Final Triumph.

SMITH-DORRIEN *by Horace Smith-Dorrien*—Isandlwhana to the Great War.

1914 *by Sir John French*—The Early Campaigns of the Great War by the British Commander.

GRENADIER *by E. R. M. Fryer*—The Recollections of an Officer of the Grenadier Guards throughout the Great War on the Western Front.

BATTLE, CAPTURE & ESCAPE *by George Pearson*—The Experiences of a Canadian Light Infantryman During the Great War.

DIGGERS AT WAR *by R. Hugh Knyvett & G. P. Cuttriss*—"Over There" With the Australians by R. Hugh Knyvett and Over the Top With the Third Australian Division by G. P. Cuttriss. Accounts of Australians During the Great War in the Middle East, at Gallipoli and on the Western Front.

HEAVY FIGHTING BEFORE US *by George Brenton Laurie*—The Letters of an Officer of the Royal Irish Rifles on the Western Front During the Great War.

THE CAMELIERS *by Oliver Hogue*—A Classic Account of the Australians of the Imperial Camel Corps During the First World War in the Middle East.

RED DUST *by Donald Black*—A Classic Account of Australian Light Horsemen in Palestine During the First World War.

THE LEAN, BROWN MEN *by Angus Buchanan*—Experiences in East Africa During the Great War with the 25th Royal Fusiliers—the Legion of Frontiersmen.

THE NIGERIAN REGIMENT IN EAST AFRICA *by W. D. Downes*—On Campaign During the Great War 1916-1918.

THE 'DIE-HARDS' IN SIBERIA *by John Ward*—With the Middlesex Regiment Against the Bolsheviks 1918-19.

LEONAUR

ALSO FROM LEONAUR
AVAILABLE IN SOFTCOVER OR HARDCOVER WITH DUST JACKET

FARAWAY CAMPAIGN *by F. James*—Experiences of an Indian Army Cavalry Officer in Persia & Russia During the Great War.

REVOLT IN THE DESERT *by T. E. Lawrence*—An account of the experiences of one remarkable British officer's war from his own perspective.

MACHINE-GUN SQUADRON *by A. M. G.*—The 20th Machine Gunners from British Yeomanry Regiments in the Middle East Campaign of the First World War.

A GUNNER'S CRUSADE *by Antony Bluett*—The Campaign in the Desert, Palestine & Syria as Experienced by the Honourable Artillery Company During the Great War .

DESPATCH RIDER *by W. H. L. Watson*—The Experiences of a British Army Motorcycle Despatch Rider During the Opening Battles of the Great War in Europe.

TIGERS ALONG THE TIGRIS *by E. J. Thompson*—The Leicestershire Regiment in Mesopotamia During the First World War.

HEARTS & DRAGONS *by Charles R. M. F. Crutwell*—The 4th Royal Berkshire Regiment in France and Italy During the Great War, 1914-1918.

INFANTRY BRIGADE: 1914 *by John Ward*—The Diary of a Commander of the 15th Infantry Brigade, 5th Division, British Army, During the Retreat from Mons.

DOING OUR 'BIT' *by Ian Hay*—Two Classic Accounts of the Men of Kitchener's 'New Army' During the Great War including *The First 100,000 & All In It*.

AN EYE IN THE STORM *by Arthur Ruhl*—An American War Correspondent's Experiences of the First World War from the Western Front to Gallipoli-and Beyond.

STAND & FALL *by Joe Cassells*—With the Middlesex Regiment Against the Bolsheviks 1918-19.

RIFLEMAN MACGILL'S WAR *by Patrick MacGill*—A Soldier of the London Irish During the Great War in Europe including *The Amateur Army, The Red Horizon & The Great Push*.

WITH THE GUNS *by C. A. Rose & Hugh Dalton*—Two First Hand Accounts of British Gunners at War in Europe During World War 1- Three Years in France with the Guns and With the British Guns in Italy.

THE BUSH WAR DOCTOR *by Robert V. Dolbey*—The Experiences of a British Army Doctor During the East African Campaign of the First World War.

CPSIA information can be obtained at www.ICGtesting.com
Printed in the USA
LVOW070729140313

324261LV00002B/113/P